THE VOICE OF FAITH

JONATHAN EDWARDS'S THEOLOGY OF PRAYER

Peter Beck's *The voice of faith* gives us more than its title implies. It masterfully presents Edwards's view on prayer by interweaving his theology of prayer (1) through a Trinitarian paradigm, (2) through Edwards's own biography, and (3) through his view of awakenings and revivals. The whole book is an enlightening, convicting and fascinating read that will move theologians, ministers and lay people to see the centrality of prayer for Christian theology and Christian living. What spiritual dwarfs in prayer we are compared to the great prayer warriors of past centuries!
JOEL R. BEEKE, *President, Puritan Reformed Theological Seminary, Grand Rapids, Michigan*

Despite the forest of research on Edwards that has arisen in recent years, there has been an empty space—Edwards's theology of prayer—where surprisingly little has emerged until this study by Peter Beck. Jonathan Edwards has a great deal to teach us about prayer, and thankfully this book has appeared to make his teaching accessible.
DONALD S. WHITNEY, *Author of* Spiritual Disciplines for the Christian Life

Jonathan Edwards is arguably the most influential theologian in American history. In this important new study, Peter Beck demonstrates that Edwards applied his theological acumen to the imminently practical topic of prayer. Beck's book is a deft combination of thoughtful scholarship and spiritual application, much like the writings of Edwards himself. *The voice of faith* is an encouragement to many contemporary evangelicals who, like Edwards, believe that God often brings about his sovereign purposes through the prayers of his people.
NATHAN FINN, *Professor, Southeastern Baptist Theological Seminary, Wake Forest, North Carolina*

Beautifully done. Edwards himself would have seen this work as aesthetically pleasing, its structural symmetry and moral usefulness perfectly complementary. The scholar will find rich insight and primary source rigour pleasing to his mind, and those who want spiritual food for the soul may ruminate the material with long-term benefit. Here we find Edwards's life contextually developed and spiritually unveiled, his full theology in its Trinitarian robustness and thickly doctrinal experimentalism carefully focused on one issue (prayer), and his abiding usefulness respectfully and expertly constructed.
TOM J. NETTLES, *Professor, The Southern Baptist Theological Seminary, Louisville, Kentucky*

COMMENDATIONS FOR *THE VOICE OF FAITH*

Prayer is the oxygen of the Christian life, and essential to effective prayer is an understanding of what exactly it is. In this book, the reader will find a clear and well-written introduction to prayer as understood by Jonathan Edwards, one of the great thinkers and pastors of the eighteenth century. A most helpful volume.

CARL R. TRUEMAN, *Professor, Westminster Theological Seminary, Philadelphia, Pennsylvania*

This a rigorous study of the doctrine of prayer through the lens and life of the greatest theologian born in the Americas, Jonathan Edwards. It is singularly unique in that it provides the historical, biblical and doctrinal considerations of prayer during one of the greatest periods of corporate revival. *The voice of faith* is a much needed antidote in our age of fluff. Your heart and soul will be blessed.

HEINZ G. DSCHANKILIC, *Executive Director, Sola Scriptura Ministries International*

Along with John Calvin, John Bunyan, Matthew Henry and others, whose treatments of prayer have gained classic status, we must now add this compendium of Jonathan Edwards. It is hard to believe that it has taken well over two centuries to appear in this format; Peter Beck has done us all a valuable service. A highly recommended volume that is sure to encourage those who read it to seek God with renewed vigour and discover afresh the joy of communion, something Edwards would be pleased with if that were the result.

DEREK THOMAS, *John E Richards Professor of Practical and Systematic Theology, Reformed Theological Seminary; Minister of Teaching, First Presbyterian Church, Jackson, Mississippi*

In addressing the teaching of Jonathan Edwards on prayer, Peter Beck has written an insightful and compelling study on this spiritual discipline. To this day, Edwards remains, arguably, America's foremost theologian and thinker. Though separated by 300 years, this New England Puritan still speaks poignantly through this excellent work, *The voice of faith*. Prayer, Edwards argues, is the burning passion of the soul, the vitality and reality of the Christian's faith. All who read this book will find themselves challenged to regularly commune with God.

STEVEN J. LAWSON, *Author of* The Unwavering Resolve of Jonathan Edwards; *Senior pastor, Christ Fellowship Baptist Church, Mobile, Alabama*

The VOICE of FAITH

Jonathan Edwards's THEOLOGY of PRAYER

Peter Beck

joshua
press

www.joshuapress.com

Published by
Joshua Press Inc., Guelph, Ontario, Canada
Distributed by
Sola Scriptura Ministries International
www.sola-scriptura.ca

First published in 2010.

———

The publication of this book was made possible by the generous support of The Ross-Shire Foundation.

© 2010 Cover and book design by Janice Van Eck.
Edited by Janice Van Eck. Proofread by Karen van Zanden.

Library and Archives Canada Cataloguing in Publication

Beck, Peter, 1965–
The voice of faith : Jonathan Edwards's theology of prayer / Peter Beck.
Includes bibliographical references and index.

ISBN 978-1-894400-32-9 (PAPERBACK)
ISBN 978-1-894400-33-6 (BOUND)

1. Edwards, Jonathan, 1703-1758. 2. Prayer--Christianity. I. Title.

BV209.B43 2010   248.3'2   C2010-901332-8

To Melanie,
my best friend and love,
and to
Alex and Karis,
living proof of God's blessings
on our home

Contents

Preface

A project of this magnitude would be impossible if it were not for the amazing grace shown by so many to one so unworthy. I must begin by thanking those scholars who have devoted their time and prayers to my academic development. Particular note should be given to Professor Michael Haykin, who provided the seed for this work during the course of a time of Christian fellowship. Professors Chad Brand and David Puckett also merit my gratitude for their wise counsel and brotherly advice. Tom Nettles, my supervising professor, deserves a special measure of thanks for guiding me into the depths of Jonathan Edwards's thought and pulling me out of the mire when I lost my way. My thanks go out to all of you.

While the task of writing a book is a solo endeavour, the writer is never truly alone. Across the country I have enjoyed the prayers of friends and family who, though they may not have truly understood "the nature of the beast," always supported me in the process. I likewise owe a debt of gratitude to the churches that hold so dear a place in my heart. Parkway Baptist in St. Louis, Missouri, was used of God to call me into the ministry, and they have faithfully supported my choice to follow God's lead ever since. The wonderful people of Van Buren Baptist in Louisville, Kentucky, tolerated my reading of Edwards's "Sinners in the hands of an angry God" and provided the funds necessary to complete my studies. Finally, Kenwood Baptist, also in Louisville, called me as their pastor in the midst of a very challenging project, allowed me the time to attend to my research and my family, and patiently loved me along the way. To all of you, and untold others I've long since forgotten, thank you.

The greatest measure of earthly thanks belongs to my family. Our children, Alex and Karis, patiently looked on as I returned over and over again to my study—while my door was never shut to them, they always honoured my commitment with their silence and blessed each night in my office with the best hugs in the world. To my wife, my best friend in the world, I owe a debt of gratitude I can never repay. She has shown great patience over the years. She displayed great grace in sheltering me in my labours. She encouraged me to continue when my thoughts were otherwise and provided a Christian example I can only hope to emulate. I could not have finished this book without the three of you—nor would I have wanted to. With all my love I say, "Thank you."

Finally, as I complete this task, I more fully understand and appreciate Augustine's own sigh of relief and wonder at the marvellous grace of God expressed when he completed his monumental *City of God*. Echoing his words, I conclude,

> I think I have now, by God's help, discharged my obligation in writing this large work. Let those who think I have said too little, or those who think I have said too much, forgive me; and let those who think I have said just enough join me in giving thanks to God. Amen.[1]

---

1 Augustine, *City of God*, XXII.30.

Introduction

A ll real and true prayer is the voice of faith."[1] Jonathan Edwards's sermon "The Terms of Prayer," preached to his congregation in the lull between the awakening in Northampton and the broader outbreak of the Great Awakening, still rings true in the ears of Christians today who desire to know the mind of God and find their repose in him. This three-century-old sermon still resonates because the eternal importance of the doctrine of prayer and its temporal relevance for believers remains unchanged. Later in the same sermon Edwards cast a vision of a loving God who hears the prayers of his children and longs to grant them great blessings in exchange for their faith: "God is as ready, and more ready, to bestow than we are to ask, and more ready to open than we are to knock."[2]

---

1 Jonathan Edwards, "The Terms of Prayer," in *Sermons and Discourses: 1734–1738*, ed. M.X. Lesser, Vol. 19 of *The Works of Jonathan Edwards* [hereafter *Works*] (New Haven: Yale University Press, 2001), 19:787.

2 Edwards, "The Terms of Prayer," *Works*, 19:783.

Thus, in his inimitable way, Edwards moved the doctrine of prayer beyond that of mere duty and responsibility to Christian privilege and joy. In doing so, Edwards offered more than simple correctives and directives, a "how-to" manual that falls short in a world of inexplicable pain, terror and challenge. Instead, he proffered a positive affirmation of God's glory, calling all true Christians to come forth in faith, voice their prayers and lean wholly upon God.

The "great duty"

Prayer seemed natural to me, as the breath, by which the inward burnings of my heart had vent.[3]

As seen in Edwards's "Personal Narrative," his commitment to and fascination with prayer found a voice at an early age. Yet, upon his conversion, prayer became not a passing fancy but a burning passion. He found himself in constant prayer. Edwards soon realized, and then regularly preached, that prayer, its power or lack thereof, evidences both the vitality and reality of the Christian's faith. "Prayer," he announced, "is as natural an expression of faith as breathing is of life."[4] The Christian has faith. The Christian prays. Otherwise, he is no Christian at all.

Prayer arises properly out of one's faith in God through Christ, according to Edwards, for "there is no other way that the heart can look to God, but only looking by faith, by faith seeking the blessing of God, and by faith depending on God for the mercy sought."[5] The prayer offered in faith, Edwards contended, serves as the only way that one may obtain such blessings.[6] In prayer, Christians access the

---

3 Edwards, "Personal Narrative," in *Letters and Personal Writings*, ed. George S. Claghorn, *Works*, 16 (1998):794.

4 Edwards, "Hypocrites Deficient in the Duty of Prayer," in *Seeking God: Jonathan Edwards' Evangelism Contrasted with Modern Methodologies*, ed. William C. Nichols (Ames, IA: International Outreach, 2001), 365.

5 Edwards, "The Terms of Prayer," *Works*, 19:787.

6 Edwards, "Justification by Faith Alone," *Works*, 19:230.

one true source of all the blessings that they stand in need of:

> [Prayer] is one of the greatest and most excellent means of
> nourishing the new nature, and of causing the soul to
> flourish and prosper. It is an excellent means of keeping
> up an acquaintance with God, and of growing in knowl-
> edge of God. It is a way to a life of communion with God.
> It is an excellent means of taking off the heart from the
> vanities of the world and of causing the mind to be con-
> versant in heaven. It is an excellent preservative from sin
> and the wiles of the devil, and a powerful antidote against
> the poison of the old serpent. It is a duty whereby strength
> is derived from God against the lusts and corruptions of
> the heart, and the snares of the world.[7]

Yet, prayer functions in Edwards's theology as more than just a
means to human ends. Faithful prayer comes before God as a "fra-
grant savour," an acceptable sacrifice of praise.[8] Prayer, offered in
humble dependence upon God, becomes the means by which the
believer can worship his Creator and Sustainer. "[Christians] have
the same language to God in prayer and praise," Edwards preached.
Prayer acts as the avenue whereby one expresses his humility and
repentance before his rightful superior. It is the proper vehicle for
expressing adoration and admiration, thanksgiving and dependence.
Prayer offers the prayer the opportunity to express his "longings
and desires after God."[9]

As such, as an act of worship before the one true God, prayer
becomes more than simply evidence of one's faith or a source of

---

7 Edwards, "Hypocrites Deficient in the Duty of Prayer," in ed. Nichols, *Seeking God*, 371–372.

8 Edwards, "God Glorified in Man's Dependence," in *Sermons and Discourses 1730–1733*, ed. Mark Valeri, *Works*, 17 (1999):200.

9 Edwards, "Christians a Chosen Generation," *Works*, 17:303. See also, "Mercy and Not Sacrifice" in *Sermons and Discourses 1739-1742*, ed. Harry S. Stout and Nathan O. Hatch with Kyle P. Farley, *Works*, 22 (2003):127.

temporal and eternal blessings. Prayer honours God and, Edwards maintained, is therefore incumbent upon all mankind, "a duty of which both the godly and the ungodly should exercise themselves."[10] Among Christians, those in a right relationship with God and recipients of his immeasurable grace, prayer is "especially becoming."[11] They are to be much in prayer, for prayer, as the ultimate act of worship, is the "great duty," the greatest of all in religion, as it ever keeps their focus on their very source and purpose for being. To ignore this duty is to "live like atheists or like brute creatures," to "live as if there were no God."[12] Such inaction and ingratitude belies the true nature of the soul, denying God the glory properly due him. Prayer, especially those of petition and supplication to which Edwards encouraged his flock, is a "great duty," even a necessity, because such prayer acknowledges the goodness and greatness of God.

The "delightful conviction"

The doctrine of God's sovereignty has very often appeared, an exceeding pleasant, bright and sweet doctrine to me.[13]

According to Edwards's account of his conversion experience, God's sovereignty served not just as the keystone but also as the key that unlocked the great mystery of salvation that had so long eluded him. Admitting that he once struggled with the concept of God's inviolable control over all things, Edwards wrote in his "Personal Narrative":

---

10 Edwards, "God's Manner is First to Prepare Men's Hearts and Then to Answer Their Prayers," in *The Glory and Honor of God*, ed. Michael D. McMullen (Nashville: Broadman & Holman, 2004), 90.

11 Edwards, "It Becomes Saints in Cases of Special Difficulty and Calamity of God's Church, to Betake Themselves in an Extraordinary Manner to Prayer to God" (1750), Beinecke Rare Book and Manuscript Library, Yale University, New Haven.

12 Edwards, "God's Manner is First to Prepare Men's Hearts and Then to Answer Their Prayers," in ed. McMullen, *The Glory and Honor of God*, 89.

13 Edwards, "Personal Narrative," *Works*, 16:792.

> My mind had been wont to be full of objections against
> the doctrine of God's sovereignty, in him choosing whom
> he would to eternal life, and rejecting whom he pleased;
> leaving them eternally to perish, and be everlastingly tor-
> mented in hell.

While he could never explain his change of heart to his own satisfaction, a change occurred nonetheless. After reading the words of 1
Timothy 1:17—"Now unto the King eternal, immortal, invisible,
the only wise God, be honour and glory forever and ever, Amen"—
Edwards found that his mind now rested in God's sovereignty.
Rather than rejecting, he was accepting. He had experienced "a
wonderful alteration in [his] mind." This alteration forever changed
his view of the world and its God. The reality of "God's sovereignty"
became to him a "delightful conviction." God's "absolute sovereignty"
no longer repulsed Edwards. Instead, such beliefs drew him to adoration and affection towards God.[14]

Given the power of his commitment to the sovereignty of God,
readers should not be surprised to find affirmations and explanations of this central doctrine throughout his theological and philosophical writings. Moreover, the reader would rightly expect to
find strains of Calvinist presuppositions in Edwards's sermons. To
find the two so closely linked in sermons on the duty of prayer,
however, can be unsettling. "The true God," he claimed, "perfectly
knows the circumstances of every one that prays to him throughout
the world."[15] "God is so perfect in knowledge, that he doth not
need to be informed by us, in order to [have] a knowledge of our
wants; for he knows what things we need before we ask him."[16]
Furthermore,

---

14 Edwards, "Personal Narrative," *Works*, 16:791–793.

15 Edwards, "The Most High a Prayer-Hearing God," in Vol. 2 of *The Works of Jonathan Edwards* [hereafter *Works* (Hendrickson)] (Peabody, MA: Hendrickson, 1998), 2:115.

16 Edwards, "The Most High a Prayer-Hearing God," *Works* (Hendrickson), 2:115.

> The business of prayer is not to direct God, who is infi-
> nitely wise, and needs not any of our directions; who
> knows what is best for us ten thousand times better than
> we, and knows what time and what way are best. It is fit
> that he should answer prayer, and, as an infinitely wise
> God, in the exercise of his own wisdom, and not ours.[17]

God's sovereign wisdom is unchangeable. That which he has determined, he has determined and he remains unmoved. In fact, one
should not mistakenly think "that God is properly moved or made
willing by our prayers."[18] Yet, God seemingly answers prayer. However, he "answers prayer" only "as though he were prevailed on by
prayer."[19] The prayers of men cannot move the unmovable.

So, why pray? Why did Edwards end a sermonic discourse on the
sovereignty of God with an appeal to a more dutiful obedience to
faithful prayer? How can Edwards encourage his congregation to
"pray with all prayer and supplication," to "live prayerful lives,"
"praying always, without ceasing, and not fainting," if God has
sovereignly predetermined the course of their lives and all history
in eternity past?[20]

A "resolution"

> Resolved, never to count that a prayer, nor to let that pass
> as a prayer, nor that as a petition of a prayer, which is so
> made, that I cannot hope that God will answer it; nor that
> as a confession, which I cannot hope God will accept.[21]

In that one "resolution," written in the early days of his nascent

---

17 Edwards, "The Most High a Prayer-Hearing God," *Works* (Hendrickson), 2:117.
18 Edwards, "The Most High a Prayer-Hearing God," *Works* (Hendrickson), 2:116.
19 Edwards, "The Most High a Prayer-Hearing God," *Works* (Hendrickson), 2:116.
20 Edwards, "The Most High a Prayer-Hearing God," *Works* (Hendrickson), 2:118.
21 Edwards, "Resolution" No. 29, *Works*, 16:755.

Christianity, Edwards envisioned a life of prayer and encapsulated his theology of prayer. Acceptable prayer is founded upon faith, to "hope" in a God who, by way of his sovereignty, can "answer" prayer. Ultimately, for Edwards the resolution of the apparent theological conundrum of God's sovereignty and man's duty required no resolution at all. Rather, it was an accepting of both: recognizing God's absolute sovereignty while praying in absolute humility.

Edwards expressed the same sentiment in a more well-rounded fashion years later in the sermon "The Terms of Prayer." "There is no other way that the heart can look to God," Edwards said, "but only looking by faith, by faith seeking the blessing of God, and by faith depending on God for the mercy sought.[22] Here Edwards again emphasized the necessity of faith, a "seeking" and a "depending on God." The faith that God seeks in human prayer, Edwards believed, amounted to no more than absolute "dependence on God, and trust in his sufficiency and mercy."[23] Note that Edwards understood there to be an important difference between faith as a trusting in God and faith as merely acknowledging of the existence of God. While belief leads to mental assent, true faith results in a "resting" and "adhering" to God.[24] Saving faith, and that which pleases God in prayer, arises only out of a wholesale dependence upon the One in whom the trust is placed.

Proper faith, Edwards believed, requires a proper understanding of God, an understanding that manifests itself in faithful prayer as expressed in humble dependence upon each person of the Trinity.

> As the Father in the economy of the persons of the Trinity is especially the Lord, sovereign, lawgiver, and judge and disposer, so prayer is especially directed to him. He is as much especially the object of prayer as he is especially Lord,

---

22 Edwards, "The Terms of Prayer," *Works*, 19:787.

23 Edwards, "The Most High a Prayer-Hearing God," *Works* (Hendrickson), 2:117.

24 Edwards, "Miscellanies" No. 339, in *The "Miscellanies": Entry a–z, aa–zz, 1–500,* ed. Thomas A. Schafer, *Works*, 13 (1994):408.

for prayer is directed to one only as Lord. Lordship and dominion and judgment belongs to the Son secondarily, viz. in the name of the Father; so prayer is to be directed to him secondarily as the Father's representative. The Spirit is Lord and disposer, and commands, …but 'tis but as the representative and messenger of both the other persons. So prayer is to be directed to him, as their representative. Thus we may pray to the Son in us, or communicating himself to us.[25]

In this way, the efficacy of prayer stands or falls upon the work and worship of the sovereign God, as manifested in Father, Son and Holy Spirit. For it is this God, and this God alone, who can and does answer the prayers of the faithful according to his good pleasure.

While they are praying, he gives them sweet views of his glorious grace, purity, sufficiency, and sovereignty; and enables them with great quietness, to rest in him, to leave themselves and their prayers with him, submitting to his will, and trusting in his grace and faithfulness.[26]

Thus, according to Edwards's theology of prayer, true prayer, that which is the voice of faith, focuses its attention wholly upon God in all his magnificent glory.

Why study Edwards?

I believe there is a prevailing impression that Edwards must be fairly met in order to make any advance in an opposite argument.[27]

---

25 Edwards, "Discourse on the Trinity," in *Writings on the Trinity, Grace and Faith*, ed. Sang Hyun Lee, *Works*, 21 (2003):143.

26 Edwards, "The Most High a Prayer-Hearing God," *Works* (Hendrickson), 2:114.

27 Henry P. Tappan, *A Review of Edwards's "Inquiry into the Freedom of the Will"*

In the century after Edwards's death, Henry Tappan perceptively recognized the long shadow that Jonathan Edwards would cast across the theological landscape. Another 100 years after Tappan, Paul Ramsey would echo his sentiments in the first volume of the fledgling critical edition of Edwards's works to come out of Yale.[28] While interpretations of Edwards's influence and influences vary, no theologian since the days of the Reformers, save perhaps Friedrich Schleiermacher and Karl Barth, has so imposed his thoughts upon the minds of those who followed as has Edwards. For a quarter of a millennium, Jonathan Edwards has stood alone as America's premier religious thinker.

Theological friends and foes, those who agree with Edwards's Reformed thinking and those who loathe it, universally recognize his genius and importance.[29] John Wesley, himself the source of an opposing theological tradition, called Edwards a "great man."[30] Samuel Hopkins, another contemporary of Edwards, could barely contain his enthusiasm for his friend:

> President Edwards, in the esteem of all the judicious, who were well acquainted with him, either personally, or by his writings, was one of the greatest—best—and most useful of men that have lived in this age.
>
> He discovered himself to be one of the greatest of divines,

---

(New York: J.S.Taylor, 1839), xi.

28 Paul Ramsey, "Editor's Introduction," in *Freedom of the Will*, ed. Paul Ramsey, *Works*, 1 (1957):12.

29 Recognizing that the Protestant Reformed tradition is broad and multiform, I use the term "Reformed" here and throughout to refer to the branch of that broader heritage with which Edwards identified, that of John Calvin and the Westminster Assembly. Of Calvinism, Edwards said, "I should not take it all amiss, to be called a Calvinist, for distinction's sake" (Edwards, *Freedom of the Will*, *Works*, 1:131).As for the Westminster Standards, Edwards acknowledged, "As to my subscribing to the substance of the Westminster Confession, there would be no difficulty" (Edwards, Letter "To the Reverend John Erskine," *Works*, 16:355).

30 John Wesley, *Works* (London, 1831), 10:475; quoted in Iain H. Murray, *Jonathan Edwards:A New Biography* (Carlisle, PA:The Banner of Truth Trust, 1987), xv.

by his conversation, preaching and writings: One of remarkable strength of mind, clearness of thought, and depth of penetration, who well understood, and was able, above most others, to vindicate the great doctrines of Christianity.[31]

Two centuries later, Perry Miller, loathing Edwards's "peculiar doctrines," still esteemed him as an "artist" and "child of genius."[32] More recently, Philip Gura dubbed him "America's evangelical,"[33] while Robert Jenson called him "America's theologian."[34]

As Iain Murray noted, "Edwards divided men in his lifetime and to no less degree he continues to divide his biographers."[35] On the one hand, Walter Eversley suggested that Edwards's "theological integrity actually undermined" his pastoral value.[36] John Gerstner, on the other hand, nearly gushed forth his approval of Edwards, calling him "the greatest philosopher-theologian ever to grace the American scene."[37] Admitting his appreciation for Edwards, Gerstner claimed that the "saint of Stockbridge" exerted a greater influence on his life than "any other human being who has ever lived outside the pages of Holy Scripture itself."[38]

The skill with which Edwards spoke and wrote still resonates today.

---

31 Samuel Hopkins, *The Life and Character of the Late Reverend Mr. Jonathan Edwards* (Northampton: S. & E. Butler, 1804; reprint of *The Life and Character of the Late Reverend Mr. Jonathan Edwards* [Boston: S. Keeneland, 1765]), iii.

32 Perry Miller, *Jonathan Edwards* (New York: William Sloane Associates, 1949), xii–xiii.

33 Philip F. Gura, *Jonathan Edwards: America's Evangelical* (New York: Hill and Wang, 2005).

34 Robert W. Jenson, *America's Theologian: A Recommendation of Jonathan Edwards* (New York: Oxford University Press, 1988).

35 Murray, *Jonathan Edwards: A New Biography*, xix.

36 Walter V.L. Eversley, "The Pastor as Revivalist," in *Edwards in Our Time: Jonathan Edwards and the Shaping of American Religion*, ed. Sang H. Lee and Allen C. Guelzo (Grand Rapids: Eerdmans, 1999), 113.

37 John H. Gerstner, *Jonathan Edwards: A Mini-Theology* (Carol Stream, IL: Tyndale House, 1987; reprint, Morgan, PA: Soli Deo Gloria, 1996), 9.

38 Gerstner, *Jonathan Edwards: A Mini-Theology*, 11.

He is recognized as one of the leading figures of a great movement that began in the sixteenth century and continues to the present. For many, he has become "a spokesman for orthodox Calvinism."[39] As such, just as Tappan believed, Edwards "must be fairly met" if one is to understand or rebut the Reformed or Calvinist interpretation of the Bible and the doctrines drawn from it.

Yet, one more reason to study Edwards remains. As Martyn Lloyd-Jones has argued, "Edwards takes you out into the depths where you begin to see man face to face with his Maker."[40] Questions of God's sovereignty and man's responsibility continue to be asked today. Answers are not easy to come by. Definitive answers are all the more rare. Therefore, they are to be coveted and pursued with the greatest of intent and treasured as precious theological jewels. In Edwards's works, the reader finds such treasure. Edwards offers the modern church more than just a comprehensive theology of prayer—he offers an all-inclusive vision of the greatness of God. "Edwards is strongest where we are weakest. He knows God," John Piper wrote. "He sees and savors the supremacy of God in all things. Our culture is dying for want of this vision and this food."[41]

Drawing on the vast *corpus* left by this great New England divine, what follows is a systematic treatment of Edwards's theology of prayer, his synthesis of the seemingly incompatible ideas of God's absolute sovereignty and man's requisite responsibility. The superstructure of Edwards's theology, a proper understanding of the nature and work of the Father, Son and Holy Spirit, will be examined as these matters relate to prayer. Likewise, consideration will be given along the way to issues such as the duty of prayer, reasons for unanswered prayer and man's vital role in the accomplishment

---

39 Ava Chamberlain, "Editor's Introduction," in *The "Miscellanies": Entry Nos. 501–832*, ed. Ava Chamberlain, *Works*, 18 (2000):2.

40 D. Martyn Lloyd-Jones, *The Puritans: Their Origins and Successors* (Carlisle, PA: The Banner of Truth Trust, 1997), 361.

41 John Piper, *God's Passion for His Glory: Living the Vision of Jonathan Edwards* (Wheaton: Crossway, 1998), 31.

of God's redemptive plans. Through the course of this study, the reader will see that the sovereignty of God is the skeleton upon which the work of flesh is hung in Edwards's theology of prayer.

Yet, as important as theology was to Edwards, it served as a means to a greater end. George Claghorn correctly identified the end for which Edwards strove: "Personal communion with the Almighty... was to be a hallmark of his theology."[42] To that end, consideration must be given to the manner that Edwards himself lived out his theology of prayer. Several chapters of "external biographies" will serve that purpose. These biographies stand, first, as homage to the impact of Perry Miller's influential biography of Edwards that offered "external biographies" of its own. However, in his biography, Miller focused on Edwards's thinking almost to the exclusion of the matters of Edwards's life, presenting tidbits related to his life only as secondary matters. Here, these external biographies are presented not as unrelated to doctrinal matters but as living proof that doctrine influenced Edwards's life in crucial ways. It will be evident that Edwards "talked the talk" *and* "walked the walk."

Conclusion

> Seeing therefore you stand in such continual need of the help of God, how reasonable is it that you should continually seek it of him, and perseveringly acknowledge your dependence upon him, by resorting to him, to spread your needs before him, and to offer up your requests to him in prayer.[43]

---

42 George Claghorn, "Editor's Introduction," *Works*, 16:745. Speaking of this experiential outworking of Edwards's theology, Lloyd-Jones wrote, "The spiritual always controlled the intellectual in him" (Lloyd-Jones, *The Puritans: Their Origins and Successors*, 356).

43 Edwards, "Hypocrites Deficient in the Duty of Prayer," in ed. Nichols, *Seeking God*, 371.

Edwards's theology of prayer proves to be quite simple in expression but profound in its implications. Christians pray; God hears. Christians need; God supplies. Christians trust; God responds. "For Christian prayer to God for a blessing is but an expression of faith in God for that blessing," he explained. "Prayer is only the voice of faith."[44] In the prayer that God accepts, the Christian humbly acknowledges and leans upon the sovereignty of God. As Edwards proclaimed in "God Glorified in Man's Dependence," prayer properly begins and ends with the character of God because "faith abases men, and exalts God."[45]

---

44 Edwards, "Justification by Faith Alone," *Works*, 19:204.
45 Edwards, "God Glorified in Man's Dependence," *Works*, 17:213.

Chapter 1

The "prayer-hearing God"

That is the character of the Most High, that he is a God
who hears prayer.[1]

The winter of 1735/1736 weighed heavy upon the hearts
of the people of Northampton. An epidemic raged
through the cultural centre of colonial Massachusetts—
Boston. Fear of that same epidemic ran rampant through
the minds of those living in the hinterlands, wondering not if but
when it would rear its ugly head among them. Contrary to the
popular image of Jonathan Edwards as a poor pastor, Edwards
recognized the symptoms of wavering faith infecting his congregation. He did what any good pastor would do. He gave them the
Word of God. He offered them hope.

Seeking to allay their concerns about an invisible foe, a foe that
might at any moment attack one and then many in Northampton,

---

1 Edwards, "The Most High a Prayer-Hearing God," *Works* (Hendrickson), 2:113.

Edwards presented his parishioners with a tightly reasoned and theologically insightful exposition of Psalm 65:2. Explaining the text, Edwards called his people to prayer to inoculate their souls with a healthy dose of dependence upon God. The prayer that he called them to offer had no guarantees of instant gratification, personal protection or certain health. Instead, it reminded them that there was something far better and far more certain: the promise of a good and mighty God who hears the prayers of his people.

In this sermon, "The Most High a Prayer-Hearing God," Edwards presented his parishioners with the hope of guaranteed access to a God who could truly remedy their concerns, if only they would cry out to him faithfully in prayer. This prayerful approach to the throne room of God, he reminded them, is a great privilege of which many in the world are destitute.[2] The majority of mankind, many of their own neighbours, would never enjoy the reality of God hearing their prayers, he argued. They would never realize the hope to which God was calling the faithful in Northampton. The problem, Edwards concluded, was not that these others were failing to pray. For, in fact, many of them prayed regularly for divine intervention and human relief. They faced a problem of a far greater nature. They were presenting their requests to deities who are deaf and dumb, gods "who cannot hear, and cannot answer prayer."[3] Their gods were creations of their own minds, the handiwork of artisans, devoid of any spiritual reality or vitality, not the God who had revealed himself in the Bible. In short, they were worshipping the wrong god.

A proper understanding of God forms the heart of Jonathan Edwards's theology of prayer. While the pulse of one's faith can be measured by one's prayer life, God does not accept just any belief as the basis for one's approach to the divine. Faith must be placed in the right God, the one and true God, recognizable by his attributes and character. "Herein," he proclaimed, "the most high God

---

2 Edwards, "The Most High a Prayer-Hearing God," *Works* (Hendrickson), 2:116.
3 Edwards, "The Most High a Prayer-Hearing God," *Works* (Hendrickson), 2:113.

is distinguished from false Gods. The true God is the only one of this character; there is no other of whom it may be said, that he heareth prayer."[4]

What follows will answer three vital questions about the centrality of God's character in relation to Edwards's robust doctrine of prayer. As to the character of God himself, one must ask, "Who is God?" Or, stated another way, "What is God like?" Having addressed the question about God's nature, the next query necessarily follows the first. "Does God answer prayer?" Acknowledging that God does indeed answer prayer, Edwards also admitted that God does not always do so. Thus, he also dealt with the difficult question, "What about unanswered prayer?" In the end it will be seen that Edwards's answers to all of these questions required his audience to ponder the majesty and the mystery of the one true and living God, the most high God who can and does answer prayer according to his great character.

Who is God?

It is of exceeding importance that we should have right notions and conceptions of the nature, attributes, and perfections of God.[5]

"Edwards's confidence in the effectiveness of prayer," Glenn Kreider rightly surmised, "was based on God's character."[6] One need not look too deeply into Edwards's vast sermonic *corpus* to find this conviction clearly proclaimed. From the outset of his ministerial career, he sought to build not just his theology of prayer, but all Christian theology, on the right understanding of God. "Now it is

---

4 Edwards, "The Most High a Prayer-Hearing God," *Works* (Hendrickson), 2:115.

5 Edwards, "God's Excellencies," in *Sermons and Discourses, 1720–1723*, ed. Wilson H. Kimnach, *Works*, 10 (1992):416.

6 Glenn Kreider, "Jonathan Edwards's Theology of Prayer," *Bibliotheca Sacra* 160 (2003):438.

impossible we should love, fear, and obey God as we ought," he taught in 1722 when he was just nineteen years old, "except we know what he is, and have right ideas of his perfections, that render him lovely and worthy to be feared and obeyed." Moreover, he reasoned, "It would be greatly to the advantage of our souls, if we understood more of the excellency and gloriousness of God." A proper understanding of God not only affords man the spiritual tools necessary for Christian living, such knowledge ultimately equips him to fulfill the very end for which he was created: "to think and be astonished [at] his glorious perfections."[7]

Historically, theologians have explored the nature of God by considering and defining his attributes; Edwards did so as well. Following his theological predecessors, Edwards believed that God possesses two kinds of attributes, or perfections, those that are moral and those that are natural.

> So divines make a distinction between the natural and moral perfections of God: by the moral perfections of God, they mean those attributes which God exercises as a moral agent, or whereby the heart and will of God are good, right, and infinitely becoming, and lovely; such as his righteousness, truth, faithfulness, and goodness; or in one word his holiness. By God's natural attributes or perfections, they mean those attributes, wherein, according to our way of conceiving of God, consists, not the holiness of moral goodness of God, but his greatness; such as his power, his knowledge whereby he knows all things, and his being eternal, from everlasting to everlasting, his omnipresence, and his awful and terrible majesty.[8]

Notice that one cannot separate Edwards's understanding of God's natural attributes from an understanding of God's moral attributes.

---

7   Edwards, "God's Excellencies," *Works*, 10:417.
8   Edwards, *Religious Affections*, ed. John E. Smith, *Works*, 2 (1959):255.

The former are derived from the latter. That is, the wonder of God's natural attributes arises out of, and displays the beauty of, his moral perfections.[9] "It seems to be a thing in itself fit and desirable, that the glorious perfections of God should be known, and the operations and expressions of them seen by other beings besides himself."[10] That is, motivated by his concern for his own glory, God reveals his infinite moral character in such a manner that these attributes may be seen in his natural attributes and appreciated by his creation.

Consideration of both categories of God's attributes, the moral and the natural, can be found throughout Edwards's sermons and writings. The moral attributes stand as the basis of what God does, while the natural are the means whereby he accomplishes his will. God's holiness and justice drive his every thought, desire and deed. To that end, Edwards's theology of prayer depends upon God's gracious and perfect character, his infallible knowledge of man's situation and his ability to remedy that situation according to his own sovereign desires. Man needs more than just a God who can hear his cries. Man needs a good God who can answer him correctly.

THE ALL-GOOD GOD

According to Edwards's estimation, God is perfect in every way. "God is infinitely, eternally, unchangeably, and independently glorious and happy."[11] These perfections are evident in the very makeup of God—his character as it is understood in light of his attributes. As Gary Crampton observed, "God is the totality of his attributes; He is identical with His attributes."[12] They are not reflections of who he is but the reality of what he is. As such, God cannot act contrary to his attributes at any point or in any way, regardless of

---

9 Edwards, *Religious Affections, Works*, 2:266.

10 Edwards, *The End for Which God Created the World*, in *Ethical Writings*, ed. Paul Ramsey, *Works*, 8 (1989):430–431.

11 Edwards, *The End for Which God Created the World, Works*, 8:420.

12 W. Gary Crampton, *Meet Jonathan Edwards* (Morgan, PA: Soli Deo Gloria, 2004), 73.

the prayer offered. To do so would be to deny himself, to undermine his deity, and to vacate his throne. Therefore, every operation
of God known to man cannot be but what God is: perfect, holy,
just and loving. All these things, and God's response to prayer, tend
ultimately to his greater glory.

"Holiness is a most beautiful and lovely thing," Edwards wrote
as he recorded the first of several hundred "Miscellanies."[13] Defining "holiness," Edwards said, "[It is the] excellency and beauty of
God's nature whereby His heart is disposed and delights in everything that is morally good and excellent."[14] Stated positively, then,
God's holiness is the totality of his own goodness and his embrace
of all that is good. Put negatively, it is his opposition to all that is
evil or antithetical to his goodness. Because God is holy, he can
only be good.

Quantitatively speaking, God's holiness is infinite, without
bounds.[15] His holiness manifests itself in his infinite hatred of sin.
This hatred finds expression in his infinite, outward opposition to
sin. "The holiness of God, which is the infinite opposition of his
nature to sin, naturally and necessarily disposes him to punish sin."[16]
God cannot but resist sin. To do otherwise, to tolerate sin or to
merely overlook evil, would be to ally himself with the enemy,
reject his own nature and cease to be God.

Qualitatively, God's holiness is complete. Thus, of God's moral
attributes, holiness ranks first, according to Edwards. God's holiness
is the "most lovely" of those attributes ascribed to him.[17] It is of the
"highest sort," greater than all the others.[18] God's holiness, he wrote,
"is to be understood in the most extensive sense for all his moral

---

13 Edwards, "Miscellanies" No. a, *Works*, 13:163.

14 Quoted in Crampton, *Meet Jonathan Edwards*, 77.

15 Edwards, "Yield to God's Word, or Be Broken by His Hand," in *Sermons and Discourses, 1743–1758*, ed. Wilson H. Kimnach, *Works*, 25 (2006):215.

16 Edwards, "Miscellanies" No. 779, *Works*, 18:437.

17 Edwards, "Yield to God's Word, or Be Broken by His Hand," *Works*, 25:215.

18 Edwards, "God's Excellencies," *Works*, 10:423.

perfection, and including his goodness and grace."[19] It is not that God is more holy than he is just. What Edwards meant is that all of God's other moral attributes are subsumed under his holiness. If God were not infinitely holy, he could not be just. If his love was tainted by the least bit of sin, it would not truly be love at all. Thus, God is holy because, by virtue of his being God, he must be holy.

Finally, Edwards's holistic view of God's attributes logically connects God's holiness to God's glory:

> GOD'S HOLINESS is his having a due, meet and proper regard to everything, and therefore consists mainly and summarily in his infinite regard or love to himself, he being infinitely the greatest and most excellent Being. And therefore a meet and proper regard to himself is infinitely greater than to all other beings; and as he is as it were the sum of all being, and all other positive existence is but a communication from him, hence it will follow that a proper regard to himself is the sum of his regard.[20]

Because God is holy, he must love what is holy. That which is most holy is God himself. Thus, God must love himself, having a higher regard for his glory than all other things. In this way, Edwards connected God's holiness with the chief end for which he created the world: to glorify himself by revealing his holiness to his creation.[21]

Intimately related to God's holiness is his justice. Edwards placed such importance on this attribute that he dedicated an entire sermon to explaining and defending it. The stated doctrine of that sermon, "The Justice of God in the Damnation of Sinners," clearly connects God's justice with his holiness: "'Tis just with God eternally to cast

---

19 Edwards, *The "Blank Bible,"* ed. Stephen J. Stein, *Works,* 24 (2006):345.

20 Edwards, "Miscellanies" No. 1077, in *The "Miscellanies": Entry Nos. 833–1152,* ed. Amy P. Pauw, *Works,* 20 (2002):460.

21 Edwards, *The End for Which God Created the World, Works,* 8:526.

off, and destroy sinners."[22] Because God is perfectly holy, he can
brook no offense against that holiness. Any violation necessarily
merits and requires just recompense:

> If God's nature be infinitely opposite to sin [that is, holy],
> then doubtless he has a disposition answerable to oppose it
> in his acts and works. If he by his nature be an enemy to
> sin with an infinite enmity, then he is doubtless disposed to
> act as an enemy to it, or to do the part of the enemy to it.[23]

If God is holy, he must react negatively against all that is not holy.
Indeed, his own glory requires it:

> If it be to God's glory that he is in his infinite nature holy
> and opposite to sin, then it is to his glory to be infinitely
> displeased with sin; and if it be to God's glory to be infi-
> nitely displeased with sin, then it must be to God's glory
> to exercise and manifest that displeasure, and act accord-
> ing to it.[24]

Thus, the first two of God's moral attributes, holiness and justice,
stand together according to his chief end, his glory, or they fall
together, neither being true of God.

God's justice does not operate in an arbitrary manner. God, as
God, always judges aright. He "weighs things in an even balance."[25]
Moreover, he judges things as they truly are and his "judgment will
be conformed to the nature of things," that of both the judge and
the judged.[26] God will deliberate, determine and reward or punish
according to his character and that of the offender. By his very

22 Edwards, "The Justice of God in the Damnation of Sinners," *Works*, 19:341.
23 Edwards, "Miscellanies" No. 779, *Works*, 18:437.
24 Edwards, "Miscellanies" No. 779, *Works*, 18:438.
25 Edwards, *Original Sin*, ed. Clyde A. Holbrook, *Works*, 3 (1970):110.
26 Edwards, *The "Blank Bible," Works*, 24:987.

character, God is obligated to do so.[27] To do otherwise would be to violate his own glory and defeat his own purposes.

God's holiness and justice require that he respond in kind, repaying man's evil actions according to the greatness of his sin. Those who have violated God's holiness will experience his justice. Sinners are "wholly without excuse before God and deserve damnation," their infinite offense worthy of infinite punishment.[28] Here God's holiness, justice and sovereignty intersect. Yet, Edwards linked another of God's moral perfections, that of his love or grace, to justice as well. "God's justice is more gloriously manifested in the sufferings of Christ for the elect than in the damnation of the wicked."[29] Jesus, taking the place of the elect, being of infinite worth and perfection, died on the cross, experiencing the infinite wrath of God in the span of six short hours. This display of God's justice occurred publicly, before the eyes of a watching world, to convince men and women of how seriously God must take their sins and the incredible depth of his love for his creation.

Edwards never tired of telling others about the love of God. His appreciation for this last perfection can be found scattered throughout his works and sermons. He preached about it in "Heaven is a World of Love." He explained it philosophically in *Charity and Its Fruit*. Regardless of the medium, however, Edwards always tied God's love to his other moral attributes. All that they are and represent, his love does as well.

Since God is infinite in all of his perfections, his love must be infinite. It is an "everlasting love."[30] The love of God, he said, "is a living spring, a spring that never fails,"[31] a bottomless ocean that

---

27 Edwards, *The "Blank Bible," Works*, 24:988.

28 Edwards, "True Grace, Distinguished from the Experience of Devils," *Works*, 25:620.

29 Edwards, *The "Blank Bible," Works*, 24:1024.

30 Edwards, "The Everlasting Love of God," *Works*, 19:477.

31 Edwards, "God's Care for His Servants in Time of Public Commotion," *Works*, 22:351.

knows no limit.[32] Moreover, because God's love is immutably connected to his very character, all that God ever says or does is
informed by his love. "God's acts which God hath done even from
eternity, have been acts of love. The things God hath done before
ever they had a being, have been acts of love; even the acts that have
been done in time, and in those acts that are in their own nature
eternal."[33] All acts of divine love are driven by God's love for himself,
the most lovely of all beings, such that he will never do anything that
violates his own righteousness, even if it were seemingly to serve to
benefit another.

God further magnifies the depth of his love in his objects of
love. While God loves all creation benevolently, sending rain on
the just and the unjust, being "kind to the unthankful and the
evil,"[34] he exercises a special love to the elect. They have been
loved from eternity past, before any acts of merit or demerit could
be done, based solely on God's own desires to communicate his
love to another.

> Now with regard to the first of the particulars mentioned
> above, viz. God's regard to the exercise and expression of
> those attributes of his nature, in their proper operations
> and effects, which consist in a sufficiency for these opera-
> tions, 'tis not hard to conceive that God's regard to himself,
> and value for his own perfections, should cause him to
> value those exercises and expressions of his perfections;
> and that a love to them will dispose him to love their exhi-
> bition and exertment: inasmuch as their excellency consists
> in their relation to use, exercise and operation; as the excel-
> lency of wisdom consists in its relation to, and sufficiency
> for, wise designs and effects. God's love to himself, and his

32 Edwards, "The Terms of Prayer," *Works*, 19:780.

33 Edwards, "The Everlasting Love of God," *Works*, 19:479.

34 Edwards, "Men's Addiction to Sin Is No Excuse, but an Aggravation," in *The
Puritan Pulpit*, ed. Don Kistler (Morgan, PA: Soli Deo Gloria, 2004), 70.

own attributes, will therefore make him delight in that which is the use, end and operation of these attributes.[35]

In other words, God loves the elect because he loves himself. To be true to himself, he must express himself. Thus, in eternity past, God chose some future sinners to be the special objects of his love—a love most profoundly expressed in the crucifixion of his Son.

Just as God revels in revealing his other attributes to his creation, he has shown his love, as well as his holiness and justice, most supremely in the gospel.

> This the gospel does, as it above all other things whatsoever exhibits to our view God's glorious beauty and love, in the contemplation of which our most perfect happiness of the soul consists. By the gospel we have by far the brightest and most excellent display of God's glory: the fullest discovery [of] all the perfections of God, and all discovered with the greatest advantage, especially on account of the union of diverse excellencies which appear in this display. Also by the gospel, God's love to us has [a] manifestation that is properly unparalleled: such discoveries of love could not have been conceived of, whether we consider [the] benefits granted or [the] means of procuring them.

God operates in this manner to show his greatness and to increase his renown.

> God's glory is manifested in a work of love to us, and a work of most transcendent love; and God's love appears in such a manner as to be consistent with the glory of all his perfections, and not only so, but so as exceedingly to manifest the glory of every perfection. Such an union

---

35 Edwards, *The End for Which God Created the World*, *Works*, 8:437.

does unspeakably heighten the sweetness and joy of the manifestation.[36]

That is to say, God has shown his love, as he does his other attributes, in the work of the cross to highlight the surpassing greatness of his majesty so that he might draw sinners to himself, who in return love him for who he is, not just for what he can do.

Being the subjects of God's love, the saints eternally enjoy the fruits of that love. God's love for himself, his desire for his own glory, has resulted in their election and their preservation. All that God has done, is doing, and will do for his children flows from that love, through its expression, back to God. "And therefore nothing that they need, nothing that they ask of God, nothing that their desires can extend themselves to, nothing that their capacity can contain, no good that can be enjoyed by them, is so great, so excellent that God begrutches it to them," Edwards reasoned.[37] God will never disappoint himself. That which leads his saints to glorify him, he will accomplish by further expressions of his love. He will respond in love out of love.

Thus, because of his moral attributes, his holiness, justice and love, the revelation of God's natural attributes, his knowledge and his sovereign acts, are never arbitrary or capricious. Instead, they are informed by, flow naturally from and display those moral qualities. "As God's perfections are things in themselves excellent, so the expression of them in their proper acts and fruits is excellent, and the knowledge of these excellent perfections, and of these glorious expressions of them, is an excellent thing, the existence of which is in itself valuable and desirable."[38] God has revealed himself in this way for he could not do otherwise. Therefore, the observation of God's natural attributes in response to prayer ought to instill faith, reverence and awe in the hearts and minds of his people.

---

36 Edwards, "Of Those Who Walk in the Light of God's Countenance," *Works*, 25:705. Note: "begrutches" is the Old English spelling of "begrudges."

37 Edwards, "The Terms of Prayer," *Works*, 19:781.

38 Edwards, *The End for Which God Created the World*, *Works*, 8:431.

THE ALL-KNOWING GOD

Edwards often referred to God's natural attributes as "God's natural perfections."[39] God's knowledge, one of those natural attributes that Edwards referred to, displays such perfection. God's wisdom is like his moral attributes, wrote Edwards, "unsearchable and boundless."[40] No limit can be found to God's knowledge because he is omniscient—he knows all things. This theological reality has a direct bearing upon one's theology of prayer. "The true God," Edwards preached, "perfectly knows the circumstances of everyone that prays to him throughout the world."[41]

If God knows all things, as Edwards held, his knowledge must be infinite. Preaching on Job 9:4, Edwards proclaimed,

> [God] sees all over this world: every man, woman, and child; every beast on earth, every bird in the air, [every] fish in the sea. There is not so much [as] a fly or worm or gnat [that is unknown to God]. [He] knows every tree, every leaf, every spire of grass; every drop of rain or dew; every single dust [mote] in the whole world. [God] sees in darkness [and] under ground. [A] thousand miles under ground [is] not hid [from his view]. [God] sees all that men [do] or say, sees their hearts [and] thoughts.
>
> [God] knows everything past, [even] things a thousand years ago. [He also knows] everything to come, [even] a thousand years to come. [He knows] all the men that will be, [and] all that they will do, say, or think.[42]

While the realization of the expansiveness of God's knowledge can be unsettling to the uninitiated, Edwards thought it to be a source of great comfort. The reality of God's omniscience calls one's

---

39 Edwards, *Religious Affections, Works*, 2:263.
40 Edwards, *Original Sin, Works*, 3:188.
41 Edwards, "The Most High a Prayer-Hearing God," *Works* (Hendrickson), 2:115.
42 Edwards, "God Is Infinitely Strong," *Works*, 25:643

attention to the fact that nothing escapes God's divine attention. Man's every need, heartache and desire, is known to God before a prayer is ever lifted up. In Edwards's words, "He knows what things we need before we ask him."[43]

Theologically speaking, the extent of God's omniscience is profound. Due to his very nature, God's knowledge of all things— past, present and future—must be perfect and free of error or even potential error. "All certain knowledge," Edwards wrote in *Freedom of the Will*, "proves the necessity of the truth known."[44] That is, that which God infallibly knows must necessarily be, for God can never be wrong.

Such a connection to things known applies to God's knowledge of the past, the present and the future. His knowledge is not bound by a linear understanding of time, each thing happening in succession, a parade of events that take place one after another, the future unknown until the present is past. Instead, God, according to Edwards, knows all things as though they are present realities. In the mind of God, the future is not unrealized potential waiting for its time to come but a present truth.

> And as he always sees things just as they are in truth; hence there never is in reality anything contingent in such a sense, as that possibly it may happen never to exist. If, strictly speaking, there is no foreknowledge in God, 'tis because those things which are future to us, are as present to God, as if they already had existence: ...future events are always in God's view as evident, clear, sure and necessary as it were.[45]

The instant that God knows something, regardless of when it may occur temporally, that thing already truly exists in the mind of God, for it flows logically from and to all other things that he knows.

43 Edwards, "The Most High a Prayer-Hearing God," *Works* (Hendrickson), 2:115.
44 Edwards, *Freedom of the Will, Works*, 1:266.
45 Edwards, *Freedom of the Will, Works*, 1:267.

The future is present to a God who knows all things completely and concurrently.

The conclusion of Edwards's rationale is unavoidable: "The connection which there is between God's knowledge and the event known, does as much prove the event to be necessary beforehand." That is, if God infallibly knows what is to come, it will certainly come. The outcome is a foregone conclusion not because of the steadfastness of the future moral agents involved but because of the steadfastness of God and the fact that in the mind of God such events have already taken place. Thus, in the future, as these events come to pass, there is no doubt in the mind of God that they will come to pass exactly as he has always known them to be. For God to be God, to be omniscient according to his moral attributes, he cannot be wrong. The future cannot be different than he has conceived in the past, "it is impossible that it should ever be otherwise."[46]

Finally, since "God made all things, he must see and know all things," Edwards told his congregation.[47] God's knowledge is perfect and all-inclusive. Rather than being an area of concern, Edwards thought, this theological premise ought to bolster the Christian's hope. The God who created all things knows all things and takes care of all things according to his good and wise plan—anything less and he would not be God.

THE ALL-POWERFUL GOD

Another of God's natural attributes, his omnipotence, or sovereignty, plays a major role in Edwards's theology of prayer as well.[48] "[God] can do what he will," he proclaimed before the people of Northampton.[49] Nothing can keep God from doing and accom-

---

46 Edwards, *Freedom of the Will, Works*, 1:267.

47 Edwards, "God Is Infinitely Strong," *Works*, 25:644.

48 Marsden in his biography of Edwards correctly diagnosed this key tenet of Edwards's theological constructs. "The central principle in Edwards' thought...was the sovereignty of God" (Marsden, *Jonathan Edwards: A Life*, 4).

49 Edwards, "God Is Infinitely Strong," *Works*, 25:644.

plishing whatever he desires as long as those desires do not violate his own character.

In 1750, Edwards called his congregation to return to the throne of God by way of prayer. In that sermon, "It Becomes Saints in Cases of Special Difficulty and Calamity of God's Church, to Betake Themselves in an Extraordinary Manner to Prayer to God," he called his people to expend themselves in a time of "extraordinary prayer." To encourage them in this spiritually arduous task, Edwards offered this hope: "God is omnipotent. With God nothing shall be impossible. He is a God that doth great things past finding out and wonders without number."[50] God is a God who hears prayer and God is a God who can answer prayer.

"The sovereignty of God is his ability and authority to do whatever pleases him," Edwards acknowledged in *Freedom of the Will*. In this rich theological treatise about the operations of the human will, he carefully sought to preserve and protect the sovereignty of God from the encroaching rationalism of those he called "Arminians." Typical of his desire to eliminate confusion and prevent his theological opponents from playing word games in their debates, Edwards carefully defined the nature and the extent of God's power. God's power, the ability to accomplish his desires, stands supreme. His power depends on no one and derives its strength from nothing external to himself. He is the source of all power. God's authority, likewise, reigns supreme. All other exercises of authority in the created universe flow from this divine fountainhead. The superlative "supreme" applies to God's will as well. It is "underived" and "independent." God's own desires, reflecting his purity of thought, direct the outworking of his will. Finally, God's wisdom stands supreme in the universe that he created, knows and reigns over.[51]

---

50 Edwards, "It Becomes Saints in Cases of Special Difficulty and Calamity of God's Church, to Betake Themselves in an Extraordinary Manner to Prayer to God" (1750), Beinecke Rare Book and Manuscript Library, Yale University, New Haven.

51 Edwards, *Freedom of the Will*, Works, 1:378–380.

Edwards drew a clear connection between God's moral perfections and the manifestation of his corresponding natural attributes. "'Tis the glory and greatness of the divine sovereignty," Edwards wrote, "that God's will is determined by his own infinite all-sufficient wisdom in everything."[52] This interaction between the attributes, Edwards maintained, flows logically from the very character of God.

> God is to be considered in this affair not merely as the governor of the world of creatures, to order all things between one creature and another, but as the supreme regulator or Rector of the universality of things, the orderer of things relating to the whole compass of existence, including himself, to maintain the rights of the whole, and decorum through the whole, and to maintain his own rights, and the due honor of his own perfections, as well as to keep justice among creatures. 'Tis fit that there should be one that has this office, and the office properly belongs to the supreme being. And if he should fail of doing justice to him[self] in a needed vindication of his own majesty and glory, it would be an immensely greater failure of his rectoral justice than if he should deprive the creatures, that are beings of infinitely less consequence, of their rights.[53]

Thus, God in all of his perfection operates according to those perfections. He is holy and just, working always to his own glory. To accomplish that purpose, God acts sovereignly over his creation, ensuring that everything happens according to his character and plan. If the exercise of his power and dominion were curtailed in any way, there would be no guarantee of success and no assurance of the rightness of the cause. In other words, he would be less than God.

---

52 Edwards, *Freedom of the Will*, Works, 1:380.
53 Edwards, "Miscellanies" No. 779, *Works*, 18:440.

Edwards recognized the sovereign hand of God at work all around him. He understood God to be operating in the manner he does so as to reveal his goodness and glorious majesty in every area of creation.

> There are many of the divine attributes that, if God had not created the world, never would have had any exercise: the power of God, the wisdom and prudence and contrivance of God, and the goodness and mercy and grace of God, and the justice of God. It is fit that the divine attributes should have exercise. Indeed God knew as perfectly, that there were these attributes fundamentally in himself before they were in exercise, as since; but God, as he delights in his own excellency and glorious perfections, so he delights in the exercise of those perfections.[54]

He admitted to the operation of God's sovereignty in the admittance of evil into the world, the subsequent fall of man, and the continued presence of sin in the world today for the ultimate purpose of showing God's greatness.

> But if by "the author of sin," is meant the permitter, or not a hinderer of sin; and at the same time, a disposer of the state of events, in such a manner, for wise, holy and most excellent ends and purposes, that sin, if it be permitted or not hindered, will most certainly and infallibly follow: I say, if this be all that is meant, by being the author of sin, I don't deny that God is the author of sin (though I dislike and reject the phrase, as that which by use and custom is

---

54 Edwards, "Miscellanies" No. 553, *Works*, 18:97. Here, too, the reader finds the perfections of God, his moral attributes, operant. God created the world for the purpose of revealing his goodness, to communicate himself, that he might be known and loved.

apt to carry another sense), it is no reproach for the most
High to be thus the author of sin.[55]

He observed it in God's merciful providence.[56]

> He hereby shows the sufficiency of his power to provide
> for all mankind all that they stand in need of. We may
> justly argue from the greatness of God's power appearing
> in providing those things that are for the support and
> comfort of our lives, that he is able to do everything that
> we need.[57]

Edwards embraced the righteousness of God's sovereignty in
salvation.

> If God deals most reasonably in choosing some and leaving
> others, then let God have the glory of his sovereignty in so
> doing. God herein doth gloriously manifest his sovereignty
> and supreme right to all his creatures, and 'tis manifested
> that we might glorify God for it, that we might adore him
> and fear him for his awful majesty.[58]

Thus, Edwards believed, God's sovereignty extends to every area of
his creation, the physical and the moral, because it magnifies God's
moral perfections at every level.

In case fallen humans should challenge the goodness of God's
sovereignty in disposing things absolutely according to his holy will
as informed by his perfect wisdom, Edwards readily offered an
answer to that challenge:

---

55 Edwards, *Freedom of the Will*, *Works*, 1:399.

56 Edwards, *The End for Which God Created the World*, *Works*, 8:508.

57 Edwards, "God's All-Sufficiency for the Supply of Our Wants," in *Sermons and Discourses, 1723–1729*, ed. Kenneth P. Minkema, *Works*, 14 (1997):474–475.

58 Edwards, "All God's Methods Are Most Reasonable," *Works*, 14:175.

God is by right, with respect to this sort of government, the sovereign ruler of the world, both by reason of his infinite greatness and excellency, by which he merits and deserves and is perfectly, and only, fit for it. He that is so excellent as to be infinitely worthy of the highest respect of the creature, he has thereby a right to that respect he deserves by a merit of condignity;[59] so that it would be injustice to deny it him. And he that is perfectly wise and true, and is only so, has a right in everything to be harkened to and to have his determinations attended and subject to.[60]

That is, by his very nature God, being of infinitely greater worth than the creature, must be sovereign and it is only proper and reasonable that such sovereignty should be expressed in his rule over the created universe in its entirety. Just as a fish must swim, a supreme God must reign supreme. Rather than rebelling against the sovereignty of God, created beings should assume and embrace it, glorifying God because of it.

Let us not therefore contend with the Almighty about this power of his, but rather fall down before his throne and acknowledge that "blessing, and honor, and glory, and power, belongs to him, that sitteth on the throne," as every creature in heaven and earth and hell will be made to acknowledge.[61]

In Edwards's estimation, God's knowledge and power stand without peer for God is without peer. His natural attributes are supreme and they are limitless because God is limitless in all of his perfection.

---

59 Theologically, "condignity" means that God deserves respect simply because he is God—it speaks to his intrinsic value and worth.

60 Edwards, "The Day of Judgment," *Works*, 14:512.

61 Edwards, "All God's Methods Are Most Reasonable," *Works*, 14:176.

There is only one true God, a God who is holy, just and loving. He is the God who reveals himself as both omniscient and omnipotent, guaranteeing that he will be glorified in his creation.

THE ALL–ENCOMPASSING GOD

Rather than being a cause for concern or theological strife, God's attributes, the moral and the natural, served as the basis of the hope Edwards put before his people. The God they needed, he explained, must be good, strong and steady. This God is without fault, perfect in character, and always motivated by what is good and fitting of a God like himself. The God to whom he pointed them is all-knowing, knowing the best way to accomplish his good and perfect will.[62] This God is also all-powerful and faithfully accomplishes all things according to his righteous will.[63] The most high God "will fulfill all his designs," Edwards cried out.[64]

To make his case, Edwards turned the Northampton church's attention from their temporal concerns to the eternal God's ever-abiding concern for their well-being. "The way of God's bringing things about in his providence is inscrutable," he noted in the pages of his "Blank Bible." "You can no more understand it than you can the cause and course of the wind and clouds."[65] Yet, Edwards believed it to be the duty of his people to humbly admit their daily dependence on God's gracious providence just as the Israelites did when they gathered their allotment of manna in the wilderness.[66] Apart from God's kind providence man has no hope of surviving.

Edwards believed that God's providential care was necessary and extended to the smallest of details, even the newly discovered

---

62 Edwards, "God Is Infinitely Strong," *Works*, 25:644.
63 Edwards, "God Is Infinitely Strong," *Works*, 25:644.
64 Edwards, "Approaching the End of God's Grand Design," Works, 25:122.
65 Edwards, The *"Blank Bible," Works*, 24:604.
66 Edwards, *Notes on Scripture*, ed. Stephen J. Stein, *Works*, 15 (1998):66–67.

atom.[67] All things, even the tiny atom, owe their existence to the preexistent God.

> That God does, by his immediate power, uphold every created substance in being, will be manifest, if we consider, that their present existence is a dependent existence, and therefore is an effect, and must have some cause: and the cause must be one of these two: either the antecedent existence of the same substance, or else the power of the Creator.[68]

As such, creation, and the providence that upholds it, gives irreproachable testimony to God's goodness and greatness. Without him the world would simply cease to be.

> It will follow from what has been observed [that all is upheld by God's sovereign power], that God's upholding created substance, or causing its existence in each successive moment, is altogether equivalent to an immediate production out of nothing, at each moment.[69]

Thus, in typical Edwards fashion, he described the necessity of God's providential care for his creation as something that must be ongoing. As such, creation itself is in effect re-created every moment.[70] Each successive moment requires and displays the same creative power that God exhibited in the beginning. Without God there would have been no creation *ex nihilo* and without God's ongoing, almighty superintendence, creation would return once

---

67 Edwards, "[Of Atoms]," in *Scientific and Philosophical Writings*, ed. Wallace E. Anderson, *Works*, 6 (1980):214.

68 Edwards, *Original Sin*, *Works*, 3:400.

69 Edwards, *Original Sin*, *Works*, 3:402. See also, "Of Being," *Works*, 6:204; and, "Miscellanies" No. 18, *Works*, 13:310.

70 Edwards, "Miscellanies" No. 346, *Works*, 13:418.

again *ad nihilo*. "As [providence] begins in God, so it ends in God."[71]

Just as Edwards saw the goodness of God's wisdom and might in creation, he observed it in the new creation. God works in the creation for one purpose, he wrote in his "Miscellanies," the redemption of his elect.[72] "And that work of God's providence to which all other works of providence," he noted elsewhere, "both in the material and the immaterial part of the creation, are subservient, is the work of redemption."[73] Thus, salvation as the great aim of providence stands as the supreme display of God's goodness to his ultimate glory.[74]

Salvation begins and ends according to the all-knowing desire of God as he, and he alone, accomplishes what he has decreed. To his former church, years after leaving Northampton, Edwards wrote,

> Sinners who are seeking converting grace, should be thoroughly sensible of God's being under no manner of obligation, from any desires, labors, or endeavors of theirs, to bestow grace upon them; ...God is perfectly at liberty, whether to show them any mercy, or not; that they are wholly in the hands of God's sovereignty.[75]

To his own fourteen-year-old son, ill and away from home, Edwards would write,

> Neither is God the more obliged to bestow [salvation] upon you, for your standing in necessity of it, your earnest desiring of it, your crying to him constantly for it, from fear of misery, and taking much pains. Till you have savingly

---

71 Edwards, *A History of the Work of Redemption*, ed. John F. Wilson, *Works*, 9 (1989):517.

72 Edwards, "Miscellanies" No. 702, *Works*, 18:296.

73 Edwards, "Miscellanies" No. 702, *Works*, 18:284.

74 Edwards, *An Humble Attempt*, in *Apocalyptic Writings*, ed. Stephen J. Stein, *Works*, 5 (1977):353.

75 Edwards, Letter "To the First Church of Christ, Northampton," *Works*, 16:482.

believed in Christ, all your desires, and pains, and prayers lay God under no obligation; and if they were ten thousand times as great as they are, you must still know, that you would be in the hands of a sovereign God, who hath mercy on whom he will have mercy.[76]

Whether one seeks the salvation of one or many, God's sovereign will reigns. Salvation accomplished according to God's sovereignty serves one great end, Edwards related: "What God aims at in the disposition of things in the affair of redemption, viz. that man should not glory in himself, but alone in God."[77]

In the same way, Edwards found prayer related to God's divine perfections. Since God desires to be glorified according to the operation of his sovereignty in the salvation of unworthy creatures, Edwards called his church, and all of New England, to pray for that glorious cause. "There is no other way that Christians…can do so much to promote the work of God, and advance the kingdom of Christ," he told his reading audience, "as by prayer."[78] Trying to sustain the fires of revival both in the colonies and in Scotland, Edwards later wrote,

> Such being the state of things in this future promised glorious day of the church's prosperity, surely 'tis worth praying for. Nor is there any one thing whatsoever, if we viewed things aright, which a regard to the glory of God, a concern for the kingdom and honor of our Redeemer, a love to his people, pity to perishing sinners, love to our fellow creatures in general, compassion to mankind under its various and sore calamities and miseries, a desire for their temporal and spiritual prosperity, love to our country, our neighbors

---

76 Edwards, Letter "To Timothy Edwards," *Works*, 16:579.

77 Edwards, "God Glorified in Man's Dependence," *Works*, 17:200.

78 Edwards, *Some Thoughts Concerning the Revival*, in *The Great Awakening*, ed. C.C. Goen, *Works*, 4 (1972):518.

and friends, yea, and to our own souls, would dispose us to
be so much in prayer for, as the dawning of this happy day,
and the accomplishment of that glorious event.[79]

Christians are to apply themselves to prayer for the lost for the good
of the lost and, more importantly, for the glory of God to be displayed in his sovereign grace over against the sinful pride of man.

> But it appears to me that the great God has wrought like
> himself, in the manner of his carrying on this work [of
> revival]; so as very much to show his own glory, and exalt
> his own sovereignty, power and all-sufficiency, and pour
> contempt on all that human strength, wisdom, prudence
> and sufficiency, that men have been wont to trust, and to
> glory in; and so as greatly to cross, rebuke and chastise the
> pride and other corruptions of men.[80]

From providence to salvation, God directs the course of history
to reveal his goodness in so construing things, his wisdom in so
determining things, and his might in so consummating things that
the world may come to know and glory in him.

SUMMARY

In keeping with his Puritan forebears, Edwards was convinced of
the thoroughly awesome character of God, his perfection in all of
his attributes. Of his moral attributes, Edwards held that God could
be and do nothing other than what accords with perfect holiness,
justice and love, to the glory of his great name. Of his natural
attributes, Edwards believed in and preached a God who is all-
knowing. This conviction led to the next: God must also be all-
powerful and able to accomplish all that he purposes according to
his irreproachable will. As Edwards saw it, "God is a Being of infinite

---

79 Edwards, *An Humble Attempt, Works*, 5:340–341.
80 Edwards, *Some Thoughts Concerning the Revival, Works*, 4:294.

greatness, of boundless might and wisdom."[81]

Yet, this God, the Creator, who is infinitely greater than the creation, has not abandoned it. He sovereignly rules over it, graciously providing the daily needs of those who depend upon him. Amazingly, this very God has "promised to hear the prayers of his people."[82] In fact, said Edwards, he invites, even encourages, the prayers of his people.[83] Why?

It is not in order that God may be informed of our wants or desires. He is omniscient, and with respect to his knowledge unchangeable. God never gains any knowledge by information. He knows what we want, a thousand times more perfectly than we do ourselves, before we ask him. ... yet it is not to be thought that God is properly moved or made willing by our prayers; for it is no more possible that there should be any new inclination or will in God, than new knowledge. The mercy of God is not moved or drawn by any thing in the creature; but the spring of God's beneficence is within himself only; he is self-moved; and whatsoever mercy he bestows, the reason and the ground of it is not to be sought for in the creature, but in God's own pleasure.[84]

The wise and mighty God who hears prayer can answer prayer because he has determined the end from the beginning and he has determined to bring it about according to his eternal perfections for his own glory. "It is the will of God to bestow mercy in this way, viz. in answer to prayer, when he designs beforehand to bestow mercy."[85]

---

81 Edwards, "All God's Methods Are Most Reasonable," *Works*, 14:188.

82 Edwards, "The Duties of Christians in a Time of War," *Works*, 25:136.

83 Edwards, "The Most High a Prayer-Hearing God," *Works* (Hendrickson), 2:114.

84 Edwards, "The Most High a Prayer-Hearing God," *Works* (Hendrickson), 2:116–117.

85 Edwards, "The Most High a Prayer-Hearing God," *Works* (Hendrickson), 2:117.

Does God answer prayer?

Again, God manifests his acceptance of their prayers, by
doing for them agreeably to their needs and supplications.[86]

Edwards realized that the fact that God hears the prayers of his
people was not sufficient to motivate them to place their faith in
him via their prayers. His people needed more encouragement than
just the affirmation that God is listening. They needed hope. This
hope Edwards offered when he assured them that not only does
God hear prayers, he answers them.

In "The Terms of Prayer," Edwards argued that "God never
begrutches his people anything they desire, or are capable of, as
being too good for 'em."[87] God "stands ready" to answer their
prayers and longs for them to humbly come to him and acknowledge their dependence on him. "God is as ready, and more ready,
to bestow than we are to ask," he noted, "and more ready to open
than we are to knock."[88] Plus, the answering of prayer delights God.
The greater the need, the more earnest the request, the greater is
God's pleasure when he answers the prayers of his people.[89]

So, in a word, "yes," God does answer prayer. Moreover, he does
so with abundant joy and goodness. Edwards's sermons and writings are peppered with myriad reasons why God answers prayer.
For the sake of this study, two such reasons will be explored, as
well as the manner that God answers prayer.

THE GOODNESS OF GOD

As Edwards related, "He knows how to do everything the best way."[90]

---

86 Edwards, "The Most High a Prayer-Hearing God," *Works* (Hendrickson), 2:114.
87 Edwards, "The Terms of Prayer," *Works*, 19:772.
88 Edwards, "The Terms of Prayer," *Works*, 19:783.
89 Edwards, "The Terms of Prayer," *Works*, 19:785.
90 Edwards, "God Is Infinitely Strong," *Works*, 25:644.

Any answer to prayer that God may give will be related to his goodness and humanity's good. As such, God's every answer to prayer must be good in and of itself.

Two very similar sermons on prayer address the goodness of God in relationship to answered prayer, "The Most High a Prayer-Hearing God" and "The Terms of Prayer." Though God is infinitely greater than his creation, Edwards said in the first, "He is graciously pleased to take a merciful notice of poor worms of the dust."[91] God reveals his goodness, his grace, in his willingness to hear the prayers of sinful men and women. He gives them "free access," allowing them entrance into the very throne room of grace.[92] There he listens to the petitions of his people most readily.[93] More than that, God extends his grace to them even while they are in the act of praying, revealing his perfections in all their manifold glory:

> While they are praying, he gives them sweet views of his glorious grace, purity, sufficiency, and sovereignty; and enables them, with great quietness, to rest in him, to leave themselves and their prayers with him, submitting to his will, and trusting in his grace and faithfulness.[94]

Further, God answers *readily*, sometimes while the prayer still prays.[95] These answers, Edwards contended, are given liberally and without condemnation: "[God] is plenteous and rich in his communications to those who call on him," often giving more than was asked.[96] Why does God do it? "Because God delights in mercy and condescension."[97] Why? Because he is merciful.

---

91 Edwards, "The Terms of Prayer," *Works*, 19:114.
92 Edwards, "The Terms of Prayer," *Works*, 19:114.
93 Edwards, "The Terms of Prayer," *Works*, 19:114.
94 Edwards, "The Terms of Prayer," *Works*, 19:114.
95 Edwards, "The Terms of Prayer," *Works*, 19:114.
96 Edwards, "The Terms of Prayer," *Works*, 19:114–115.
97 Edwards, "The Terms of Prayer," *Works*, 19:116. Edwards noted in another sermon this same gracious tendency in the character of God. "God delights in the

In the second of these sermons, "The Terms of Prayer," Edwards further expands upon the idea of God's grace. "God stands ready to fulfill all their petitions," he proffered.[98] Pointing to Romans 9:23 and Ephesians 1:5–7, Edwards argued that God does so to highlight the infinitude of his grace.[99] "God's goodness is without bounds," he added.[100] If only people would truly understand the gospel, they would grasp the goodness of the God who awaits their prayers.

> 'Tis true those things are too good and too great for them
> to deserve, but not too great for the grace of God to bestow
> on those that are so undeserving. Their meanness and un-
> worthiness can be no impediment to him whose declared
> design it is to magnify his free grace, by doing great things
> for the mean and unworthy. A sufficient acquaintance
> with the gospel, where this design of God is revealed,
> would remove all such objections.[101]

To display his goodness once more to an unworthy people, to highlight the depth of his grace and the greatness of his mercy, "God stands ready to fulfill all their petitions in anything that they ask that is for their good,"[102] the good which he alone determines according to his own good and wise plans.

THE PURPOSES OF GOD
The wisdom of God, as revealed in the manifest goodness of God,

---

welfare and prosperity of his creatures; he delights in making of them exceeding happy and blessed, if they will but accept of the happiness he offers" (Edwards, "God's Excellencies," *Works*, 10:424).

98 Edwards, "The Terms of Prayer," *Works*, 19:783.

99 Edwards, "The Terms of Prayer," *Works*, 19:776. Or, as he stated in a different sermon, "God often manifests in his Word that his delight is showing mercy, and not exercising judgment towards his people" (Edwards, "Undeserved Mercy," *Works*, 19:639).

100 Edwards, "The Terms of Prayer," *Works*, 19:780.

101 Edwards, "The Terms of Prayer," *Works*, 19:782–783.

102 Edwards, "The Terms of Prayer," *Works*, 19:782–783.

Edwards linked inextricably to the sovereignty of God. "They reflect glory one on the other," he declared, "and 'tis the glory of God that those attributes should always be exercised and expressed in a consistence and harmony one with the other."[103] Mercy and majesty, Edwards believed, go hand in hand. God answers prayer according to his good pleasure, moved by nothing more than his own sovereign desires which are necessarily good because God is good.

> Though there be no goodness in natural men's earnestly praying, yet 'tis their best way to pray, because 'tis the way that God has appointed for them to find mercy in. God is sovereign. He may bestow mercy upon men in what way he pleases and he has, in wisdom, seen cause to appoint this: that men should wait for mercy in this way.[104]

In case someone should suggest that what brings God pleasure is anything less than holy, Edwards reminded his hearers that God can do no wrong.[105] Finally, as with all things in Edwards's theology, God answers prayer to bring himself glory.

> God's end in the creation of the world consists in these two things, viz. to communicate himself and to glorify himself. God created the world to communicate himself, not to receive anything. But such was the infinite goodness of God that it was his will to communicate himself, to communicate of his own glory and happiness; and he made the world to glorify himself, [as it is] fit that God should glorify himself.[106]

---

103   Edwards, "God Makes Men Sensible of Their Misery," *Works*, 17:159.

104   Edwards, "There Is No Goodness in Praying, Though It Be Never So Earnestly, Merely Out of Fear of Misery" (1728), Beinecke Rare Book and Manuscript Library, Yale University, New Haven.

105   Edwards, "All God's Methods Are Most Reasonable," *Works*, 14:194.

106   Edwards, "Approaching the End of God's Grand Design," *Works*, 25:116.

God most commonly communicates himself, that is, reveals himself, and answers prayer through his providential care of the universe. Providence, Edwards contended, is a public display of God's perfection in all his glory.

> He thereby shows the sufficiency of his power to provide for mankind all that they stand in need of. We may justly argue from the greatness of God's power appearing in providing those things that are for the support and comfort of our lives, that he is able to do everything that we need. His power in those things appears plainly infinite.
>
> He shows his infinite power in creating those things which subserve to our necessity and delight....
>
> He shows his almighty strength in forming and fixing those vast globes over our heads....
>
> And God shows that nothing is too hard for him to do for us by the strength [of his arm] in so ordering, moving and directing those things so as to make them administer to our good, particularly in moving and managing the heavenly bodies so that they may be under advantages in the best manner to diffuse their light and heat all over the face of the earth.[107]

Thus, in the greatness of his sovereignty, God provides for the meanest of man's needs.

Edwards connected providence to answered prayer as well. "God manifests his acceptance of their prayers, by doing for them agreeably to their needs and supplications," outwardly displaying his mercy in the workings of providence. There is "an agreeableness between [God's] providence and [man's] prayers," he said.[108] Every prayer need not be answered supernaturally. Instead, God often provides

---

107 Edwards, "God's All-Sufficiency," *Works*, 14:474–475.
108 Edwards, "The Most High a Prayer-Hearing God," *Works* (Hendrickson), 2:114.

the answers to prayer by way of providence. Prayers in a time of drought are answered with rain. Prayers for healing find God's response in the provision of medicine. In this way, God provides answers to many prayers, answers that may go unnoticed by those expecting divine intervention of a more mysterious nature. Regardless of man's expectations of the miraculous, he is in no position to challenge the goodness of God's sovereign will, questioning God's answering prayer via common grace or providence. God has determined beforehand to respond to prayer in this fashion. It is in vain that one should seek otherwise.[109] Since man cannot alter the appointment of God's providential answers to prayer, he should "consider their nature, and accommodate [him]self to 'em."[110] Moreover, "Seeing you can't bring events to your spirit, bring your spirit to events on a thorough weighing of those events, that you may rightly discern their nature and aspect."[111] In other words, one should look for, recognize and rejoice at the kind hand of God as he works in creation through providence.[112]

The manner that God operates providentially, answering prayer through the common things of life, adheres to Edwards's understanding of the use of means. God uses various things, means, to accomplish his will. The preaching of the gospel is a means appointed by God to be used of the Spirit to bring about the salvation of men. God ordains the attending of weekly worship services as a

---

109   Edwards, *The "Blank Bible," Works*, 24:586–587.

110   Edwards, *The "Blank Bible," Works*, 24:594.

111   Edwards, *The "Blank Bible," Works*, 24:584.

112   Providence, said Edwards, is best pictured as a wheel. Like a wheel, all things revolve around a central point, the hub. At the centre, turning the wheel via providence, is God (Edwards, *Notes on Scripture, Works*, 15:373–379). God does this for a good reason. "The revolutions by which God's great design is brought to pass are doubtless chiefly revolutions among them, and that concern their state and not the state of things without life or reason. And therefore surely 'tis requisite that they should know something of it; especially seeing that reason teaches that God has given his rational creatures reason and a capacity of seeing God in his works for this, that he may see God's glory in them and give him the glory of them" (Edwards, *A History of the Work of Redemption, Works*, 9:521).

means of preparing the soul for hearing and responding to the gospel message. If the sinner does not take advantage of these means, he will not hear the sermon explaining his condition nor will he have the opportunity to respond to the gospel call as offered by the preacher. In the same way, prayer has been determined by God to be the means whereby he providentially provides for man's needs. Moreover, it is not that God needs these things to accomplish his will but that he calls for them that they might be used to direct the attention of the believer to the God who requires them.

God has also appointed prayer as the means by which he will accomplish the supernatural as well, whether the salvation of the saints or delaying the judgement of the damned. God has decreed that he will save souls, individually and en masse, and that he will do so only in a visible response to the prayers of people.

> So [it] is God's will, through his wonderful grace, that the prayers of his saints should be one great and principal means of carrying on the designs of Christ's kingdom in the world. When God has something very great to accomplish for his church, 'tis his will that there should precede it the extraordinary prayers of his people.[113]

In response to the decline in the awakenings experienced in Northampton, Edwards called his people to renewed vigour in praying for revival. "God seems now, at this very time, to be waiting for this from us."[114] Continuing, he added, "There is no way that Christians in a private capacity can do so much to promote the work of God, and advance the kingdom of Christ, as by prayer."[115] Thus, God has determined not only what will happen, but when and how it will happen, using the prayers of his people as the means to his righteous purposes, revealing both his sovereignty and his glory in the process.

---

113 Edwards, *Some Thoughts Concerning the Revival, Works*, 4:516.
114 Edwards, *Some Thoughts Concerning the Revival, Works*, 4:517.
115 Edwards, *Some Thoughts Concerning the Revival, Works*, 4:518.

GOD'S WAY OF ANSWERING PRAYER

Edwards knew that speaking of how God answers prayer might appear to be in direct contradiction to his conviction concerning God's transcendent sovereignty. If God needs no new information, has already determined the course of history and will unfailingly accomplish his goals, how can it legitimately be said that God answers the prayers of his people? Edwards foresaw this objection and had an answer:

> For though, speaking after the manner of men, God is sometimes presented *as if* he were moved and persuaded by the prayers of his people; yet it is not to be thought that God is properly moved or made willing by our prayers; for it is no more possible that there should be any new inclination or will in God, than new knowledge. The mercy of God is not moved or drawn by any thing in the creature; but the spring of God's beneficence is within himself only; he is self-moved; and whatsoever mercy he bestows, the reason and ground of it is not to be sought for in the creature, but in God's own good pleasure. It is the will of God to bestow mercy in this way, viz. in answer to prayer, when he designs beforehand to bestow mercy [emphasis mine].[116]

The key to Edwards's answer lies in the words "as if." From man's perspective, it appears that God has been overcome by his prayers. God operates in this manner, Edwards maintained, as yet another act of grace, thereby encouraging man to come boldly to him.[117]

---

116 Edwards, "The Most High a Prayer-Hearing God," *Works* (Hendrickson), 2:116–117.

117 In *An Humble Attempt*, Edwards wrote, "God, in wonderful grace, is pleased to represent himself as it were at the command of his people, with regard to mercies of this nature, so as to be ready to bestow them whenever they shall earnestly pray for them" (Edwards, *An Humble Attempt*, *Works*, 5:353).

Edwards pointed to Scripture to justify his use of language like "as if" and "as though" for the purpose of encouragement. Jacob's wrestling with and his apparent

From God's perspective, however, the prayers of men are ultimately lifted up in response to his sovereign will. "When the people of God are stirred up to prayer," he continued, "it is the effect of [God's] intention to show mercy."[118] They pray not to bring about God's grace but because God has already determined to reveal it. Thus, while God has determined the course of events, he has done so in such a way that both the prayers of volitional agents and his answers to them are part of his larger, predetermined plan for history.

In so arguing, Edwards preserved the theocentric character of his theology of prayer. Yet, he did not miss the potential implications of such a high view of God's wisdom and power and the illusory nature of his "as if" language. If God already knows all things, and such knowledge provides the absolute certainty of all things according to his will, why pray at all? Or, if God isn't really answering man's prayers according to the prayer but according to his own will, what purpose does prayer really serve? To these questions Edwards would answer, "There may be two reasons given why God requires prayer in order to the bestowment of mercy":

1. With respect to God, prayer is but a sensible acknowledgment of our dependence on him to his glory....
2. With respect to ourselves, God requires prayer of us in order to the bestowment of mercy, because it tends to prepare us for its reception.[119]

---

overcoming of God, Edwards said, was not to belittle the power of God but to put in human terms the greatness of Jacob before his people (Genesis 32:28). Likewise, Moses' intervention on behalf of Israel at the foot of Mount Sinai was not intended to show the power of Moses nor the passability of God but his grace in staying the hand of punishment due at the behest of his divinely-appointed mediator (Exodus 32:9f.) [Edwards, "The Most High a Prayer-Hearing God," *Works* (Hendrickson), 2:115].

118 Edwards, "The Most High a Prayer-Hearing God," *Works* (Hendrickson), 2:116.

119 Edwards, "The Most High a Prayer-Hearing God," *Works* (Hendrickson), 2:116.

God requires prayer because it displays his sovereignty. Given that God is concerned for his glory, he has so constructed the universe and its operation that he is to be given glory by the creature in all things. Prayer forces fallen man to see his failings and consider the exalted position of God.

> This is God's ordinary manner before any great and signal expression of his mercy and favor. He very commonly so orders it in his providence and so influences men by his Spirit, that they are brought to see their miserable condition as they are in themselves, and to despair of help from themselves or from an arm of flesh, before he appears for them, and also makes them sensible of their sin and unworthiness of God's help.[120]

Prayer brings the individual praying to humble himself and approach God with an attitude of complete submission. Prayer "is but a suitable acknowledgment of our dependence on the power and mercy of God for that which we need," Edwards said.[121] It is the "proper honour done to God, a suitable acknowledgment of God's perfection [and] a proper expression of a sense of our Emptiness."[122] Connected to the humility that an individual must display before God is the conviction of man's sinfulness.

> Earnest and constant prayer to God is one great means by which God carries on a conviction of sin and makes man sensible [of] what they are, whereby he humbles and abases them before him. They think ignorantly who think that it is

---

120   Edwards, "God Makes Men Sensible of Their Misery," *Works*, 17:143.

121   Edwards, "The Most High a Prayer-Hearing God," *Works* (Hendrickson), 2:116.

122   Edwards, "It Becomes Saints in Cases of Special Difficulty and Calamity of God's Church, to Betake Themselves in an Extraordinary Manner to Prayer to God" (1750), manuscript.

not worth the while for them to pray, for this is a principal means to prepare their hearts for the mercies they seek.[123]

Such importance does Edwards place on the abasement of man in light of God's glory that he urged his congregation to beg for it from the hand of God.[124] In true prayer—prayer that pleases God—man admits that God is God and he is not.

God also requires prayer because it prepares men to accept his sovereignty and enjoy his mercy. Prayer prepares the heart for both the encounter with and the blessings of God, Edwards proclaimed. Edwards spent a great deal of time working out the implications of the preparatory nature of prayer. In "The Most High a Prayer-Hearing God," Edwards gave more attention to this aspect of prayer than to its humbling effect. He presented his congregation with six ways in which prayer prepares the heart to accept and enjoy God's sovereignty: (1) Prayer highlights the greatness of man's needs and the mercy being sought; (2) Prayer increases one's desires for that mercy; (3) Prayer prepares the mind "to prize it, to rejoice in it" and to be "thankful for it" when bestowed; (4) Prayer reminds man of his unworthiness to receive the mercy sought; (5) Prayer places man in the immediate presence of God, revealing his majesty; and (6) Prayer is used by God to "excite in us a suitable sense and consideration of our dependence on God for the mercy we ask, and a suitable exercise of faith in God's sufficiency." All this, Edwards said, prepares the individual praying "to glorify [God's] name when the mercy is received."[125]

Two months after preaching "The Most High a Prayer-Hearing God" in January 1735, Edwards devoted another sermon, "God's

123 Edwards, "God's Manner is First to Prepare Men's Hearts and Then to Answer Their Prayers," in ed. McMullen, *The Glory and Honor of God*, 94.

124 Edwards, "It Becomes Saints in Cases of Special Difficulty and Calamity of God's Church, to Betake Themselves in an Extraordinary Manner to Prayer to God" (1750), manuscript.

125 Edwards, "The Most High a Prayer-Hearing God," *Works* (Hendrickson), 2:116.

Manner Is First to Prepare Men's Hearts and Then to Answer Their Prayers," solely to prayer's preparatory role. "God's manner is first to prepare men's hearts and then to answer their prayers." In this sermon, Edwards explained four more ways that prayer prepares the heart. First, prayer prepares the individual to enjoy the mercy sought when it is bestowed. "They are not capable of tasting the sweetness of and reaping the benefit of [the mercy given] unless God first makes an alteration in them to prepare them for it." Prayer is the means by which God makes that alteration.[126] Second, prayer readies the individual to acknowledge God's hand in the answer of their prayers.[127] Third, prayer guides the individual to acknowledge God's sovereignty in the answering of prayer.[128] And, finally, prayer prepares the person to make good use of the mercy given. "What God gives is not only for our enjoyment but for our improvement."[129] God uses prayer as a preparation of the heart, Edwards explained, "to secure his own glory and to promote their good."[130]

Implicit in Edwards's preaching is another reason why God requires prayer: God, according to his absolute sovereignty, has ordained that prayer will precede the exercise of that sovereignty. Prayer serves as the means to God's ends, the bestowment of his mercy. "God has been pleased to constitute prayer to be antecedent to the bestowment of mercy; and he is pleased to bestow mercy in consequence of prayer, as though he were prevailed upon by prayer."[131] God has ordained prayer as the antecedent to his blessings. "For though God has

---

126   Edwards, "God's Manner is First to Prepare Men's Hearts and Then to Answer Their Prayers," in ed. McMullen, *The Glory and Honor of God*, 79–81.

127   Edwards, "God's Manner is First to Prepare Men's Hearts and Then to Answer Their Prayers," in ed. McMullen, *The Glory and Honor of God*, 81–82.

128   Edwards, "God's Manner is First to Prepare Men's Hearts and Then to Answer Their Prayers," in ed. McMullen, *The Glory and Honor of God*, 82.

129   Edwards, "God's Manner is First to Prepare Men's Hearts and Then to Answer Their Prayers," in ed. McMullen, *The Glory and Honor of God*, 82.

130   Edwards, "God's Manner is First to Prepare Men's Hearts and Then to Answer Their Prayers," in ed. McMullen, *The Glory and Honor of God*, 84.

131   Edwards, "God's Manner is First to Prepare Men's Hearts and Then to Answer Their Prayers," in ed. McMullen, *The Glory and Honor of God*, 86.

appointed the time for these things in his own counsels, yet he will be enquired of for them before he accomplishes them."[132]

Even God's determination to use prayer as a means to his ends benefits man and serves the purposes outlined by Edwards. As Stephen Nichols helpfully explained, "God ordains the end or the results, and he ordains the means. Prayer is a God-ordained means to carrying out his will. Although this humbles us, God ordains the means of the prayers of his people in the carrying out of his will."[133] Thus, the union of prayer, preparation, and providence answers the challenge of Edwards's critics: Why pray when God has already decided the outcome? Christians are not to pray hoping to change the perfect God. Christians are to pray because prayer changes them.

> They should see themselves not only to pray for the mercy but also to seek to be prepared for it and therefore should first examine themselves [as to] what they need to fit them for it and should seek that they may be more humbled. Sense of unworthiness. Repentance. Contrition. Dependence on God. That they may have an holy appetite after a sense of the excellencies of those spiritual mercies they seek. The sweetness and the happiness. And that they seek divine love actively, they have a disposition to give God the glory, to be ready to bless his mercy and to improve to his glory.

Prayer is "one of the greatest duties of religion" because prayer glorifies God.[134]

---

132 Edwards, "Value of Salvation," *Works*, 10:336.

133 Stephen J. Nichols, *Jonathan Edwards: A Guided Tour of His Life and Thought* (Phillipsburg, NJ: Presbyterian & Reformed, 2001), 210. Michael Haykin has interpreted the sermonic evidence in the same manner: "Prayer is also designed to put those who pray in a proper frame of mind and heart to receive answers to their requests. Prayer changes those who pray, preparing them to be the sort of people through whom God can work" (Michael A.G. Haykin, *Jonathan Edwards: The Holy Spirit in revival* [Webster, NY: Evangelical Press, 2005], 139).

134 Edwards, "God's Manner is First to Prepare Men's Hearts and Then to Answer Their Prayers," in ed. McMullen, *The Glory and Honor of God*, 89.

SUMMARY

So, in the end, Edwards readily acknowledged that God does answer prayer. God's ability to answer prayer, Edwards taught, arises properly out of God's good desire to answer prayers according to his holy purposes. That is, God in his sovereignty has determined that the accomplishment of his wise will shall occur according to his wise plans using prayer as a means to those ends. Thus, he argued, God awaits the cries of his people and then responds mightily with lovingkindness. Edwards spoke of God being "overcome" and "conquered" by prayer, describing God's answering prayer in anthropomorphic terms, the language of the "as if," language he understood to be true to the Bible, that he might encourage his congregation not to begrudge God's sovereignty but to accept it and submit themselves prayerfully to it.

The problem of unanswered prayer

> It is no argument, that God is not a prayer-hearing God,
> if he give not to men what they ask of him to consume
> their lusts.[135]

Edwards placed his undying faith in the knowledge that God hears the prayers of his people. God always hears the prayer of faith, he taught his people. He revelled in the fact that God even answers the prayers of his people often beyond the measure of the request itself. He readily acknowledged, however, that God does not always answer. That hard lesson he learned as he repeatedly prayerfully sought deliverance from turmoil in both Northampton and Stockbridge. Nonetheless, the reality of unanswered prayer did not shake Edwards's faith. Instead, he argued, God's refusal to answer serves as further proof of God's goodness and greatness.

---

135   Edwards, "The Most High a Prayer-Hearing God," *Works* (Hendrickson), 2:117.

In his many sermons on prayer, Edwards often answered the unspoken but ever-present rhetorical question: Why does God not answer my prayers? To respond, Edwards leaned upon his understanding of God's character. There he found great solace in the goodness of God as he exercises his omniscience and omnipotence, displaying those great attributes in his dealings with fallen men, in prayers both answered and unanswered.

GOD'S OMNISCIENCE

The first reason given by Edwards as to why God does not answer prayer is the greatness of God's knowledge. God possesses a perfect knowledge of all things. Rather than allowing the profundity of that theological premise to unsettle his faith, Edwards saw God's omniscience as foundational for the faith exercised in prayer. It is to the God who knows all that the believer lifts his voice. "The business of prayer is not to direct God, who is infinitely wise, and needs not any of our directions; who knows what is best for us ten thousand times better than we, and knows what time and what way are best," he explained. "It is fit that he should answer prayer, and, as an infinitely wise God, in the exercise of his own wisdom, and not ours."[136] Or, as he stated elsewhere, even when God appears to respond to man's pleas,

> 'Tis not intended [when God appears to respond to man's present situations] that God takes up any purpose or resolution in time that he did not purpose from all eternity: God is an unchangeable being... And therefore there can be nothing new in God, and so no new purpose. 'Tis not with God as 'tis with men, who alter their purposes, and come to new resolves upon occasion. This cannot be, because [God] knows all things from all eternity.[137]

---

136 Edwards, "The Most High a Prayer-Hearing God," *Works* (Hendrickson), 2:117.

137 Edwards, "The Dreadful Silence of the Lord," *Works*, 19:114.

God's wisdom, his infinite knowledge, gives the one who prays the grand hope that God's answers, or lack thereof, will be guided by his holy, immutable goodness and his eternal knowledge of all things, past, present and future, not man's temporal desires. Because God knows all things and because God orders all things, Edwards said, he and he alone knows his plan for mankind. Thus, sometimes the prayers placed before the throne of God go unanswered for no other reason than that the timing of the request fails to coincide with the timing of God's plan.

When God defers for the present to answer the prayer of faith, it is not from any backwardness to answer, but for the good of his people sometimes, that they may be better prepared for the mercy before they receive it, or because another time would be the best and fittest on some other account.[138]

God knows what is best. Moreover, his infinite goodness predisposes him to answer prayers, whether in the positive or the negative, according to that which is good for both God and man in accordance with his perfect plan. Thus, the thing requested has not fallen on deaf ears but on benevolent and patient ears.

It is no argument that he is not a prayer-hearing God, that he exercises his own wisdom as to the time and manner of answering prayer. Some of God's people are sometimes ready to think, that he doth not hear their prayers, because he doth not answer them at the times when they expected; when indeed God doth hear them, and will answer them, in the time and way to which his own wisdom directs.[139]

---

138 Edwards, "The Most High a Prayer-Hearing God," *Works* (Hendrickson), 2:114.

139 Edwards, "The Most High a Prayer-Hearing God," *Works* (Hendrickson), 2:117.

In so operating, God actually causes all things, including prayers and answers, to work together for the good of those who love him.

In pointing to God's knowledge and the timing of his answers, Edwards counselled his congregation to exercise patience. The lack of an answer in the present does not necessarily mean that God will not answer in the future. Instead, he urged them, learn from the process of waiting and build your faith.

> That you don't know that God will never bestow it. 'Tis no argument that God is unwilling to bestow this mercy on you as too good for you, because he don't bestow it in your time. He may bestow it in his own time, and it may be most for his glory, and also best for you. For ought you know, the dispensation you are now under, though very sorrowful for the present, may in the end be for your humbling, and be more abundantly fitted for comfort, and fitted for greater comfort; so that spiritual comfort may be both sweeter and more profitable.

In this way, Edwards married faith and prayer so as to accomplish the ends discussed above: the preparation of God's saints for greater things. While causing the believer to wait, God prepares him to receive the blessing sought and nourishes a faith that as yet may be too little or too immature to enjoy the fullness of God's goodness. God operated this way, Edwards thought, in the lives of Abraham and Sarah who waited decades before the birth of the desired child. The people of Israel toiled and prayed for 400 years before God sent Moses to deliver them. Thousands of years passed between the giving of the promise to Abraham and its fulfillment in Christ. Scripture, he said, presses upon believers "to wait and to hope." To see God's ultimate answer, the faithful must persevere in faith until the end when his wisdom will prove correct and his goodness undeniable.[140]

---

140   Edwards, "The Terms of Prayer," *Works*, 19:786.

GOD'S OMNIPOTENCE

Just as unanswered prayer does not reveal a failing in God's knowledge but the perfection of it, Edwards saw unanswered prayer as unassailable proof of the sovereignty of God. In choosing to answer some prayers as they have been prayed and pass over others, God reveals his sovereignty. In his sermons, Edwards described what he believed were at least three occasions when God might choose not to answer the prayers of the faithful for the purpose of showing his sovereignty.

First, God so orchestrates the providential circumstances of life to humble men and therefore exalt himself. "This is God's ordinary manner before any great and signal expression of his mercy and favor," Edwards announced in his sermon "God Makes Men Sensible of Their Misery before He Reveals His Mercy and Love."[141] When a man finds himself in the dark pit of despair, the bright light of God's glory shines brightest. Joseph found himself in an Egyptian dungeon long before God delivered him to Pharaoh's throne room. Joseph's brothers were brought low before he lifted them up at his banquet table. Only after Pharaoh had increased their workload did God unburden his people. The apostle Paul admitted that God allowed him and his companions to face the immediate threat of death to break them of their self-sufficiency and turn their hearts to the only God who raises the dead. In all of these biblical cases, Edwards saw the merciful hand of God at work in not answering their cries until such a time as he saw fit. "God leads them through the wilderness to prove them and let them know what is in their hearts," leaving them in their sin so "that he may afterwards turn it to their good, when he in infinite wisdom sees meet so to do."[142] He withholds his sweet mercies so that they might know and appreciate him all the more.

---

141   Edwards, "God Makes Men Sensible of Their Misery," *Works*, 17:143.
142   Edwards, "God Makes Men Sensible of Their Misery," *Works*, 17:148–149.

'Tis the will of God that the discoveries of his terrible
majesty, and awful holiness, and justice, should accompany
the discoveries of his grace and love, and that he would
glorify himself and make discoveries of himself as he is,
and give to his creatures worthy and just apprehensions of
himself.[143]

He does this, Edwards said, to glorify himself by displaying the
majesty of his nature.

The second occasion for God's temporarily staying his blessings
echoes the larger principle mentioned immediately above. God
lingers in his answers until such a time as his people acknowledge
his goodness. The prayer properly offered in faith and exercised
with patience teaches the believer to depend on one greater than
himself. God keeps them waiting, he does not answer, until such a
time as they gain a proper sense of their weakness in light of his
greatness. Whether Christians pray for deliverance from death or
evil, whether they pray for faith or revival, God often leaves them
waiting in agonizing anticipation, voicing a continuous litany of
seemingly worthless prayers, not to test their faith *per se*, but to
temper them by fire and to turn their eyes wholly to him.

If it be thus [not to depend on ourselves, but God], then
let us ascribe all the glory, of the promoting of religion
amongst us, to God only. We may infer from the doctrine
[of the sermon], that 'tis God only that has done it, inas-
much as we are without strength, and are unable to do
anything of ourselves. It would be highly offensive to God,
and justly so, if we should assume any of the honor of such
a work to ourselves. All means and endeavors were in vain,
till God was pleased to set in. The same means were used
before, as have been used now; but yet of late there has

---

143 Edwards, "God Makes Men Sensible of Their Misery," *Works*, 17:159.

been more done in a week than used, at some other times, to be done in some years; whereby God makes it most evident, how the work is his, and not man's, that we may ascribe all the glory to him.[144]

Thus, by making men wait upon himself, the Lord forces them to recognize and acknowledge his perfections in the answers given.

The third occasion in which God waits to answer prayer, Edwards thought, follows necessarily upon the first two. God waits so that he might bend the will of man to his own. Man's illegitimate prayers rise up before God and rather than answering them as voiced and bolstering man's defective faith with undue cause for hope, God refuses to answer until that faith and its connected desires are brought into line with his righteous purposes. The problem is not that God lacks the will to answer but that man possesses the wrong will. "[God is] able to do all things for us, if we yield to him under affliction and comply with his will."[145] The struggles of men, Edwards reasoned, are given of God to correct the errors of their ways. Though a man may lift his prayers to God, not only is God under no compulsion to answer those supplications but he may, in fact, prolong the affliction so as to steer his heart to a course set by God's good will. Until God's desires become those of man as well, man's prayers will remain unanswered and God's goodness and greatness unchallenged.

MAN'S WEAKNESS

In addition to the revelation of God's perfect character, unanswered prayer may reflect poorly upon a man's character. From the obvious, the presence of sin, to the more sublime, the building of faith, the weakness of man further highlights the greatness of God when it comes to his refusing to answer according to man's prayer.

Speaking of the dreadful silence of the Lord, Edwards reminded

---

144 Edwards, "Our Weakness, Christ's Strength," *Works*, 19:384.
145 Edwards, "God's Use of Affliction," *Works*, 25:651.

his flock that God's answers are often tied to spiritual rebellion. Even the prayers of the faithful for sinners fall on deaf ears. Pointing to the biblical account of Jeremiah when God forbade him to pray for Israel because of their sin, Edwards argued that God still refuses to hear the prayers of and for the sinful (Jeremiah 7:13,16). "He refuses to hear any prayers for them. If the godly pray for them, God don't answer them in the thing they ask. Though [they] pray often [and] earnestly, [though they be] persons of eminent piety, none are heard." Thus, withholding his blessings, God seeks to correct the wayward walk of the sinful. In addition to explaining the reality of unanswered prayer, Edwards believed this harsh fact to be ample motivation for godly living. The great danger for sinners is that God may choose to leave them forever in their sin because they are guilty of violating his infinite holiness.[146]

The content of prayers betrays the sinful nature of the one who prays. God will not answer prayers so that men may feed their lusts. They pray for no good purpose. Instead, they approach the holy God and seek that which will "gratify their pride or sensuality." Doing so, they reveal that they see God, not as the God of the Bible, but as a "worldly spirit." They attempt to use God as an "idol." To answer such prayers as these, said Edwards, would place God at odds with his own holy character. If he were to answer prayers offered with such a lowly conception of himself, one of human construct and vain imaginings, for the purpose of fulfilling sinful intent, God would be acting as his own enemy. If he answered sinful prayers, he would surrender his glory to another. God would become the servant and man would become the sovereign.[147]

Since aiding and abetting the enemy would be at odds with God's divine purposes, he does not answer the prayers of the sinful. He who knows all things, the omniscient God, knows the hearts of those who pray to him. "God looketh not at words, but at the heart."

---

146 Edwards, "The Dreadful Silence of the Lord," *Works*, 19:116.
147 Edwards, "The Most High a Prayer-Hearing God," *Works* (Hendrickson), 2:117.

Sinners come before God not seeking blessing but expecting it. "They show in words as though they are beggars," he explained, "but in heart they come as creditors, and look on God as their debtor." Such prayer is no prayer at all.[148] Preaching to the people of Northampton when the colonists had gathered an army to attack the French stronghold at Louisbourg, Edwards warned that God does not seek words but worship. Prayer offered in any fashion other than humble dependence on God is an affront to God.

> Our provocations have been very great: if we don't turn from our evil way, we can't pray with the spirit of prayer— we shall not look towards God's holy temple in our prayer. There is no true praying in the name of Christ without repentance of sin, for Christ is the savior of sinners. As long as we continue in the worship of idols, we shall trust in idols to deliver [us] and look to them [for our strength]. They that are devoted to the creature trust in the creature. This will not be such a fast as God has chosen: our fasting and praying will be but mocking.[149]

In so arguing, Edwards explained that God refuses to answer the prayers of the unrepentant to illustrate his holiness and magnify his glory, to remind them that he, and he alone, is God.

Just as outright sinfulness usually results in unanswered prayer, so too does the lack of true faith. Of such prayers Edwards would say, "That prayer which is not of faith, is insincere." Of the spiritually malnourished he would add, "Where this trust or faith is wanting, there is no prayer in the sight of God."[150] While Edwards did

---

148   Edwards, "The Most High a Prayer-Hearing God," *Works* (Hendrickson), 2:117.

149   Edwards, "The Duties of Christians in a Time of War," *Works*, 25:139.

150   Edwards, "The Most High a Prayer-Hearing God," *Works* (Hendrickson), 2:117.

acknowledge that God occasionally seems to answer the prayers of the wicked, he does so always according to his own sovereign desires, not theirs. The prayers of the lost are offensive to God. "All that is done by natural men in an attendance on religious duties is done wrong," he said. "There is nothing that they do right" because they do not truly know God.[151] Connecting prayer to faith, Edwards reasoned that when the lost pray they worship God "ignorantly, not knowing what they worship."[152]

> But natural men, when they come before God, they don't know who he is that they come before. They are ignorant of his perfection. When they come to pray to him, they don't know that they are in the presence of God, or that God sees them and knows what they ask for. They don't know that he is able to give 'em their requests.[153]

Thus, like the unrepentant, the unbeliever approaches God too boldly, acting as though he is dependent upon God, when in reality he presumes to tell God what God must do. When God refuses to answer their prayers, the faithless petitioner reveals his heart. He is offended that God has not responded according to his wishes. These, too, Edwards would say, are not praying to the God of the Bible but one of their own making. "They don't believe that [he] is the true and sovereign bestower of his own grace."[154] They fail to realize that a righteous God answers to no man but as befits his perfect plans. Until they do, they should not expect to find their prayers answered.

Those of weak or insufficient faith also find their prayers unanswered for the time being. God has heard their prayers and he may yet be pleased to answer them. He is ready but they are not. "When

---

151 Edwards, "All That Natural Men Do Is Wrong," *Works*, 19:527.
152 Edwards, "All That Natural Men Do Is Wrong," *Works*, 19:528.
153 Edwards, "All That Natural Men Do Is Wrong," *Works*, 19:528.
154 Edwards, "All That Natural Men Do Is Wrong," *Works*, 19:529.

God thus seems for a while to turn a deaf ear to persons' cries," he said, "it is oftentimes only for a trial of their resolution and steadfastness in seeking."[155] In instances such as these, it is not that God has not heard the prayer, nor is he unwilling to answer the prayer. It is the individual who is found wanting. Moreover, in times of unanswered prayer the believer should not be shocked. Instead, he should be all the more alert to God searching his heart. In such times, God not only remains silent, he may send further trials and tribulations. He may exercise "them with frowns of providence," testing their resolution. God does this, Edwards explained, to test the thoroughness of their faith in him.

> Those trials that God exercises [those that seek his blessing], tend to their humiliation {and despair}. [The] wisdom of God much appears in thus ordering and dispensing upon this account; [for it] tends to bring 'em to a sight of themselves, {to bring them to} show what they be, {to bring them to} know [their] own hearts, {to bring them to} despair in themselves, {and to bring them to} empty them of themselves.

> Thus, for instance, when God seems to turn a deaf ear, [and makes] no answer {to their cries for mercy}, it tends to bring persons to reflect on themselves, and consider how they have offended [and] provoked him, thus to refuse to answer; how just [to] take notice of what is in [their] hearts, how poor their prayers, how little to be depended on. And again, when things laid in the way [make it] difficult and hard to be gone through, {it tends to bring persons to} find [their] own weakness, find {their own} strength of corruption, [and] how much [it is] against this

---

155 Edwards, "Blessed Struggle," *Works*, 19:427. In "Persevering Faith," Edwards argued, "God is wont to exercise professors with difficulties and trials, to that end that he may prove their sincerity, and whether they will cleave to God or no" (Edwards, "Persevering Faith," *Works*, 19:606).

constant self-denial. When persons come to have occasion violently to resist corruption, then they will find the strength {of resolution}. But by their having those things that are most contrary to corruption, they will find {God's blessing}.

By God's deferring long to bestow {his blessing}, they learn by more and more experience, how far 'tis out of their reach, how impossible they should {obtain it}; and are led more and more to consider their dependence on God for it, and to consider their own unworthiness of it.[156]

By not answering the prayers of the weak-kneed, God is teaching them. He reveals himself in new glories to them. They discover that he is truly good. They find that God, and God alone, is the source of their joy and not the blessing sought. "Hereby," said Edwards, "they will most be likely to find their insufficiency to reach the good they seek of themselves; and how dependent are they on the power, and arbitrary pleasure, of God for the bestowment; and so are best prepared to acknowledge God on it, when bestowed."[157] In other words, they are brought to worship God as he desires and deserves to be worshipped.

SUMMARY

Edwards did not believe that it was cruel or unusual that God should choose to refuse or delay answers to prayers. According to his theology of prayer, unanswered prayers are neither a challenge to nor a rejection of God's character. Rather, such decisions proceed according to his character. Withholding the blessing sought, he believed, reinforces the reality and importance of these godly attributes in the mind of man.

---

156 Edwards, "Blessed Struggle," *Works*, 19:432. (Note: The use of {—} follows that of the editors of the Yale Edition of Edwards's *Works*, indicating where the editors have made an assumption about an illegible word in the handwritten manuscript.)

157 Edwards, "Blessed Struggle," *Works*, 19:425.

The lost must first come to know and trust the God of the universe and they must embrace his will as their own before he will answer. They must seek God according to God's desires or he will be no God of theirs. If, in due time, God chooses to hear and answer their prayers, he will do so according to his "sovereign mercy."[158] Likewise, the faithful are schooled by their unanswered prayers. They learn that they must become ever more faithful in their prayers, trusting the God who knows what is best for them and does only what is best for them according to his own kind intent.[159] When he refuses to answer the prayers of his elect, God displays his eternal lovingkindness toward them.

> The faith and holiness of the saints is so far from being the foundation of the eternal love of God that 'tis the fruit of it. God has loved them from all eternity, and that is the reason that he has given them faith and holiness, and has brought them home to himself truly to believe in, and love, and fear, and serve God.[160]

Thus, all that God has ordained and does, all that he gives and all that he withholds, issue forth from his perfect knowledge and sovereign reign as those attributes reflect glory upon his unblemished holiness.

Conclusion

God always hears the prayer OF FAITH.[161]

---

158 Edwards, "The Most High a Prayer-Hearing God," *Works* (Hendrickson), 2:117.

159 Edwards, "The Terms of Prayer," *Works*, 19:785.

160 Edwards, "The Everlasting Love of God," *Works*, 19:479.

161 Edwards, "The Most High a Prayer-Hearing God," *Works* (Hendrickson), 2:117.

Edwards's theology of prayer contained more than a simple acknowledgement of God's ability to hear prayer. He believed the true comfort offered in prayer is the hope that God not only hears one's cry but that he responds in the manner most befitting his greatness and their greatest needs. Thus, the beginning of any sound theology of prayer must be a proper understanding of the God to whom one prays. This God who hears prayers, Edwards said, displays his goodness and majesty in response to prayer. Thus, according to Edwards, God's unchanging character acts not as an impediment to prayer but as the basis of one's hope in prayer as God can be trusted to act according to his flawless character.

Theological truth, however, is insufficient in and of itself. The possessor of such knowledge must embrace and act upon it. The fact that God does hear prayer, Edwards thought, should be an incentive to prayer. Only by acting upon one's faith in these truths does one gain access to God.

> How distinguished are we from them [the lost], in that we have the true God made known to us; a God of infinite grace and mercy; a God full of compassion to the miserable, who is ready to pity us under all our troubles and sorrows, to hear our cries, and to give us all the relief which we need; a God who delights in mercy, and is rich unto all that call upon him![162]

Thus, one must know God in all his glory and seek him as he has ordained, if he has any hope of being blessed by him.

Therein lies the true heart of Edwards's theology of prayer—the seeking and finding of God. God is the centre of prayer. "The good, that shall be sought by prayer," Edwards wrote, "is God himself."[163] He is not just the bestower of blessing but the blessing

---

162 Edwards, "The Most High a Prayer-Hearing God," *Works* (Hendrickson), 2:116.

163 Edwards, *An Humble Attempt, Works,* 5:315.

itself. Speaking of the prophet Zechariah's call to prayer, Edwards said,

> But certainly that expression of "seeking the Lord," is very commonly used to signify something more than merely, in general, to seek some mercy of God: it implies, that God himself is the great good desired and sought after; that the blessings pursued are God's gracious presence, the blessed manifestation of him, union and intercourse with him; or, in short, God's manifestations and communications of himself.[164]

In so doing, pursuing God in prayer by faith, the believer proves his faith and glorifies his God. If this is the desire of his heart and the goal of his prayer, the faithful will see his every prayer answered, for this is the end to which God is directing all things. On the basis of that blessed hope, Edwards called his struggling congregation to return to their first love in prayer.

> Seeing we have such a prayer-hearing God as we have heard, let us be much employed in the duty of prayer: let us pray with all prayer and supplication: let us live prayerful lives, continuing instant in prayer, watching thereunto with all perseverance; praying always, without ceasing, earnestly, and not fainting.[165]

---

164 Edwards, *An Humble Attempt*, *Works*, 5:315.
165 Edwards, "The Most High a Prayer-Hearing God," *Works* (Hendrickson), 2:118.

Chapter 2

His early life

Being sensible that I am unable to do anything without God's help, I do humbly entreat him by his grace to enable me to keep these Resolutions, so far as they are agreeable to his will, for Christ's sake.[1]

Jonathan Edwards penned those words in 1722 within months of graduating from Yale at the age of eighteen. Edwards desired to become a solid Christian, to have the kind of Christian testimony that marked the revivals in his father's parish, to enjoy those experiences that would mark him as a true Christian, too. To that end, he resolved,

On the supposition, that there never was to be but one individual in the world, at any one time, who was properly a complete Christian, in all respects of a right stamp, having

---

1 Edwards, "Resolutions," *Works* 16:753.

Christianity always shining in its true luster, and appearing excellent and lovely, to act just as I would do, if I strove with all my might to be that one, who should live in my time.[2]

These longings as expressed in "Resolution" No. 63 represent nothing new in Edwards's constitution. He had been striving toward that end for years. In fact, he had been praying for it since childhood.

An awakened interest

Young Edwards knew something of the awakening work of the Spirit. "I had a variety of concerns and exercises about my soul from my childhood," he recalled years later. Two such "remarkable seasons of awakening" would precede his conversion at Yale. The first of these seasons occurred when Edwards was but a young boy. As the fires of revival swept through his father's congregation in East Windsor, Connecticut, Edwards's soul was warmed by the spiritual enthusiasm surrounding him. "I was then very much affected," he remembered, "concerned about the things of religion, and my soul's salvation." He would often withdraw from his parents' watchful eyes to pray about these things. This he did as often as five times a day with much great delight and pleasure.[3]

At this time, Edwards enlisted several of his schoolmates in his religious exercises as well. In addition to spending time in spiritual discourse, they "built a booth in the swamp" for the purpose of private prayer. Even this course of corporate prayer with his peers, however, could not satisfy Edwards's spiritual appetites. He had several other secret places to which he would retire to spend more time in individual prayer. Doing so, Edwards found himself "much affected." "I seemed to be in my element," he recalled, "when engaged in religious duties."[4]

While spiritual matters, particularly time spent in prayer, brought

---

2   Edwards, "Resolutions," *Works* 16:758.
3   Edwards, "Personal Narrative," *Works*, 16:790.
4   Edwards, "Personal Narrative," *Works*, 16:791.

Edwards great delight, hindsight proved that this had been but a season of awakening not regeneration. "In the process of time, my convictions and affections wore off." He lost those desires for things spiritual and "left off secret prayer." Unconverted, Edwards's passions cooled and he returned to his sinful ways like a dog to its vomit.[5]

Edwards had, according to his own confession, mistaken self-righteousness for the work of God. The religious duties he pursued with pleasure brought only temporary reprieve because they were self-centred. Instead, the experience that Edwards so desperately sought, and needed, had to be God-centred. Until he recognized that simple spiritual reality, his much heralded early efforts at Christianity, now the stuff of Christian legend, were wasted, sacrificed on the altar of works, as lost as the young boy who so eagerly longed for spiritual release.

During the latter days of his time at Yale, Edwards continued to struggle with uneasy thoughts about the condition of his soul. In the midst of his spiritual turmoil, "it pleased God" to bring Edwards to the precipice of life and death, showing him the depths of his despair, shaking him "over the pit of hell." Thus, Edwards experienced another remarkable season of awakening. And, yet, this too fell short of bringing him to saving faith. "It was not long after my recovery," he wrote, "before I fell again into my old ways of sin."[6]

By the grace of God, however, Edwards was not left in the sin he so enjoyed. "God would not suffer me to go on with any quietness." Instead, his spiritual struggles intensified. New vows of self-righteousness were made and the duties of religion were rejoined. This time, however, the joy of earlier years was not to be found. His seeking after salvation in this fashion became miserable. He began to doubt even the possibility of his own salvation.[7]

Then something happened—a seismic shift occurred in his thinking. Edwards finally saw that his struggle with God was one

---

5 Edwards, "Personal Narrative," *Works*, 16:791.
6 Edwards, "Personal Narrative," *Works*, 16:791.
7 Edwards, "Personal Narrative," *Works*, 16:792.

of priority. Who was going to be the God of his life? God or Edwards? This struggle "against the doctrine of God's sovereignty" was not new; it had followed Edwards from his childhood. Now the matter came to a head. He was forced to come to a conclusion. Finally, he acquiesced. He admitted God's greatness in all things, including his own salvation. While he could not at that time explain how God's sovereignty operated, nor the change of heart he had experienced, Edwards knew that he had experienced "a wonderful alteration [of the] mind" nonetheless. The self-righteous rebel finally laid down his arms and rested in God's.[8]

The change of heart that led to Edwards's salvation also produced a change in religious exercise. He now worshipped the sovereign God who had chosen him, not the god of his own choosing. "The doctrine of God's sovereignty has very often appeared, an exceeding pleasant, bright and sweet doctrine to me: and absolute sovereignty is what I love to ascribe to God." This realization, then, changed his prayer life. "I kept saying, as it were singing these words of Scripture (1 Timothy 1:17) to myself; and went to prayer, to pray to God that I might enjoy him; and prayed in a manner quite different from what I used to do; with a new sort of affection." Edwards now prayed asking that God would change him rather than hoping that he could change himself.[9]

The new sense of the divine, born in Edwards at salvation, continued to blossom and kindled a "sweet burning" in his heart. Seeking to understand the manner of his salvation, he spoke to his father and meditated on his advice. Walking alone, in a "solitary place," pondering these great matters, Edwards enjoyed a renewed vision of God's glory.

> And as I was walking there, and looked up on the sky and clouds; there came into my mind, a sweet sense of the glorious majesty and grace of God, that I know not how to

---

8 Edwards, "Personal Narrative," *Works*, 16:792.
9 Edwards, "Personal Narrative," *Works*, 16:792–793.

express. I seemed to see them both in a sweet conjunction: majesty and meekness joined together; it was a sweet and gentle, and holy majesty; and also a majestic meekness; an awful sweetness; a high, and great, and holy gentleness.[10]

The effect of this realization on Edwards was total; "the appearance of everything was altered." He could look at nothing in the same way ever again. The glory of God, his moral and natural attributes, became his passion and the purpose of his prayer.

My mind was greatly fixed on divine things; I was almost perpetually in the contemplation of them. Spent most of my time in thinking of divine things, year after year. And used to spend abundance of my time, in walking alone in the woods, and solitary places, for meditation, soliloquy and prayer, and converse with God. And it was always my manner, at such times, to sing forth my contemplations. And was almost constantly in ejaculatory prayer, wherever I was. Prayer seemed to be natural to me; as the breath, by which the inward burnings of my heart had vent.[11]

Edwards was a new man and prayer was the avenue through which he would seek God and find his fill.

The New York state of mind

My sense of divine things seemed gradually to increase, till I went to preach at New York, which was about a year and a half after they began.[12]

Edwards arrived in New York City late in the summer of 1722.

10 Edwards, "Personal Narrative," *Works*, 16:793.
11 Edwards, "Personal Narrative," *Works*, 16:794.
12 Edwards, "Personal Narrative," *Works*, 16:795.

Yet to turn nineteen years old, he was there to take charge of his first pastorate, an interim preaching position at a small Presbyterian church meeting near the wharfs. It was during this brief time in New York that Edwards experienced a time of spiritual maturation, both by election and necessity. Biographer Sereno Dwight remarked in his account of Edwards's life: "Probably, in no part of his life, had he higher advantage for spiritual contemplation and enjoyment" than during this period.[13] Edwards did just that.

> My longings after God and holiness, were much increased. Pure and humble, holy and heavenly Christianity, appeared exceeding amiable to me. I felt in me a burning desire to be in everything a complete Christian; and conformed to the blessed image of Christ: and that I might live in all things, according to the pure, sweet and blessed rules of the gospel. I had an eager thirsting after progress in these things. My longings after it, put me upon pursuing and pressing after them. It was my continual strife day and night, and constant inquiry, how I should be more holy, and live more holily, and more becoming a child of God, and disciple of Christ.[14]

And so Edwards dedicated himself to honing the spiritual disciplines, pursuing the grace that he had been given by God. While his time there was short, just eight months, the lessons that he learned in New York would exert a lasting influence on his life and ministry.

---

13 Sereno E. Dwight, *Life of Edwards* (New York: G. & C. & H. Carvill, 1830), 64. Ola Winslow remarked, "This eight-month period [when Edwards was serving in New York] was an opportunity for spiritual refreshment and further cultivation of the inner life" (Ola E. Winslow, *Jonathan Edwards: 1703–1758* [New York: Macmillan, 1940], 85). Henry Bamford Parkes, too, saw this time as one of great spiritual use for Edwards, during which he "schooled" himself "in the ways of Christianity" (Henry B. Parkes, *Jonathan Edwards* [New York: Minton, Balch & Company, 1930], 77).

14 Edwards, "Personal Narrative," *Works*, 16:795.

When Edwards arrived in New York City, the former Dutch colony was already a booming international hub. Her 7,000 citizens represented many European heritages including those of Jewish, English, Scottish and Irish descent. The latter two had only recently formed the first Presbyterian church in the city and were led by the Reverend James Anderson. In addition to the Scots-Irish adherents, the little congregation began to attract New Englanders to its fold. These newcomers found it difficult to fit in with their Old World brothers and sisters in Christ with their rigid traditions and strange accents. The New England Presbyterians ultimately withdrew to form their own church just a few blocks away. These upstarts contacted Yale through one of their own members who served there as a trustee requesting pulpit help. Young Edwards was the answer to that request.

Among his fellow New Englanders Edwards found a kindred spirit. The congregation was both spiritually rigorous and pious and, even better, the family who served as Edwards's hosts were all the more so. They were everything Edwards aspired to be. During his time in the home of Madame Smith and her son, John, Edwards enjoyed an "abundance of sweet religious conversation." The boys became soulmates, fellow seekers after the same spiritual experience, praying for the same glory of God.

> I very frequently used to retire into a solitary place, on the banks of Hudson's River, at some distance from the city, for contemplation on divine things, and secret converse with God; and had many sweet hours there. Sometimes Mr. Smith and I walked there together, to converse of the things of God; and our conversation used much to turn on the advancement of Christ's kingdom in the world, and the glorious things that God would accomplish for his church in the latter days.

Even after his heartrending departure from New York in April 1723, the two young men, bound together in their love for God, maintained contact for at least another twenty years.[15]

The freshness of his faith, the vigour of daily theological discourse and the challenge of spiritual responsibility, set Edwards upon a course of reflection and self-discipline that would guide him throughout the remainder of his days. Beginning in New York Edwards committed his ideas and thoughts to paper with regularity and surprising profundity. There within the confines of the Smith family sanctuary Edwards began to flesh out his faith and his ideas about it. He started many of his various notebooks of biblical and prophetic reflections. He penned the first of his "Miscellanies." He plotted his spiritual course in his "Resolutions" and he kept track of his faithfulness in his "Diary."

Edwards's driving question in his diary seems to be, as he records every joyous moment and tortured doubt, "Am I saved?" The "Resolutions" ask, "What must I do to prove that I am saved?"[16] Thus, the two pieces run parallel courses, one asking and the other answering antiphonally. In both, prayer plays a central role in the definition and development of Edwards's spiritual life.

Prayer stands at the beginning of the "Resolutions" as the basis for Edwards's belief in their ability to affirm his faith. The preface to these written goals begins with his entreaty that God grant him "by his grace to enable me to keep these Resolutions."[17] Having thus begun his quest with prayer, Edwards proceeds not with Quixotic naïveté but a strong faith in God's ability to hear prayer. In the first "Resolution," Edwards determined to "do whatever I think

---

15 Edwards, "Personal Narrative," *Works*, 16:797.

16 Marsden explained the purpose of the "Resolutions" in this manner, arguing that using them Edwards "kept score of how well he did" (Marsden, *Jonathan Edwards: A Life*, 52). Claghorn described the "Resolutions" as "instructions for life" and "guidelines for self-examination" ("Editor's Introduction," Claghorn, ed. *Works*, 16:741). Summarizing their purpose, Claghorn added, "The ultimate intention of the 'Resolutions' was to produce a soul fit for eternity with God, they served as a set of practical day-to-day guidelines for achieving that end" (*Works*, 16:743).

17 Edwards, "Resolutions," *Works*, 16:753.

to be most to God's glory." He resolved "to do whatever I think to be my duty."[18] The fourth "Resolution" echoes the first, resolving "never to do any manner of thing, whether in soul or body, less or more, but what tends to the glory of God."[19] Edwards's sixty-second "Resolution" adds that he intended to attend to these duties "willingly and cheerfully."[20] Whenever Edwards would outline religious duties in his other writings, he always included the practice of prayer. Thus, prayer, by way of implication of his concern for duty, finds its way into several of Edwards's "Resolutions."

If Edwards included prayer in a number of the "Resolutions" as a means whereby his goals would be accomplished and his faith proven, he did so more overtly in others. The twenty-ninth "Resolution" speaks directly to how a true Christian must pray. "Resolved, never to count that a prayer, nor to let that pass as a prayer, which is so made, that I cannot hope that God will answer it."[21] The true faith of a believer, Edwards resolved, would be proven by his steadfastness in prayer, a dedication driven by the firm conviction that God can answer his prayers.

> Resolved, when I find those "groanings which cannot be uttered," of which the Apostle speaks [Romans 8:26], and those "breakings of the soul for the longing it hath," of which the Psalmist speaks, Ps. 119:20, that I will promote them to the utmost of my power, and that I will not be weary of earnestly endeavoring to vent my desires, nor of the repetitions of such earnestness.[22]

The true Christian prays and he prays with purpose, passion and, if necessary, perseverance. If not, he is no Christian at all.

---

18 Edwards, "Resolutions" No. 1, *Works*, 16:753.
19 Edwards, "Resolutions" No. 4, *Works*, 16:753.
20 Edwards, "Resolutions" No. 62, *Works*, 16:758.
21 Edwards, "Resolutions" No. 29, *Works*, 16:755.
22 Edwards, "Resolutions" No. 64, *Works*, 16:758.

Whereas the resolutions are powerful and upbeat, Edwards's diary entries written at the same time prove that his spiritual life was often more about longsuffering than victory. During this period he struggled with two pieces of evidence that seemed to undermine the reality of his conversion experience just a year-and-a-half earlier. The first had to do with the manner of his salvation. His conversion had failed to follow the paradigm set forth by his New England forebears and his father. Salvation, according to their model, followed a prescribed course wherein one stage or event prepared the individual for the next, oftentimes over the course of a year or more. Edwards, on the other hand, came to the point of conversion in a more direct fashion, skipping some steps altogether. His first diary entry reflects the angst caused by this incongruity: "I cannot speak so fully to my experience of that preparatory work, of which the divines speak." Continuing, he wrote, "I do not remember that I experienced regeneration, exactly in those steps, in which divines say it is generally wrought."[23]

As if the idea that his conversion might be false because it violated the teaching of those whom he revered was not disconcerting enough, Edwards found little consolation in his reflection on his faith: "I do not feel the Christian graces sensibly enough, particularly faith. I fear they are only such hypocritical outside affections, which wicked men may feel, as well as others."[24] Thus, on the same day that he recorded those concerns, he resolved that "whenever I so much question whether I have done my duty, as that my quiet and calm is thereby disturbed, to set it down, and also how the question was resolved."[25] In other words, when disturbed by doubts, Edwards would acknowledge their existence in his diary and, once settled, note the resolution to that particular dilemma.

The resolution to Edwards's doubts would not come easily nor would it come based solely on his efforts. He knew that God alone

---

23 Edwards, "Diary," *Works*, 16:759.
24 Edwards, "Diary," *Works*, 16:759.
25 Edwards, "Resolutions" No. 35, *Works*, 16:755.

could allay his concerns. "It is to no purpose to resolve, except we depend on the grace of God."[26] To that end, Edwards prayed for God's continuing grace. By the grace of God, Edwards recorded a number of these prayers in his diary.

One Saturday in January 1723, Edwards found himself awakening from a period of spiritual malaise. In the morning he rededicated himself to his Christian calling through prayer.

> I have been before God; and have given myself, all that I am and have to God, so that I am not in any respect my own: I can challenge no right in myself, I can challenge no right in this understanding, this will, these affections that are in me; neither have I any right to this body, or any of its members: no right to this tongue, these hands, nor feet; no right to these senses, these eyes, these ears, this smell or taste. I have given myself clear away, and have not retained anything as my own. I have been to God this morning, and told him that I gave myself wholly to him.[27]

He knew that his conversion had been a result of the sovereign outworking of God's grace and now he sought that grace anew by acknowledging that same sovereignty again. Such was his prayer for renewal:

> And I pray God, for the sake of Christ, to look upon it as a self-dedication; and to receive me now as entirely his own, and deal with me in all respects as such; whether he afflicts me or prospers me, or whatever he pleases to do with me, who am his.[28]

This prayer concern also found a tangible voice in his resolutions.

---

26 Edwards, "Diary," *Works*, 16:760.
27 Edwards, "Diary," *Works*, 16:762.
28 Edwards, "Diary," *Works*, 16:762.

There Edwards determined that "never henceforward, till I die, to act as if I were anyway my own, but altogether God's."[29]

By mid-February of the same year, Edwards's spiritual condition ebbed and flowed again. "I do certainly know that I love holiness, such as the gospel requires," he gushed. Yet, in the same entry, he acknowledged that he had failed to maintain a proper commitment to divine worship. He was "not applying [himself] with application enough to the duty of secret prayer."[30]

Struggles, such as those he encountered that winter, continued to the end of his time in New York. Just weeks before his painful departure on April 23, 1723, Edwards wrote, "This week I found myself so far gone, that it seemed to me, that I should never recover more." How did Edwards respond? Not with the melancholic, emotional self-flagellation that his detractors see when they read his diary but with an abiding faith in the God who hears the prayers of his saints. Edwards wrote: "Let God of his mercy return unto me, and no more leave me thus to sink and decay! I know, O Lord, that without thy help, I shall fall innumerable times, notwithstanding all my resolutions, how often so ever repeated."[31]

Edwards struggled with the emotional pain of his departure from New York as he left behind those he had come to love with such Christian affection during his brief time there. He had already been comforted once by the grace of God at Westchester as he walked alone in another field communing with God.[32] Later, in a flash of painful honesty, he admitted that each new struggle encountered always seemed greater than those that preceded it and that he knew this must continue throughout the course of the human life. Again, his response to such agonizing spiritual torment began and ended with prayer and praise.

29 Edwards, "Resolutions" No. 43, *Works*, 16:756.
30 Edwards, "Diary," *Works*, 16:766.
31 Edwards, "Diary," *Works*, 16:768.
32 Edwards, "Personal Narrative," *Works*, 16:798.

Lord, grant that from hence I may learn to withdraw my thoughts, affections, desires and expectations, entirely from the world, and may fix them upon the heavenly state; where there is fullness of joy; where reigns heavenly, sweet, calm and delightful love without alloy; where there are continually the dearest expressions of their love: where there is enjoyment of the persons loved, without ever parting: where those persons, who appear so lovely in this world, will really be inexpressibly more lovely, and full of love to us. How sweetly will the mutual lovers join together to sing the praises of God and the Lamb! How full will it fill us with joy to think, this enjoyment, these sweet exercises, will never cease or come to an end, but will last to all eternity.[33]

A prayer manual

I think it best commonly to come before God three times a day, except I find a great inaptitude to that duty.[34]

The "Diary" continues for little more than another year after Edwards's departure from New York. In it the reader finds glimpses into his life in East Windsor, back in the home of his parents, his rejection of a call to pastor a church in Bolton and his removal to Yale for a tutorship that would cause him much grief. Interspersed throughout this period are new resolutions and desires for holiness. Buried among these familiar longings are several notes on the proper way to pray and two beautiful examples of Edwards's worshipful approach to prayer.

Edwards began recording his thoughts concerning his method of prayer in the days and months after his return from New York. The advice that he gives himself is both practical and insightful. For example, in response to the realization that his mind was prone to

---

33 Edwards, "Diary," *Works*, 16:768.
34 Edwards, "Diary," *Works*, 16:769.

wander during corporate prayer, he noted that one ought to pray three times per day, unless, of course, one finds himself to be spiritually distracted, unprepared to encounter God.[35] In another entry, he lamented that he had failed to follow his own advice, becoming "slight" in his exercises of secret prayer.[36] Weeks later, obviously still struggling with what he perceived to be spiritual sloth, he noted that "it is best to be careful in prayer."[37] Care must be exercised to make sure that one is truly sincere in his prayers and not merely going through the motions. The source of his sluggishness, Edwards knew, was the continued presence of sin in his life.

> As a help against that inward shameful hypocrisy, to confess frankly to myself all that which I find in myself, either infirmity or sin; also to confess to God, and open the whole case to him, when it is what concerns religion, and humbly and earnestly implore of him the help that is needed; not in the least to endeavor to smother over what is in my heart, but to bring it all out to God and my conscience.[38]

Once again, the particular infirmity that drew Edwards's attention on that morning was his inability to capture his thoughts and focus them on God. God must always be the centre of prayer or it is no prayer at all.

To help his wandering mind, Edwards set himself to praying as if publicly for others to hear. He determined, "For the time to come, when I am in a lifeless frame in secret prayer, to force myself to expatiate, as if I were praying before others more than I used to do."[39] Moreover, he would intentionally note at the beginning of his prayer the nature of his petition to help himself remain attentive to the

---

35 Edwards, "Diary," *Works*, 16:769.
36 Edwards, "Diary," *Works*, 16:771.
37 Edwards, "Diary," *Works*, 16:773.
38 Edwards, "Diary," *Works*, 16:778.
39 Edwards, "Diary," *Works*, 16:782.

prayer itself. To help himself accomplish this goal, he "determined, when I am indisposed to prayer, always to premeditate what to pray for."[40] If all that did not keep his mind on the subject at hand, Edwards reminded himself, it is better to keep the prayer short than to sin by allowing his mind to wander while in the presence of God.

As prayer focuses one's attention on God and his holiness in comparison to man's smallness and sin, Edwards thought, worship should flow naturally from the heart of the faithful. In this way, Edwards often moved effortlessly from one duty to the other, ever blurring the lines of distinction between prayer and praise.

The attentive reader discovers that Edwards's recorded prayers in the latter portion of his diary are more worship than petition. In these examples of his prayer life, Edwards leaned upon the character of God, praising him, both directly and indirectly, acknowledging that God alone could answer his needs. On one such occasion, he prayed,

> I have abundant cause, O my merciful Father, to love thee ardently, and greatly to bless and praise thee, that thou hast heard me in my earnest request, and hast so answered my prayer for mercy to keep from [spiritual] decay and sinking. O, graciously, of thy mere goodness, still continue to pity my misery, by reason of my sinfulness. O my dear Redeemer, I commit myself, together with my prayer and thanksgiving into thine hand.[41]

Shortly thereafter he was spiritually listless again. He made further resolutions to attempt to correct his wayward spiritual course. Finally, three weeks to the day after he first prayed that prayer, he prayed it again, repeating verbatim its contents.

> I have abundant cause, O my merciful Father, to love thee ardently, and greatly, to bless and praise thee, that thou hast

---

40 Edwards, "Diary," *Works*, 16:787.
41 Edwards, "Diary," *Works*, 16:771–772.

heard me, in my earnest request, and so hast answered my
prayer, for mercy, to keep me from decay and sinking. O,
graciously, of thy mere goodness, still continue to pity my
misery, by reason of my sinfulness. O, my dear Redeemer,
I commit myself, together with my prayer and thanksgiving, into thine hand![42]

The most high God who had heard and answered the prayers of
his faithful servant in the past was worthy of continued trust and
worship. He had proven himself worthy of Edwards's trust and
praise.

Amen and amen

The early days of Jonathan Edwards's Christian life were full of
jubilation and tribulation. He experienced spiritual highs filled
with delight. He sunk to spiritual lows, bordering on melancholy.
These peaks and valleys reveal not a manic form of Christianity but
the sincere efforts of a young believer trying to understand and live
out the implications of God's converting grace.

Throughout the 1720s Edwards attempted to improve his walk
with the Lord, resolving to make the most of every opportunity.
His "Resolutions" came to be the standard of how he measured his
growth. When he triumphed, he rejoiced. When he failed, he
became disheartened. Yet, through it all it was his faith in God's
gracious abilities expressed in his prayers that carried him through
the difficult years of transition from pastor's son to child prodigy
to young pastor. Years later, at the end of the decade, Edwards found
himself as the sole pastor of a legendary church, filling the great
pulpit of his grandfather Solomon Stoddard in Northampton, Massachusetts. There he reflected on the goodness and greatness of the
God who had graciously carried him through many dark nights of
the soul:

---

42 Edwards, "Diary," *Works*, 16:772.

Since I have come to this town, I have often had sweet complacency in God in views of his glorious perfections, and the excellency of Jesus Christ. God has appeared to me, a glorious and lovely being, chiefly on the account of his holiness. The holiness of God has always appeared to me the most lovely of all his attributes. The doctrines of God's absolute sovereignty, and free grace, in showing mercy to whom he would show mercy; and man's absolute dependence on the operations of God's Holy Spirit, have very often been much my delight. God's sovereignty has ever appeared to me, as great part of his glory. It has often been sweet to me to go to God [in prayer], and adore him as a sovereign God, and ask sovereign mercy of him.[43]

---

43 Edwards, "Personal Narrative," *Works*, 16:799.

Chapter 3

The excellent Christ

So that if we choose Christ for our friend and portion, we shall hereafter be so received to him, that there shall be nothing to hinder the fullest enjoyment of him, to the satisfying [of] the utmost cravings of our souls.[1]

Twenty-three sermon manuscripts survive from Jonathan Edwards's brief time in New York. These early sermons trace his own spiritual journey as he preached through text after text on the necessity and nature of salvation and the course of the Christian's walk. Of particular interest to the young Edwards was the person and work of Jesus as they related to those matters that weighed so heavily on his own soul. The "sweet hours" he spent contemplating these things in the fields surrounding New York found their voice in his diary and these sermons. In the former, the young preacher twice noted that he

---

1   Edwards, "The Excellency of Christ," *Works*, 19:592.

had enjoyed "higher thoughts than usual of the excellency of Jesus Christ and his kingdom."[2] Of the latter, four sermons are dedicated to examining and explaining the wonders of Christ and encouraging fellow believers to join him in admiring the Saviour. The theological presuppositions formed during his first pastorate would follow Edwards throughout his ministry. He continued to proclaim the greatness of Christ to all who would listen. Notably, among the only collection of pastoral sermons published in his lifetime, *Discourses on Various Important Subjects* (1738), Edwards purposely included a sermon on this topic, "The Excellency of Christ."[3] Second in length only to his now famous "Justification by Faith Alone," also published in that collection, this sermon plumbs the depths and scales the heights of orthodox Christology. Considering Christ, he observed, "There is an admirable conjunction of diverse excellencies in Jesus Christ."[4] There is both "infinite highness" and "infinite condescension," "infinite justice" and "infinite grace," "infinite majesty" and "transcendent meekness."[5] In Christ, Edwards declared, man finds his all in all.

> And here is not only infinite strength and infinite worthiness, but infinite condescension; and love and mercy, as great as power and dignity. If you are a poor distressed sinner, whose heart is ready to sink for fear that God never will have mercy on you, you need not be afraid to go to Christ, for fear that he is either unable or unwilling to help you: here is a strong foundation, and an inexhaustible treasure,

---

2 Edwards, "Diary," *Works*, 16:760–761.

3 The choice to include this sermon in the collection was Edwards's alone. That he decided to do so reflects the pastoral concern of his heart for his readers. "[I was] thinking that a discourse on such an evangelistic subject, would properly follow others that were chiefly legal and awakening, and that something of the excellency of the Savior, was proper to succeed those things that were to show the necessity of salvation" (Edwards, "Preface" to *Discourses on Various Important Subjects, Works*, 19:797).

4 Edwards, "The Excellency of Christ," *Works*, 19:565.

5 Edwards, "The Excellency of Christ," *Works*, 19:565–567.

to answer the necessities of your poor soul; and here is infinite grace and gentleness to invite and embolden a poor unworthy fearful soul to come to it. If Christ accepts of you, you need not fear but that you will be safe.[6]

Convinced of these truths, Edwards spent himself extolling the virtues of Christ, calling others to trust and worship the Saviour.

As Edwards noted in this sermon and others, the believer's relationship with Christ does not end at faith. Rather, faith is but the beginning of a life of wondrous joy and great consequence, all of which are intrinsically related to the person and work of Christ. The benefits obtained through faith are of both eternal and temporal value. In addition to one's hope for eternal life, Edwards included hope for life here and now. The sacrifice that purchased the former ensures the latter. Among the Christian's present hopes so intimately connected to Christ stands the privilege of prayer. "The smoke of [Christ's] sacrifice has perfumed the souls of believers and has made them and their prayers and praises sweet in the nostrils of God, so that now he smells a sweet savor in their prayers which were most offensive to him before."[7] To that end, one must grasp Edwards's understanding of Christ, if he hopes to understand his theology of prayer.

To appreciate the interrelatedness of Edwards's Christology and his theology of prayer two questions must be answered. First, "Who is Jesus?" Christ must be more than a mere man to play a role in prayer. Edwards's answer to the first question begs the second: "What has Jesus done?" Perhaps, as it relates to prayer, a better question would be, "What is Jesus doing?" While one part of Christ's work was truly finished at the cross, Edwards would argue, Christ's work in the life of the believer continues in the present and into the future. Thus, Edwards forces his audience, both then and now, to consider the excellency of Christ, the God who came to man that he might take man to God, in salvation and in prayer.

---

6 Edwards, "The Excellency of Christ," *Works*, 19:583–584.
7 Edwards, "Christ's Sacrifice," *Works*, 10:600.

Who is Jesus?

For God glorifies himself in communicating himself, and he communicates himself in glorifying himself. Jesus Christ, and that as God-man, is the grand medium by which God attains his end, both in communicating himself to the creatures and [in] glorifying himself by the creation.[8]

One cannot fully comprehend or appreciate Edwards's conception of the person and work of Christ apart from considering the way Christ fulfills God's doxological purposes. This passion, this all-consuming concern for God's glory, expressed itself throughout Edwards's career. In his "Resolutions," among Edwards's earliest writings, he resolved, "Never to do any manner of thing, whether in soul or body, less or more, but what tends to the glory of God."[9] He dedicated many sermons and "Miscellanies" to exploring the ramifications of God's glory. Finally, at the end of his days, Edwards summarized a lifetime of theological musings in *The End for Which God Created the World*:

> Thus we see that the great and last end of God's works which is so variously expressed in Scripture, is indeed but one; and this one end is most properly and comprehensively called, "the glory of God."[10]

For that reason, Edwards's Christology must begin where his theology proper ends—the glory of God.

God "delights in glorifying himself" Edwards argued.[11] God's desire for his own glory, however, represents not a flaw in his

---

8 Edwards, "Approaching the End of God's Grand Design," *Works*, 25:117.

9 Edwards, "Resolutions," *Works*, 16:753.

10 Edwards, *The End for Which God Created the World*, *Works*, 8:530.

11 Edwards, "Miscellanies" No. 1151, *Works*, 20:525.

character but its perfection. "God don't seek his own glory for any happiness he receives by it, as men are gratified in having their excellencies gazed at, admired and extolled by others. But God seeks the display of his own glory as a thing in itself excellent."[12] God, being perfect in every way, must love what is lovely and good. And as he himself is preminently lovely and good, he loves most his own love and admiration.

> 'Tis good that glory should be displayed. The excellency of God's nature appears in that, that he loves and seeks whatever is in itself excellent. One way that the excellency of God's nature appears is in loving himself, or loving his own excellency and infinite perfection; and as he loves his own perfection, so he loves the effulgence or shining forth of that perfection, or loves his own excellency in the expression and fruit of it.[13]

Thus, God by his very nature seeks his own glory for his own glory.

God does not merely seek his own glory; he desires to propagate it as well. As Edwards reasoned, the glory of God implies two things, "manifestation and communication."[14] To accomplish the former God created all things that his glory might be seen and honoured by others.[15] Having displayed his attributes in creation, he created beings that might wonder at that creation, beings to which he might communicate "his own glory and happiness."[16] The fall of those beings, however, interrupted the chorus of praise that God sought in his creation. Therefore, God, in a still greater manifestation of his glory, communicated his grace to creation through the supreme display of that grace in the person and work of his Son, Jesus Christ.

---

12 Edwards, "Miscellanies" No. 699, *Works*, 18:282.
13 Edwards, "Miscellanies" No. 699, *Works*, 18:282.
14 Edwards, "Miscellanies" No. 1094, *Works*, 20:483.
15 Edwards, "Miscellanies" No. 448, *Works*, 13:496.
16 Edwards, "Approaching the End of God's Grand Design," *Works*, 25:116.

Indeed, God's communicating himself and glorifying {himself} ought not to be looked upon as though they were distinct ends, but as what together makes one last end, as glorifying God and enjoying {God} make one chief end of man. For God glorifies himself in communicating himself, and he communicates himself in glorifying himself. Jesus Christ, and that as God-man, is the grand medium by which God attains his end, both in communicating himself to the creatures and [in] glorifying himself by the creation.[17]

God has revealed himself in the person of Jesus Christ for his glory in such a way as to magnify that glory through Christ's works so that his creation, the recipients of his lovingkindness, might give God the glory as they enjoy his happiness.

Sereno Dwight summarized Edwards's argument in this manner:

From the purest principles of reason, as well as from the fountain of revealed truth, he demonstrates that the chief and ultimate end of the Supreme Being, in the works of Creation and Providence, was the manifestation of his own glory, in the highest happiness of his creatures."[18]

God has revealed his glory in the deity of Christ, bridged the creator-creation gap in the humanity of Christ, and accomplished his purposes through the work of Christ. Through this person, Jesus Christ, who is God, man and mediator, God the Father shares his glory and basks in it. Joining theology and Christology, Edwards held to a theology of prayer that is both God-centred and Christ-dependent.

---

17 Edwards, "Approaching the End of God's Grand Design," *Works*, 25:116-17.
18 Dwight, *Life of Edwards*, 542.

JESUS IS GOD

As Edwards argued in many places and many ways, God delights in glorifying himself. He does so ultimately and most supremely in the person of Jesus Christ. Christ is "the grand medium by which God attains his end."[19] For it is in and through Jesus that God has revealed himself in such a way as to express his own perfections to a creation incapable of enjoying those perfections in their supernatural state. In order to fulfill this lofty purpose, Christ must be more than just a mere reflection of God. Created man already possesses in himself the *imago Dei*, the image of God. That image in man, however, is insufficient to reveal the full glory of God. Thus, Christ must of necessity be more. He must be God himself, the second person of the Trinity, if he is to manifest the fullness of God. As such Christ reveals God's manifold goodness, possesses God's perfect attributes and shares God's great glory. Christ accomplishes all this according to the glory of God for the good of man.

As spirit, God is supposed but unseen. That is, as Paul expresses in Romans 1, man knows intuitively that there is a God but he knows little else about him. If God is to receive the glory he desires and deserves, he must reveal himself in such a manner as to be more fully grasped by lower creatures. His perfections need to be expressed, to be seen *and* comprehended by those who are to give him that glory. That expression, the manifestation of God's glory, is Jesus Christ— God's "declarative glory."[20] Christ is the vehicle by which God reveals himself to man. Once revealed and known, God can and will be properly glorified. All this he does in and through Christ because "all the attributes of [God's] glory come through [Jesus'] hands."[21]

In Christ, God translates his glory into a language, or form, that man may understand rightly according to his own limited abilities. Moreover, man's knowledge of God remains incomplete until revealed and interpreted in light of Jesus Christ. "It signifies nothing

---

19 Edwards, "Approaching the End of God's Grand Design," *Works*, 25:117.
20 Edwards, "Miscellanies" No. 1099, *Works*, 20:485.
21 Edwards, "Approaching the End of God's Grand Design," *Works*, 25:116.

for us to know anything of any one of God's perfections," Edwards remarked, "unless we know them as manifested in Christ."[22] But, as manifested in Christ, God can be known for Christ is the communication of God's happiness,[23] the expression of his goodness,[24] and the declaration of God's glory.[25] In these things Christ acts not simply as the vehicle of God's revelation, a mere purveyor of the goods of another, but as God himself. "In the Son the Deity, the whole Deity and glory of the Father, is as it [were] repeated or duplicated," said Edwards. "Everything in the Father, is repeated or expressed again, and that fully, so that there is properly no inferiority."[26] Hence, Jesus is no less than God. He is God, God made manifest, a clear communication of all that God is and all that he wishes to be made known.

If Christ is in no way inferior to God because he is God, he will possess all the perfection, the moral and natural attributes, of God. Such is the case, Edwards argued. "There is an admirable conjunction of diverse excellencies in Jesus Christ."[27] In him is the very nature of God. All that God is, Christ is. Moreover, the traits of God are in no way diminished in the person of Christ. He possesses all of God's traits in their fullness, "in an infinite degree."[28] As God the Son, Jesus wants for nothing the Father possesses.

It necessarily follows, then, that Christ possesses the attributes of God. "All the attributes of God," Edwards reasoned, "do illustriously shine forth in the face of Jesus Christ."[29] These attributes, both moral and natural, are found in Christ in their fullness as well. "God the Father hath no attribute or perfection, that the Son hath not, in

---

22 Edwards, "Miscellanies" No. 837, *Works*, 20:53.

23 Edwards, "Miscellanies" No. 104, *Works*, 13:272.

24 Edwards, "Miscellanies" No. 461, *Works*, 13:502.

25 Edwards, "Miscellanies" No. 1099, *Works*, 20:485.

26 Edwards, "Miscellanies" No. 1062, *Works*, 20:430.

27 Edwards, "The Excellency of Christ," *Works*, 19:565.

28 Edwards, "Thy Name Is as Ointment Poured Forth," in *The Blessing of God*, ed. Michael D. McMullen (Nashville: Broadman & Holman, 2003), 166.

29 Edwards, "Glorious Grace," *Works*, 10:395. See also "The Excellency of Christ," *Works*, 19:565.

equal degree, and equal glory."[30] Of those attributes, Edwards loved to single out certain attributes for special consideration. He referred often to those attributes belonging to both God and Christ, notably their omniscience and omnipotence.[31] More than that, however, Edwards singled out the divine, moral attribute of holiness with the greatest frequency. "And the beauty of his divine nature, of which the beauty of his human nature is the image and reflection, does also primarily consist in his holiness."[32] This must be so, Edwards argued elsewhere, to fulfill God's purposes in revealing himself. "If there was any merit in Christ's suffering and death, it must be because there was an excellent righteousness or holiness in that act of laying down his life."[33] Without the holiness of God in the sacrifice of Christ, there would have been no merit in his death, for common man lacks the necessary holiness to please God. Thus, Edwards connected the person of Christ, his divine character, with the work of Christ and the glory of God.

> For the better understanding of this matter [salvation], we may observe that God in the revelation that he has made of himself to the world by Jesus Christ, has taken care to give a proportionable manifestation of two kinds of excellencies or perfections of his nature, viz. those that especially tend to possess us with awe and reverence, and to search and humble us, and those that tend to win and draw and encourage us.[34]

God has revealed himself in Christ in order that he might woo man, calling him back to the Father.

---

30 Edwards, "The Excellency of Christ," *Works*, 19:570.
31 Edwards, *Notes on Scripture*, *Works*, 15:588, and "Christ the Supernatural Sun," *Works*, 22:55, respectively.
32 Edwards, *Religious Affections*, *Works*, 2:259.
33 Edwards, "Miscellanies" No. 532, *Works*, 18:77.
34 Edwards, *Some Thoughts Concerning the Revival*, *Works*, 4:463.

These two kinds of attributes [God's holiness and mercy] are as it were admirably tempered in the revelation of the Gospel: there is proportionable manifestation of justice and mercy, holiness and grace, majesty and gentleness, authority and condescension. God hath thus ordered that his diverse excellencies, as he reveals himself in the face of Jesus Christ, should have a proportionable manifestation, herein providing for our necessities.[35]

That is, God has revealed himself pursuant to his desire to glorify himself in the person of Christ in such a way as to instill awe and affection in the creature so that he, the creature, might see and know God.

Clearly Edwards believed that God does all things, including his self-revelation, for his own glory. God communicated that glory in Christ. "He is the shining forth of the Father's glory in himself in his eternal proceeding from the Father, or which is the same thing, he eternally proceeds from the Father as the shining forth of his glory."[36] Christ does not simply reflect that glory as a mirror might reflect the sun. No, he is more than that. He is the shining forth of God's glory. That is to say, Jesus Christ is the glory of God itself. Therefore, he possesses "all the glory of the Father."[37] Moreover, he shares that glory with the Father he so gloriously reveals. "The honor of God is that he is the fountain of the Deity, or he from whom proceed both divine wisdom and also excellency and happiness. The honor of the Son is equal, for he is himself the divine wisdom, and is he from whom proceeds the divine excellency and happiness."[38] Thus, for these reasons and many more, Edwards

---

35 Edwards, *Some Thoughts Concerning the Revival, Works*, 4:463–464.

36 Edwards, "Jesus Christ Is the Shining Forth of the Father's Glory," in ed. McMullen, *The Glory and Honor of God*, 226.

37 Edwards, "Jesus Christ Is the Shining Forth of the Father's Glory," in ed. McMullen, *The Glory and Honor of God*, 227.

38 Edwards, "Discourse on the Trinity," *Works*, 21:135–136.

would say, man would do well to remember with whom he deals when it comes to the matter of saving faith.

This admirable conjunction of excellencies appears in the acts and various passages of Christ's life. Though Christ dwelt on the earth in mean outward circumstances, whereby his condescension and humility especially appeared, and his majesty was veiled; yet his divine dignity and glory did in many of his acts shine through the veil, and it illustriously appeared that he was, not only the Son of man, but, the great God.[39]

JESUS IS MAN

The revelation of God in the deity of Christ falls short of accomplishing God's grand plan. The failure, however, comes not through any deficiency of the communicator, God, nor the translator, Christ, but the receptor, man. In his fallen condition man may admit that there is a God and mentally acknowledge that Christ may be the perfect image of that God in all his fullness, but his sinful condition blinds his spiritual eyes. In his sin, fallen man can neither fully see Christ for all that he is or respond to the grace of God as revealed in Christ because the barrier of his own dreadful sin remains. This barrier man cannot remove or breech. "There is an infinite distance between the human nature and the divine," wrote Edwards[40] So then, fallen man needs more than just a clear revelation of God's glory. He needs an avenue by which he might respond to that glory in a manner pleasing to God, an acceptable way of communicating with a holy God. He needs a go-between, someone who can overcome his inability and approach the perfect holiness of God. He needs someone like himself yet without the encumbrances of a sinful nature. He needs someone who can both speak to man and for man.

---

39 Edwards, "The Excellency of Christ," *Works*, 19:574.
40 Edwards, "Miscellanies" No. 741, *Works*, 18:366.

Thus is Christ. Though he be the great God, yet he has as it were brought himself down to be upon a level with you, so as to become man as you are, that he might not only be your lord, but your brother, and that he might be under advantages for a more familiar converse with him, than the infinite distance of the divine nature would allow of.[41]

What man needs can be found only in Jesus Christ, Edwards believed, for he is the God-man, fully God and fully man.

In man's original condition, that of Adam in the Garden of Eden before the Fall, his heart was disposed only to what was good for he knew no other. In man, the *imago Dei* shone brightly.

As there are two kinds of attributes in God, according to our way of conceiving of him, his moral attributes, which are summed up in his holiness, and his natural attributes, of strength, knowledge, etc. that constitute the greatness of God; so there is a twofold image of God in man, his moral or spiritual image, which is his holiness, that is the image of God's moral excellency (which image was lost by the Fall); and God's natural image, consisting in men's reason and understanding, his natural ability, and do-minion over the creatures, which is the image of God's natural attributes.[42]

As a result, the sinless man knew more of God because he was truly able to know God.

God created man in his own image, inspired him with a heavenly ray, gave him noble and excellent powers. This is evident to reason. And the beasts are left without those faculties that man has, whereby he is able to meditate on

---

41 Edwards, "The Excellency of Christ," *Works*, 19:589.
42 Edwards, *Religious Affections*, *Works*, 2:256.

God, or the first cause of all things, to see him who is invisible, and see future and eternal things.[43]

Adam walked with God and he talked with God. Yet, for a moment of sensual gratification, he rebelled and lost his soul and the hope of his progeny. Adam and each succeeding generation have since been rendered insensate, unwilling and unable to change spiritually. Edwards explained the depths of man's depravity and the darkness of his heart in *The Freedom of the Will*. "[Man's] heart is wholly under the power of sin, and he is utterly unable, without the interposition of sovereign grace, savingly to love God, believe in Christ, or do anything that is truly good and acceptable in God's sight."[44] Sin has turned man's affections from God to himself. Self-love now dominates the heart. This understanding of the human heart Edwards further described in *Original Sin*:

> These things together signify, that man is as it were all-over corrupt, in every part. And not only is the total corruption thus intimated, by enumerating the several parts, but by denying all good; any true understanding or spiritual knowledge, any virtuous action, or so much as truly virtuous desire, or seeking after God.... And in general, by denying all true piety or religion in men, in their first state.... The expressions [used in Scripture] are evidently chosen to denote a most extreme and desperate wickedness of heart.[45]

His soul eternally lost, fallen man lives without hope, forever separated from God by a vast chasm of evil of his own making.

The infinite distance that separates the creature from his Creator,

---

43 Edwards, "Nothing Upon Earth Can Represent the Glories of Heaven," *Works*, 14:148.

44 Edwards, *Freedom of the Will*, *Works*, 1:432.

45 Edwards, *Original Sin*, *Works*, 3:291.

that great gulf of sin, can be crossed by neither. God cannot sully his holiness by coming to man for he can tolerate no evil in his presence. Conversely, man cannot sufficiently overcome the evil of his infinite sins and guilt to approach an infinitely righteous God. In essence, the Fall of man caused a creation conundrum. Eternally separated in this manner, man cannot fulfill the end for which he was created, glorifying God. Nor can God fulfill his desire, glorifying himself.

Left with no other recourse but to rectify the desperate situation himself, God committed the act of "infinite condescension." He, in the second person of the Trinity, became man. He did so for one reason, said Edwards. "His condescension is great enough to become their friend: 'tis great enough to become their companion, to unite their souls to him in spiritual marriage: 'tis great enough to take their nature upon him, to become one of them, that he may be one with them."[46] Humbling himself, taking on human nature, Christ united himself to mankind in every way but in their guilt.

> And not only so, but that he might conform himself to his people, he became subject to affliction and temptation as they; lived in the same evil world as they do; was subject to the changes and vicissitudes of time as they are; dwelt in a frail body with them; took the human nature in its weak, broken state to be like them, and took it with those disadvantages that are the fruits of sin; was subject to hunger, and thirst, and weariness, pain, and death as they are; and liable to the afflicting, trying influences of evil spirits as they are, to be conformed to them.[47]

Becoming man's equal, he assumed their nature and their problems. While Jesus was no less a man than Adam, his divinity was in no way diminished either. Thus, Edwards argued, there is an "admirable

---

46 Edwards, "The Excellency of Christ," *Works*, 19:566.
47 Edwards, "The Sweet Harmony of Christ," *Works*, 19:443.

conjunction of excellencies," both divine and human, in Christ. He is the God-man, possessing the fullness of both natures. "Everything that is lovely in God is in him, and everything that is or can be lovely in man is in him," Edwards proclaimed, "for he is man as well as God, and he is the holiest, meekest, most humble, and every way the most excellent man that ever was."[48] It could not have been otherwise for at no time did Christ become somehow less than God. The divine was part of his eternal constitution. "It was impossible," Edwards explained, "that the acts of the will of the human soul of Christ should, in any instance, degree or circumstance, be otherwise than holy, and agreeable to God's nature and will."[49]

Christ's two natures coexist in the man named Jesus by the power of the Holy Spirit. "The Holy Spirit is the bond of union by which the human nature of Christ is united to the divine, so as to be one person," he wrote.[50] Due to the presence of the Spirit the divine attributes are communicated to the human so as to be the real attributes of that nature as well.[51] Thus, what belonged to the divine, preexistent Christ also belonged to the man Jesus in the incarnation. In this way, Christ remained all that God is and became all that man should have been.

Thus, for Edwards, the incarnation represents both the manifestation of God's glory and its communication as well. Christ became man to display God's perfections to an imperfect creation and restore the created order by calling man back to God.

> For Christ being united to the human nature, we have advantage for a far more intimate union and conversation with him, than we could possibly have had if he had remained only in the divine nature. So we, being united to

---

48 Edwards, "Children Ought to Love the Lord Jesus Christ," *Works*, 22:172.

49 Edwards, *Freedom of the Will*, *Works*, 1:281.

50 Edwards, "Miscellanies" No. 764b, *Works*, 18:411. See also "Miscellanies" No. 766, Works, 18:411–414 and No. 1043, *Works*, 20:383.

51 Edwards, "Miscellanies" No. 766, *Works*, 18:413.

a divine person, can in him have more intimate union and conversation with God the Father, who is only in the divine nature, than otherwise possibly could be. Christ, who is a divine person, by taking on him our nature, descends from the infinite distance between God and us, and is brought nigh to us, to give us advantage to converse with him.[52]

Christ has bridged the divide that separates sinful man from a holy God. Crossing the distance between the divine and the human by being both, the incarnation of Christ marks the temporal beginning of the restoration of the created order. God can now reveal himself to man through a man, a man truly after his own heart. Doing so, God in Christ has taken the first step toward bringing together heaven and earth.[53]

JESUS IS OUR MEDIATOR

"We have proved that the end of creation must needs be happiness and the communication of the goodness of God," remarked Edwards. "The Father's begetting of the Son is a complete communication of all his happiness."[54] Yet, for the communication to be complete and God's happiness to be operative in the creation, Christ must necessarily be more; he must fulfill yet one more role. Not only is he fully God, capable of communicating with God, he is also fully man capable of communicating with man. To that end, the incarnate Christ stands between these two warring parties, the righteous God on the one hand and the rebellious sinner on the other, mediating an eternal peace. In fact, Edwards said, that is the

---

52 Edwards, "Miscellanies" No. 571, *Works*, 18:110.

53 Commenting on Psalm 144:5, he wrote: "This was never so remarkably fulfilled as in the incarnation of Jesus Christ, when heaven and earth were as it were brought together. Heaven itself was as it were made to bow that it might be united to the earth. God did as it were come down and bring heaven with him. He not only came down to the earth, but he brought heaven down with him to men and for men" (Edwards, *The "Blank Bible," Works*, 24:539).

54 Edwards, "Miscellanies" No. 104, *Works*, 13:272.

purpose of the incarnation and the uniting of Christ's two natures in one person. "Therefore I suppose the name of our Mediator, 'Messiah,' or 'Christ,' or 'Anointed,' signifies the union of the divine nature to the human."[55] Thus, as the God-man, Christ can do for man what no one else could. As the perfect Mediator he alone can bring fallen men into God's perfect happiness.

When it comes to communion with a holy God, Edwards told his congregation, sinful man suffers a great disadvantage. Sin has not only blemished his soul but has metastasized and infected every area of his being, head to toe, heart to soul.

> They are full of sin; full of principles of sin, and full of acts of sin: their guilt is like great mountains, heaped one upon another, till the pile is grown up to heaven. They are totally corrupt, in every part, in all their faculties; and all the principles of their nature, their understandings, and wills; and in all their dispositions and affections, their heads, their hearts, are totally depraved; all members of their bodies are only instruments of sin; and all their senses, seeing, hearing, tasting, etc. are only inlets and outlets of sin, channels of corruption. There is nothing but sin, no good at all.[56]

Even worse, sin presents man with a threefold danger. First, sin leaves man in need of a merciful God who can and desires to remove the burden of his guilt. Second, that same sin drives man to flee from that merciful God into the dark corners of the Garden rather than running to him. Third, even if he would seek God, the sinful man cannot find him for God tolerates no challenges to his righteous authority. Forever stained by sin, fallen man cannot approach the throne of God for the mercy he needs because the cause of that very need, sin, forever blocks his way. Should fallen

---

55 Edwards, "Miscellanies" No. 487, *Works*, 13:530.
56 Edwards, "The Justice of God in the Damnation of Sinners," *Works*, 19:344–345.

man stand before God in his present condition he will experience not the grace but the wrath of God, the God who would "prove [to be] a consuming fire to 'em."[57] Therein lays the crux of sinful man's dilemma. He must approach God for mercy but he will not and cannot. He needs help. "For God the Father would have nothing to do with fallen man in a way of mercy, but by a mediator."[58]

Given that the notion of a mediator plays such a central role in soteriology (the doctrine of salvation), Edwards returned to this theme often. Moreover, he did not leave his audience wondering what he meant by his use of such a term. In one sermon, he clearly defined "mediator" as a "middle person between God and man." The mediator "takes upon him the work of a mediator between God and man, he puts himself in man's stead, he becomes man's representative."[59] Such was what man needed and such was what God provided.

Having determined that he would glorify himself in all ways, God decreed that he would display his glory in the most magnificent ways possible. First among those ways stands Jesus Christ, the embodiment of all that God is. To that end, God appointed Christ to the role of mediator in eternity past.

> Christ is the chosen of God both as to his divine and human nature. As to his divine nature he was chosen of God, though not to any addition to his essential glory or real happiness which is infinite, yet to [his] great declarative glory. As he is man, he is chosen of God to the highest degree of real glory and happiness of all creatures. As to both, he is chosen of God to the office and glory of the Mediator between God and man, and the head of all the elect creation.[60]

---

57 Edwards, *A History of the Work of Redemption*, *Works*, 9:188.

58 Edwards, *A History of the Work of Redemption*, *Works*, 9:358.

59 Edwards, "Even As I Have Kept My Father's Commandments," in ed. McMullen, *The Glory and Honor of God*, 212.

60 Edwards, "Miscellanies" No. 769, *Works*, 18:415.

God has done so out of his love for the Son[61] and the creature.[62] Moreover, revealing the great depths of God's mercy, the mediating work of Christ began not at the moment of his physical incarnation but at the moment of man's fall. "'Tis manifest that Christ began to exercise the office of mediator between God and man as soon as man fell," Edwards wrote, "because mercy began to be exercised towards man immediately."[63] Thus, even Adam, unbeknownst to himself, benefitted from the mediated mercy of God as Christ in some way interceded on his behalf, and that of his children, insuring that God would not execute instantaneous punishment on the deserving sinner and guaranteeing that the day would come when Christ would be fully revealed and his church saved for the glory and honour of God.[64]

That day did come, Edwards rejoiced. God has fulfilled his plan. The Mediator has come; the issue was never in doubt. As the God-man, Christ was perfectly suited to the role of mediator, a role only he could fill.

> The business of a mediator is as a middle person between two parties, at a distance and a variance, to make peace between them. Christ is the Mediator between God and man to make peace between them, by reconciling God to man [and man] to God. He alone is fit to be the Mediator.

---

61 Edwards, *Charity and Its Fruit, Works*, 8:144.

62 Edwards, *A History of the Work of Redemption, Works*, 9:130.

63 Edwards, *A History of the Work of Redemption, Works*, 9:130. Edwards also said: "After man fell, [Jesus] actually took on him[self] the work of the Mediator, and began to govern the world as mediator, and as actually fulfilling the work of such an office" (Edwards, "Miscellanies" No. 833, *Works*, 20:45).

64 "From this day [of the Fall] forward Christ took on him the care of the church of the elect, he took here the care of fallen man in the execution of all his offices. He undertook henceforward to teach mankind in the exercise of his prophetic office and to intercede for fallen man in the {exercise of the} priestly {office} and he took on him as it were the care and burden of the government of the church and of the world of mankind from this day forward" (Edwards, *A History of the Work of Redemption, Works*, 9:130).

> He only of the persons of the Trinity is fit, being the middle person between the Father and the Holy Ghost, and so only is fit to be a mediator between the Father and sinners, in order to their holiness and happiness.[65]

Perfect in two natures, he was more than adequate for the task for which he was appointed; he was the perfect Mediator. Being holy in every way, Christ enjoyed eternal access to God. Moreover, as a man, where Adam had fallen so miserably short, Christ accomplished perfect obedience to all of God's commands. Perfect in every way, Christ's sacrifice on the cross appeased the wrath of God. In one sermon, Edwards remarked, "The excellency of this person [Jesus] gives value to his blood, hence its atoning nature that 'tis the blood of an infinitely exultant person."[66] In another, he said,

> Fallen man is in a state of exceeding great misery, and is helpless in it; he is a poor weak creature, like an infant cast out in its blood, in the day that it is born: but Christ is the Lion of the tribe of Judah; he is strong, though we are weak; he hath prevailed to do that for us, which no creature else could do. Fallen man is a mean despicable creature, a con-

---

65 Edwards, "Miscellanies" No. 772, *Works*, 18:419. Edwards used this same language when he preached to his flock (Edwards, "Jesus Christ Is the Great Mediator and Head of Union," in ed. McMullen, *The Blessing of God*, 315). In this sermon, Edwards clarified his comments about Christ's fitness for mediation being a result of his being the second person of the Trinity, perfectly situated between the Father and the Spirit. "For in acting the part of a middle person between the Father and sinners in spiritual concerns, he acts the part of a middle person between the Father and the Holy Spirit in them" (ibid.). Edwards does not mean to suggest that the other two persons of the Trinity need mediation between themselves. Instead, he said, "What Christ does for men in the office of a mediator between God and men is to procure the Holy Ghost for man and bestow it upon him, and the whole may be summed up in that" (Edwards, "Jesus Christ Is the Great Mediator and Head of Union," in ed. McMullen, *The Blessing of God*, 316). Thus, Christ's mediation between God and man procures the gift of the Spirit of the former for the benefit of the latter.

66 Edwards, "Thy Name Is as Ointment Poured Forth," in ed. McMullen, *The Blessing of God*, 173–174.

temptible worm; but Christ, who has undertaken for us, is infinitely honorable and worthy. Fallen man is polluted, but Christ is infinitely holy: fallen man is hateful, but Christ is infinitely lovely: fallen man is the object of God's indignation, but Christ is infinitely dear to him. We have dreadfully provoked God, but Christ has performed that righteousness that is infinitely precious in God's eyes.[67]

Christ, the God-man, was precious in the eyes of God because he honoured God. More than that, however, he is precious because of the relationship that exists between Father and Son. "God doth necessarily love, even Jesus Christ. Jesus Christ is God's own Son, the same in substance with the Father; and God necessarily loves him."[68] Moreover, all that Christ would accomplish in mediation, all good that would come to the redeemed of God, would come by way of the supreme purchasing power of the Redeemer, the merit of their Mediator. For, as Edwards argued, the value of the sacrifice made depends upon the value of the sacrifice given. In his Mediator, the Christian finds all he needs to be restored to the grace of God because of the resident excellencies so sweetly united in Christ, the only one who is both God and man.

SUMMARY

Amy Pauw has rightly said, "The work of redemption reveals the depth and ultimate triumph of God's desire that the creation participate in the beauty and excellency of the Trinity."[69] In the work of redemption God has fulfilled the purpose of self-glorification. He has revealed himself, manifesting himself in the person of Christ. The second person of the Trinity possesses all the divine attributes in their perfection. He wants for nothing found in God. Moreover,

---

67 Edwards, "The Excellency of Christ," *Works*, 19:583.

68 Edwards, "The Everlasting Love of God," *Works*, 10:484.

69 Amy P. Pauw, "The Trinity," in *The Princeton Companion to Jonathan Edwards*, ed. Sang H. Lee (Princeton: Princeton University Press, 2005), 54.

God communicated his goodness in the man Jesus. Dwelling among men, Jesus expressed the love of God in human terms. Possessing all that could have been excellent in man, he fulfilled God's purposes for mankind by living a sinless life and glorifying God in all that he did. Finally, Christ as Mediator paid the human sin debt, removed the barrier between God and creation and, standing in the breech, brought heaven and earth together. For that, "God begrutches nothing to him."[70]

What is Jesus doing?

We have a glorious Mediator, who has prepared the way, that our prayers may be heard consistently with the honor of God's justice and majesty.[71]

Arguing for the infinite worth of Christ, Edwards told his congregation that they may approach the throne of God only "through him." He gave three reasons to substantiate his claim. First, in his substitutionary death, Jesus Christ paid the sin debt of the elect, "so that our guilt need not stand in the way, as a separating wall between God and us, and that our sins might not be a cloud through which our prayers cannot pass." Second, Christ's fulfillment of God's commands purchased for believers the privilege of having their prayers heard by God. Third, Christ now intercedes before the Father on their behalf, making "continual intercession for all that come to God in his name; so that their prayers come to God the Father through his hands." Thus, Edwards carefully connected his theology of prayer with the work of Jesus Christ.[72]

As Christ is God, man and Mediator, perfect in every way, so too his work will be perfect and accomplish everything God the Father has ordained. Christ's person and work must be related to each other.

---

70 Edwards, "The Terms of Prayer," *Works*, 19:778.
71 Edwards, "The Most High a Prayer-Hearing God," *Works* (Hendrickson), 2:116.
72 Edwards, "The Most High a Prayer-Hearing God," *Works* (Hendrickson), 2:116.

Just as God's moral nature is reflected in his natural attributes, Christ's character is revealed in his actions. These truths, Edwards maintained, find their expression in the doctrine of prayer. Those for whom Christ came to save, he saves. These he then unites to himself, sharing his happiness and perfection with them. And, having been united to them, he intercedes on their behalf before the Father. In this way, Edwards connected Christology with his theology of prayer for without the perfect nature of Christ, his works (salvation, union and intercession) are worthless and prayer impossible.

SALVATION

"All that a wicked man doeth is sin," Edwards explained to his congregation.[73] In that statement he included every action of the unbeliever. While he admitted that the merit or demerit of any given action might be different from that of another, ultimately all actions of the nonbeliever do not please God for they fail to render the honour due him. Man's sin nature produces acts that are self-motivated and driven by self-love. Even the prayers to which Edwards called the lost (because it put them in the frame of mind to consider God's mercy) offend the Creator because they focus on the individual not God. The prayers of the lost, he said, are "good for nothing." Speaking analogically, such prayers make God sick to his stomach. "They stink in his nostrils."[74] The abiding presence of sin in the life of the unbeliever places him at odds with God. He stands, as it were, a person *incommunicado*. He cannot speak to God because of the insurmountable barrier of his sin, that "cloud through which our prayers cannot pass."[75]

Man needs the mediator that God has provided in the person of Jesus Christ—the only One who can open the way to the throne of God. Jesus Christ did this on the cross.

---

73 Edwards, "There Is No Goodness in Praying, Though It Be Never So Earnestly, Merely Out of Fear of Misery" (1728), manuscript.

74 Edwards, "Envious Men," *Works*, 17:108.

75 Edwards, "The Most High a Prayer-Hearing God," *Works* (Hendrickson), 2:116.

By his atonement he hath made the way to the throne of grace open. God would have been infinitely gracious if there had been no Mediator; but the way to the mercy-seat would have been blocked up. But Christ hath removed whatever stood in the way. The veil which was before the mercy-seat "is rent from the top to the bottom," by the death of Christ. If it had not been for this, our guilt would have remained as a wall of brass to hinder our approach. But all this is removed by his blood. [76]

All this, Edwards reasoned, Christ accomplished through his sacrificial death, taking the just punishment of guilty men upon his guiltless self. Doing so, he satisfied God's wrath and made possible the renewal of relationships between God and man. Thus, Christ's death on the cross makes efficacious prayer possible.

Christ, in his role as mediator, unlocked the gates of heaven and paved the way to God with his blood. Doing so, he fulfilled his earthly reason for being, said Edwards.

The Messiah came to save men from their sins, and deliver them from their spiritual enemies; that they might serve him in righteousness and holiness before him: he gave himself for us, that he might redeem us from all iniquity, and purify unto himself a peculiar people, zealous. And therefore his success consists in gaining men's hearts to virtue, in their being made God's willing people in the day of his power. His conquest of his enemies consists in his victory over men's corruptions and vices. [77]

Or, as he noted in his notebook on Scripture,

---

76 Edwards, "The Most High a Prayer-Hearing God," *Works* (Hendrickson), 2:116.
77 Edwards, *Freedom of the Will, Works,* 1:246.

So Christ, God-man, Mediator, was made for the salvation of his church, to save it from that destruction and woe that is denounced against this wicked world, and that deluge of wrath that will overwhelm all others. The way in which persons were saved by the ark was by taking warning from Noah, the preacher of righteousness, to fly from the wrath to come, and hearkening to the call, and flying for refuge to the ark, and getting into the ark. So the way which we are saved by Christ is by flying from the deluge of God's wrath, and taking refuge in Christ, and being in him.[78]

Through his mediatorial death, Jesus Christ reconciles man to God by delivering him from his sin and into God's grace. He came to earth to be the Mediator and he fulfilled that calling.

Only Christ could have done this great work. Only he could mediate true peace between rebellious men and women and their holy King. He can do this, Edwards said, because of who he is. More specifically, he argued, "He only can answer the purpose who is both God and man."[79] Because of the "diverse excellencies" that reside coeternally in Christ, his every act proves to be of infinite value, the very "life and soul" of all that he did.[80] There is great "value and efficacy," Edwards wrote, in his humiliation and death.[81] Thus, Christ's death on the cross sufficiently atones for the combined guilt of all who would trust in him, seeking their refuge from the storm of God's wrath. The death of no other man would have sufficed.

Standing with Luther and Calvin, Edwards believed that all men and women bear the guilt of Adam's sin. Moreover, that guilt brings upon its bearer the unmitigated anger of God. This anger, Edwards said, must be "infinitely great and powerful" because it is God's

---

78 Edwards, *Notes on Scripture*, *Works*, 15:268.
79 Edwards, "Christ's Sacrifice," *Works*, 10:597.
80 Edwards, "Miscellanies" No. 483, *Works*, 13:524.
81 Edwards, "Miscellanies" No. 487, *Works*, 13:530.

anger.[82] Such is God's anger that no one can withstand it.[83] Man can neither tolerate God's wrath nor satisfy his justice. There was only one recourse—God had to provide a scapegoat, a sacrifice worthy of his acceptance. To that end, God in Christ became man, the Mediator, so that he might suffer God's just punishment in the sinner's place.

> But especially was it of rich and boundless grace that he gave his only Son for our restoration. By our fall, we are cast down so low into sin and misery, so deeply plunged into a most miserable and sinful condition, that it may truly be said, although all things are infinitely easy to God [with] respect to his omnipotency, yet with respect to God's holiness and justice, God himself could not redeem us without a great deal of cost, no, not without infinite costs; that is, not without the presence of that, that is of infinite worth and value, even the blood of his Son, and in proper speaking, the blood of God, of a divine person.
>
> This was absolutely necessary in order to our redemption, because there was no other way of satisfying God's justice.[84]

Uniting himself to the creature, assuming their nature, Christ assumed their guilt as well that he might satisfy God's requirement of holiness and his demand for justice.[85]

Christ's death served two great purposes in God's grand plan, Edwards said. "The death of Christ is both satisfactory and meritorious."[86] Satisfaction of God's wrath occurred when Christ took upon himself the sin debt of those who would find their salvation

---

82 Edwards, "God's Excellencies," *Works*, 10:426.
83 Edwards, "Life through Christ Alone," *Works*, 10:524.
84 Edwards, "Glorious Grace," *Works*, 10:393.
85 Edwards, "Miscellanies" No. 764a, *Works*, 18:410.
86 Edwards, "The Free and Voluntary Suffering and Death of Christ," *Works*, 19:513.

in him. The merit in his death, Edwards proclaimed, comes from the voluntary nature of his suffering. Because Christ died willingly, extra value accrued to his account. Since man remains "destitute of any righteousness in himself," salvation necessarily involves more than just the pardon of sin.[87] Christ may have atoned for his guilt but man still possesses no positive righteousness of his own. Thus, the believer still needs to access those merits of Christ. His righteousness must become their righteousness by means of justification.

Therein lays the close connection between satisfaction and justification. Justification, or imputation, results in the application of another's God-pleasing righteousness, in this case Christ's, to man's spiritual account. "God of his sovereign grace is pleased in his dealings with the sinner," Edwards declared, "to take and regard, that which is indeed not righteousness, and in one that has no righteousness, so that the consequence shall be the same as if he had righteousness."[88] Edwards presented this same thought to his readers in *Religious Affections*:

> And this is the notion of justification without works that it is not the worthiness or loveliness of our works, or anything in us, which is in any wise accepted with God, as a balance for the guilt of sin, or a recommendation of sinners to his acceptance as heirs of life. Thus we are justified only by the righteousness of Christ, and not by our righteousness.[89]

87 Edwards, "Justification by Faith Alone," *Works*, 19:148.

88 Edwards, "Justification by Faith Alone," *Works*, 19:148.

89 Edwards, *Religious Affections*, *Works*, 2:455. This concept was not limited to Edwards mature thought. He argued for the same definition of justification in his master's "Quæstio" at Yale in 1723: "By justification we mean an act of divine favor towards the sinner which forgives sins and approves him as righteous....But there can be no doubt that justification is a certain act of positive favor that not only frees a person from sin but is also understood in fact as the approval of him as righteous through the righteousness of Christ, both active and passive in both obedience and satisfaction" (Edwards, "A Sinner Is Not Justified in the Sight of God Except Through the Righteousness of Christ Obtained by Faith," *Works*, 14:60).

Elsewhere Edwards added, "We are justified only by faith in Christ, and not by any manner of virtue or goodness of our own."[90] Thus, justification comes entirely from God through Christ's merit. Now justified, fallen man now stands by the grace of God, leaning upon the works of Christ, "approved of God as free from the guilt of sin, and its deserved punishment."[91] Furthermore, justification serves as the means by which men may be admitted into communion with Christ, the presence of God and the rewards found only there.

Not only did it please God to so order salvation, the outcome pleased him as well. "God is well-pleased with Christ as mediator," Edwards commented. "He is well-pleased in him as high priest and sacrifice upon his own account."[92] Moreover, God glorified himself by so construing things.[93] Likewise, salvation by way of substitution and imputation glorifies Christ as well. Drawing upon Ephesians 4:6 and echoing his own language in *The End for Which God Created the World*, Edwards remarked in *A History of the Work of Redemption*: "And therefore the Work of Redemption being, as it were, the sum of God's work of providence, this shows the glory of our Lord Jesus Christ as being above all, and through all, and in all."[94] Hence, salvation in and through Christ alone communicates the glory of God, garnering glory for Father and Son just as God always desired.

---

90 Edwards, "Justification by Faith Alone," *Works*, 19:149.

91 Edwards, "Justification by Faith Alone," *Works*, 19:150.

92 Edwards, "The Sacrifice of Christ Acceptable," *Works*, 14:449.

93 "'Tis manifest from Scripture that God's glory is the last end of that great work of providence, the work of redemption by Jesus Christ" (Edwards, *The End for Which God Created the World*, *Works*, 8:485).

94 Edwards, *A History of the Work of Redemption*, *Works*, 9:518. Moreover, those that refuse to give Christ the glory due him have no part in the salvation that brings him such honour. "And that because God would glorify his Son as mediator, as the glory of man's salvation belongs to Christ, so 'tis the will of God that all the people of Christ, all that are saved by him, should receive their salvation as of him, and should attribute the glory of it to him, and that none that won't give the glory of salvation to Christ should have the benefit of it" (Edwards, "God Makes Men Sensible of Their Misery," *Works*, 17:162).

Having fulfilled every letter of the law, honouring God in every perfect act of obedience, Christ has mediated a lasting peace between God and man. He has made possible the restoration of fallen man to his former place of blessing, returning all that had been lost in Adam's fall.

> Christ is the Procurer of the inherent good that is in a Christian. He has purchased conversion and sanctification for the fallen creature. Christ has purchased for the elect light in their understanding and divine love in their hearts. All the graces of God's Spirit are things purchased and given in no other way than as being bought by His blood. By his suffering and obedience, Christ has purchased faith for them. He has not only purchased pardon of sin, justification, and eternal life, but He has purchased that they should come to Him and put their trust in Him for those things. He has purchased that they should live holy lives; all their qualifications and every holy act is the fruit of His purchase.[95]

More specifically, as it relates to the present study, Christ, by way of his role in salvation, makes meaningful communication between God and man possible.

> Christ, by his obedience, has purchased this privilege, viz. that the prayers of those who believe in him should be heard. He has not only removed the obstacles to our prayers, but has merited a hearing of them. His merits are the incense that is offered with the prayers of the saints, which renders them a sweet savour to God, and acceptable in his sight. Hence the prayers of the saints have such power with God; hence at the prayer of a poor worm of

---

95 Edwards, "Christ Is the Christian's All," in ed. Kistler, *The Puritan Pulpit*, 197–198.

the dust God has stopped the sun in his course for about the space of a whole day; hence Jacob as a prince had power with God, and prevailed. Our prayers would be of no account, and of no avail with God, were it not for the merits of Christ.[96]

In salvation, through the amazing grace of God and the inimitable works of Christ, man may now approach the throne of God.

UNITION

To approach God's throne requires something special, an intimate, personal knowledge of the saving work of Christ and faith in the sufficiency of that work. As Edwards said, "Justification is by the first act of faith."[97] While a full discussion on the nature of faith will come later, it is appropriate and necessary to mention the role of faith as it relates, looking backward, to salvation and, looking forward, to the blessings to be bestowed on the people of God through Christ. For in Edwards's theology of prayer, faith, or "unition" as he often called it, forms the connective tissue between soteriology and spiritual blessings—past, present and future. Without faith, the death of Christ on the cross was a senseless act of violence perpetrated on an innocent man. With faith, his sacrifice becomes the freeing gift of grace that God intended it to be.

"Unition" played a key role in Edwards's understanding of faith. He used the words "faith" and "unition" interchangeably. Edwards defined faith differently than many do today. Rather than believing faith to be simply a passive resting in Christ in the past, faith meant more to him. For Edwards, faith as expressed in "unition" should be ever present and active. "God don't give those that believe, an union with, or an interest in the Savior, in reward for faith, but only because faith is the soul's active uniting with Christ, or is itself the

---

96 Edwards, "The Most High a Prayer-Hearing God," *Works* (Hendrickson), 2:116.
97 Edwards, "Justification by Faith Alone," *Works*, 19:201.

very act of unition, on their part."[98] Unition, he argued, is an active state of being not just a past act or thought; unition must be an ongoing reality in the life of the believer or he is no believer at all. Using unition as an active verb, not a static noun, Edwards proceeded to describe the act of faith itself, portraying unition as the intersection of *notitia* and *assensus*.

It is fit that, seeing we depend so entirely and universally, visibly, and remarkably, on God, in our fallen state, for happiness, and seeing the special design of God was to bring us into such a great and most evident dependence; that the act of the soul, by which it is interested in this benefit, bestowed in this way, should correspond; viz. a *looking* and *seeking* to, and *depending* on God for it; that the unition of the heart, that is the proper term, should imply such an application of the soul to God, and *seeking* his benefits only and entirely, and with full sense of dependence on him, that as the condition before was obedience, or rendering to God, so now it should be *seeking* and *looking* to him, *drawing* and *deriving* from him, and with the whole heart *depending* upon him, on his power and free grace, &c. Faith is the proper active union of the soul with Christ as our Saviour, as revealed to us in the gospel. But the proper active union of the soul with Christ as our Saviour, as revealed to us in the gospel, is the soul's active *agreeing*, and *suiting* or *adapting* itself, in its act, to the exhibition God gives us of Christ and his redemption; to the nature of the exhibition, being pure revelation, and a revelation of things perfectly above our senses and reason; and to Christ himself in his person as revealed, and in the character under which he is revealed to us; and to our state with regard to

98 Edwards, "Justification by Faith Alone," *Works*, 19:158. Edwards believed salvation as explained in the Old Testament also depended upon "an active unition of the heart to Christ" (Edwards, "Miscellanies" No. 1353, *Works*, 21:493).

him in that character; and to our need of him, and concern with him, and his relation to us, and to the benefits to us, with which he is exhibited and offered to us in that revelation; and to [the] great design of God in that method and divine contrivance of salvation revealed. But the most proper name for such an action, union, or unition of the soul to Christ, as this, of any that language affords, is faith [emphasis mine].[99]

Notice the repeated use of the present active participle in this lengthy passage. Unition, Edwards argued, begins with a knowledge of the facts and results in action. Moreover, speaking of Christ's perfections as they relate to unition, Edwards said, "A seeing the sufficiency of Christ as our high priest, the sufficiency of the sacrifice he offered us, and the sufficiency and acceptableness of his mediation and intercession, implies a seeing his divine beauty consisting in his moral excellency."[100]

Assent to facts alone, however, does not equal saving faith, either. God requires more of the would-be believer. The truths revealed in Christ must move the true believer as well. To express the emotional truth of unition, Edwards used many beautiful word pictures, sometimes bordering on the sensual, that reflect the biblical language of Christ as the groom and the church as his bride.[101] Coming to Christ, he said, requires the recognition of Christ's loveliness, admitting to the excellencies of his person and his works, and longing for a union with him.[102] Those who unite with Christ find "soul-

---

99 Edwards, "Miscellanies Remarks Concerning Faith" §54, *Works* (Hendrickson), 2:585.

100 Edwards, "'Controversies': Justification," *Works*, 21:358.

101 In this way, Edwards interpreted the Canticle, otherwise known as The Song of Solomon or The Song of Songs, entirely Christologically. He read every interaction between the bride and her groom as a portrayal of that special relationship between the church and her Saviour. For example, see "Justification by Faith Alone," *Works*, 19:201.

102 Edwards, "What Is Meant by Believing in Christ," in ed. McMullen, *The*

satisfying delight" in him.[103] Unition, he said, is a "mutual love" wherein "the heart of Christ and the true Christian are united in love" toward one another.[104] Bound to Christ in love, the true believer finds his fulfillment in all that Christ is and does.

> The believer has also a complacence in Christ: he has complacence in the person of Christ, and hath complacence in his offices. He approves of him as a Redeemer. His soul acquiesces in the way of salvation by him, as a sweet, and excellent, and suitable way: it loves the way of true grace by Christ and by his righteousness, and is well-pleased in it, that Christ should have all the glory of his salvation. He takes full contentment in Christ as a Savior. Having found Christ, he desires no other: having found the fountain, he sits down by it: having found Christ, his hungry and thirsty soul is satisfied in him. His burdened soul is eased in him: his fearful soul is confident: his weary soul is at rest.[105]

In this loving relationship, true love continues. "Christ and the true Christian have [present tense] desires after each other."[106] Moreover, like a husband and wife who at marriage became one, the marriage remains vital so long as true love continues to exist between both parties. Saving faith, true unition, lasts forever. The moment of faith is never just in the past but always in the present. Thus, "Faith gives a title to salvation as it gives an union to Christ," Edwards wrote, "or is in its nature an actual unition of the soul to Christ."[107] True

---

Blessing of God, 240.

103   Edwards, "The Dying Love of Christ," in ed. McMullen, *The Blessing of God*, 292.

104   Edwards, "The Sweet Harmony of Christ," *Works*, 19:440.

105   Edwards, "The Sweet Harmony of Christ," *Works*, 19:441–442.

106   Edwards, "The Sweet Harmony of Christ," *Works*, 19:441–442.

107   Edwards, "Miscellanies" No. 729, *Works*, 18:354–355. Edwards continued, "But there is the same reasons why 'tis necessary that the union between Christ and

faith, that state of perpetual unition, forever weds the believer to Christ and continues to manifest itself throughout the eternal duration of the relationship.

Just as unition continues from the moment of salvation onward, the blessings associated with the believer's new love also continue, in both the present and the future. The fact that Christ has been resurrected and sits at the right hand of God proves to be the key to these blessings. "It is a matter of great comfort and rejoicing to any person, whatever circumstances that he is in, when he can say that he knows that his Redeemer lives."[108] Those united to Christ in a living faith presently enjoy the fruits of their relationship with him. "The believer lives," Edwards proclaimed, "by His life."[109]

Those who live in love to Christ enjoy many blessings and benefits. Indeed, theirs is the most pleasant life in the world. Being counted as one with the King, they in effect possess all things—all the riches of the world are theirs by association.[110] Edwards, however, saw those blessings as fleeting. Of momentary significance, earthly blessings pale in comparison to the yet greater riches found in unition with Christ. Edwards placed great emphasis upon the happiness the believer enjoys in Christ. The happiness that he pointed to amounted to more than passing temporal pleasure. "The

---

the soul should remain in order to salvation, as that is should once be, or that it should [be] begun: for it is begun to that end that it might remain, and if it could be begun without remaining, the beginning would be in vain. The soul is saved no otherwise than in union with Christ, and so is fitly looked upon [as] his. 'Tis saved in him; and in order to that, 'tis necessary that the soul should now be in him, even when salvation is actually bestowed, and not only that it should once have been in him. In order to its being now saved, it must now be one of Christ's; and in order to being fitly or congruously looked on as now one of Christ's, it is necessary that is should now be united, and not only that it should be remembered that he once was united. And there is the same reason why believing, or the quality wherein the unition consists, should remain in order to the union's remaining, as why the union should once be in order to the union's once being" (*Works*, 18:354–355).

108 Edwards, "He Knows His Redeemer," in ed. McMullen, *The Blessing of God*, 47.

109 Edwards, "Christ Is the Christian's All," in ed. Kistler, *The Puritan Pulpit*, 199.

110 Edwards, "Miscellanies" No. ff, *Works*, 13:183.

happiness with which the Christian is blessed, he has all in and by Christ, and that in three respects: all is communicated by Him, all is enjoyed in fellowship with Him, and He Himself is the Christian's objective happiness."[111] That is, the greatest happiness that man may know is that happiness obtained when man knows Christ. All true happiness, he continued, comes from the hand of Christ. Jesus procures and distributes happiness to those who find their delight in him. Moreover, he is, even now, carrying them along through life, transporting them from this earthly existence to that rest promised in heaven. Along the way, "It is He who clothes them with robes of glory and satisfies the soul with rivers of pleasure."[112] Furthermore, as his friend, his lover, and his spouse, the believer shares all that presently belongs to Christ, his glory included.[113] He and Christ are truly counted as one in all ways. In Christ, they enjoy that happiness that so eluded Adam in the Garden.

When Adam fell, he lost more than the earthly blessings associated with the Garden of Eden. He was rejected by God and lost his immediate access to and relationship with the Father. In Christ, believers are restored to that place of favour: "And through Christ they stand in a nearer relation to God the Father, and are partakers of a greater love of the Father, as partaking with Christ of his relation and love and partaking with him in the rewards of his obedience."[114] Because Christ, being the God-man, fulfilled all righteousness in his mediatorial role, he brings the redeemed with him to the Father. Like the prodigal son, they are welcomed back into the family of God and once more enjoy all the blessings associated with that great position of privilege because they stand positionally in Christ, by way of imputation, through active faith.

The saints, being united to Christ, shall have a more glorious

---

111 Edwards, "Christ Is the Christian's All," in ed. Kistler, *The Puritan Pulpit*, 200.
112 Edwards, "Christ Is the Christian's All," in ed. Kistler, *The Puritan Pulpit*, 201.
113 Edwards, "Miscellanies" No. 571, *Works*, 18:107.
114 Edwards, "East of Eden," *Works*, 17:344.

union with and enjoyment of the Father, than otherwise could be, for hereby their relation becomes much nearer. They are children of God in a higher manner than otherwise they could be; for being members of God's own natural Son, they are partakers of his relation to the Father, or of his sonship. Being members of the Son, they are partakers of the Father's love to the Son and his complacence in him.[115]

All that was the Son's, particularly his intimate relationship with the Father, now belongs to the believer, both in the present and for eternity. In unition, the believer has become once for all one with the Father and the Son, enjoying all the fruit of that relationship. He has become, by means of his unity with Christ, a member of the "blessed Trinity."[116]

Since the wall of separation was torn down at Calvary and the benefits thereof secured by faith, the believer may now freely access God in prayer. In fact, said Edwards, prayer gives evidence of faith. "Faith is that inward sense and act of which prayer is the expression," he commented.[117] Moreover, he argued, "The same expressions that are used in Scripture for faith may be well used for prayer also, such as coming to God or Christ, and looking to him."[118] As Edwards continued,

Faith in God is expressed in praying to God. Faith in the Lord Jesus Christ is expressed in praying to Christ and praying in the name of Christ, and the promises are made to asking in Christ's name in the same manner as they are to believing in Christ.[119]

---

115   Edwards, "Miscellanies" No. 571, *Works*, 18:109.

116   Edwards, "Thy Name Is as Ointment Poured Forth," in ed. McMullen, *The Blessing of God*, 179.

117   Edwards, "Faith," *Works*, 21:438.

118   Edwards, "Faith," *Works*, 21:438.

119   Edwards, "Faith," *Works*, 21:439.

By faith, the believer comes to a saving relationship with Christ and a renewed relationship with God, one of open communication because the death of Christ as God, man and Mediator merits his hearing.[120]

INTERCESSION

"Christ enforces the prayers of his people, by his intercession at the right hand of God in heaven," Edwards gratefully announced.[121] Not only has Christ provided the sacrifice sufficient to cover the sins of the elect and appease the anger of an offended God, not only does he reconcile alienated sinners with that holy God bringing those united in faith with him to the Father, Christ even now intercedes before the throne of God on their behalf.

Christ's ongoing ministry of intercession reveals the greatness of God's grace. Without this ministry, the prayers of man would not be heard "because God treats with fallen man only by this second Person, who is the Mediator."[122] Rather than being a point of consternation, however, this is great news. Believers have a Mediator who is the source of their great hope, both in salvation and in prayer. As the Son of God, fully divine and fully human, Christ's excellencies stand as the basis of the Christian's hope. He came to earth for this purpose[123] and he has returned to heaven for this purpose.[124] As man's perfect high priest Christ has entered into the holiest of places interceding on his behalf, both for eternal salvation and present blessing. This he can do because of the inestimable value of his self-sacrifice, his own blood cleansing both the saints and their

---

120   Edwards, "The Most High a Prayer-Hearing God," *Works* (Hendrickson), 116.

121   Edwards, "The Most High a Prayer-Hearing God," *Works* (Hendrickson), 116.

122   Edwards, "Seeing God Makes Men Sensible What They Are," ed. Kistler, *The Puritan Pulpit*, 132. See also, "Children Ought to Love the Lord Jesus Christ," *Works*, 22:177.

123   Edwards, "Miscellanies" No. 571, *Works*, 18:108.

124   Edwards, "The Threefold Work of the Holy Ghost," *Works*, 14:392.

prayers. Interacting with Song of Songs 4:3 and attributing the groom's words to Christ, Edwards wrote,

> There is probably a special respect to the speech of the saints in prayer, which is dyed in the blood of Christ, and by this means becomes pleasant, and acceptable, and of an attractive influence, like a scarlet cord, to draw down blessings. The prayers of the saints are lovely and prevalent only through the incense of Christ's merits.[125]

Accepted of God, Christ offers the believer the confident hope that his prayers will be heard because Christ, and Christ alone, can deliver the petitions of his people to the Father. His perfections ensure their hearing.

Not only is Christ the basis of the believer's every hope, Edwards reasoned, he guarantees their spiritual success.

> Seeing Christ is our only priest and sacrifice, let us offer up all our prayers, petitions, confessions, and praises in his name. He is our Mediator; wherefore, let us always come unto God by him. We are sure that we shall be accepted when we come in his name. Our prayers are loathsome till they are presented by him in his intercession for us, till they ascend up before God with this incense. When we ask mercy, let us hope for receiving only upon the account of an intercessor. Let us plead with his blood, for our prayers must be purified thereby before God will receive them. Christ has promised that we shall receive whatever we ask in his name.[126]

Christ serves as both the basis and the guarantee of prayerful success; he is God's appointed "medium of mercy."[127] As such, he intercedes

---

125 Edwards, *Notes on Scripture*, *Works*, 15:582–583.
126 Edwards, "Christ's Sacrifice," *Works*, 10:602.
127 Edwards, "Christ's Sacrifice," *Works*, 10:602.

in heaven, fighting, if you will, for his people.[128] Moreover, with
sure victory already his, Christ stands as Lord over all with all that
the believer truly needs at his disposal. Referring specifically to the
kingdom of Christ, Edwards argued that Christ, as mediator, "rules
over all events, every change, and every part of the universe so as
to conduce to the good of his church, and to bring to pass the ends
of his mediation, and to suit the purposes of his kingdom of grace."[129]
The prayers of believers pass through the one who has the ability
to give them their heart's desires.

   To encourage his flock to pray, Edwards reminded them that
Christ offers them all that belongs to him. As Christ is the Vine and
they are the branches, all the good that he possesses can be theirs
as it passes through him to them. He is the fountain of all that is
good, the source of their blessings.

> They that have found Christ have a fountain that is ex-
> ceeding full, full of that which they stand in need of for
> the supply of the wants, and satisfying the cravings of their
> souls; a fountain of that happiness that is true happiness,
> that which is exquisitely sweet, a fountain of living waters
> from whence rivers are continually flowing. They that
> find him find rivers of waters in a dry place.
>   Here they find an inexhaustible treasure. Here they find
> balm to heal the wounds of their souls, excellent food, "fat
> things full of marrow, and wines on the lees well refined"
> [Isaiah 25:6]. Here they find that fruit that is sweet to the
> taste. Here they find gold tried in the fire. Here is white
> raiment to clothe them. Here are crowns of glory.
>   Here they have enough, enough to live upon as long as
> they live in this world, and to all eternity. Here is enough;
> they can desire no more. The fountain is inexhaustible
> and never can be diminished. And has not a poor, ragged,

---

128 Edwards, *Notes on Scripture, Works,* 15:129.
129 Edwards, "Miscellanies" No. 86, *Works,* 13:250.

naked beggar, a wretched outcast, a wandering, famish-
ing, lost creature, cause of exceeding great joy when,
after it has long wandered in the wilderness, it finds such
a fountain?[130]

Having all their benefit in and through Christ, believers want for
nothing. The only appropriate response is to trust this mediator and
offer him their prayers. After all, commented Edwards, God awaits
the prayers of the faithful, ready to answer the cries of them that
love Christ.[131] In fact, he told his church, "[God] not only allows, but
encourages, and frequently invites them" for the prayers of his
people bring him great delight.[132]

As man's prayer partner, the believer's intercessor, Christ makes
their prayers a "sweet savour" in God's nostrils.[133] Without him their
prayers have no hope of ascending to heaven and pleasing God.
With him their prayers are assured a proper hearing. Therefore, the
only true prayer and communication with God comes through the
intercessory work of Christ. Those that know him and love him,
those that trust him with their eternal souls, need to look no further
than their Saviour for their temporal well-being. They need no
further encouragement to pray but to look upon his wonderful face
and trust his intercession. Thus, Edwards encouraged believers,
young and old, to pray without ceasing. "Come and cast yourself
down at his feet and kiss 'em, and pour forth upon him the sweet
perfumed ointment of divine love, out of a pure and broken heart,
as [Mary Magdelene] poured her precious ointment out of her pure,
alabaster, broken box."[134]

---

130   Edwards, "Seeking After Christ," *Works*, 22:292.
131   Edwards, "Miscellanies" No. 1283, in *"Miscellanies": Entry Nos. 1153–1360*,
ed. Douglas A. Sweeney, *Works*, 23 (2004):230.
132   Edwards, "The Most High a Prayer-Hearing God," *Works* (Hendrickson),
2:114.
133   Edwards, "Christ's Sacrifice," *Works*, 10:600.
134   Edwards, Letter "To Deborah Hatheway," *Works*, 16:93.

SUMMARY

According to Edwards's theology of prayer, the believer's prayers and the works of Christ are inextricably linked. One cannot enjoy the former without benefitting from the latter. "He hath entered for us into the holy of holies, with the incense which he hath provided," Edwards proclaimed, "and there he makes continual intercession for all that come to God in his name; so that their prayers come to God the Father through his hands."[135] In this way, the work of Christ plays a vital role in that theology of prayer. The second person of the Trinity, fully divine, became man so that he could stand in as humanity's proxy. He suffered. He died. He rose again. And, now, he is seated at the right hand of God, once more in his rightful place, basking in God's glory, fulfilling God's plan and sharing God's happiness.

Conclusion

> If you had loved Christ, you would love to go to him by prayer.[136]

A complete apprehension of the nature of prayer, Edwards held, begins with a proper sense of who God is and what he is like. The God to whom the Christian prays is perfectly holy, right in all his ways. In his mercy, God responds to the prayers of the saints because he is omniscient, knowing the end from the beginning, and omnipotent, fully able to bring his will to pass. Moreover, the God of the Bible is a prayer-hearing God. As such the believer ought to give God the glory due him, worshipping him in thought and deed, including their daily prayers.

Edwards's strong theology of prayer, however, only begins with an acknowledgement of the goodness and greatness of God. As

---

135   Edwards, "The Most High a Prayer-Hearing God," *Works* (Hendrickson), 2:116.

136   Edwards, "Children Ought to Love the Lord Jesus Christ," *Works*, 22:176.

Kreider has argued, Edwards's view of prayer is thoroughly Christ-centred as well.[137] The Christian must possess, he believed, a vision of the excellency of Christ and an acceptance of his labours on man's behalf, both in salvation and in prayer. Recognition of Christ's excellencies starts with a realization of who Christ is: God, man and mediator. Additionally, the would-be believer, and prayer, must have a grasp of what Christ has done in salvation, making atonement for the sins of those who will call upon his name, and unite with him, not in a singular act of faith but in an active faith. While Christ's work on the cross is complete, his ministry for the church continues in the form of his ongoing intercession for the saints. This work, too, Christ will complete fully, pleasing God in every way, because the perfect Son of God can do no other.

Those who see these things and rejoice in them place their faith in Christ and increase their prayers knowing that God can now hear them. Christ is the source of all good in the life of the believer and deserves to be the focus of their prayers. "If Christ is your all, then trust in Him alone," said Edwards. "Don't trust in yourself, nor in any man of the flesh; but have respect to Him only as your confidence. And whatever you do in prayer or praise, do all in His name."[138] Thus, for Edwards, prayer becomes a proper act of worship directed toward Christ as well as God.

As the believer directs his prayer to and through Christ, and God answers those prayers, he glorifies both Father and Son. In fact, Christ's glory, particularly as displayed in the salvation of wayward souls, should be the central focus of the church's prayer.

> Such being the state of things in this future glorious day of the church's prosperity, surely 'tis worth praying for. Nor is there any one thing whatsoever, if we viewed things aright, which a regard to the glory of God, a concern for the

---

137 Kreider, "Jonathan Edwards's Theology of Prayer," *Bibliotheca Sacra* 160 (2003):454.

138 Edwards, "Christ Is the Christian's All," in ed. Kistler, *The Puritan Pulpit*, 206.

kingdom and honor of our Redeemer, a love to his people, pity to perishing sinners, love to our fellow creatures in general, compassion to mankind under its various and sore calamities and miseries, a desire of their temporal and spiritual prosperity, love to our country, our neighbors and friends, yea, and to our own souls, would dispose us to be so much in prayer for, as the dawning of this happy day, and the accomplishment of that glorious event.[139]

These prayers, unlike any other, tend most directly to his glory by seeking the fulfillment of God's desires to manifest and communicate his own glory.

Finally, in Edwards's Christocentric theology of prayer, the love of Christ in prayer reigns supreme. If believers truly knew Christ, they would love Christ and they would love those things that Christ loves. They would seek his glory in all things and for all things go to him in prayer. For, as Edwards explained, prayer proves one's faith. "Prayer is only the voice of faith to God through Christ."[140]

---

139 Edwards, *An Humble Attempt, Works*, 5:340–341.
140 Edwards, "Faith," *Works*, 21:437.

Chapter 4

EXTERNAL BIOGRAPHY II
Awakening and revival

So [it] is God's will, through his wonderful grace, that the
prayers of his saints should be one great and principal
means of carrying on the designs of Christ's kingdom in
the world. When God has something great to accomplish
for his church, 'tis his will that there should precede it the
extraordinary prayers of his people.[1]

The 1720s presented Jonathan Edwards with great spiritual victories and struggles. He came to know his Saviour intimately and he came to doubt his salvation frequently. This decade also brought him great joy as he moved from the interim pastorate in New York through New Haven and East Windsor to Northampton, the locale of his greatest days as a pastor. There, on the western frontier of colonial Massachusetts, Edwards moved from obscurity to celebrity.

---

1 Edwards, *Some Thoughts Concerning the Present Revival of Religion in New England*, in *The Great Awakening, Works*, 4:516.

Northampton itself lacked no celebrity. The church there exerted great influence throughout New England through the voice and pen of its venerable pastor, Solomon Stoddard. In nearly sixty years of holding forth from the pulpit there, Stoddard oversaw five seasons of spiritual harvest and remarkable revival. His views on the qualifications for admission to the Lord's Supper caused a great theological disturbance when he opened the communion table to all citizens of the community who held no disagreement with the church's confession or its people, regardless of their own profession of faith or lack thereof. Moreover, through familial connections and sheer force of personality, Stoddard virtually controlled the practice of religion in the region. For that reason, contemporaries Cotton and Increase Mather, who opposed Stoddard and his communion innovations, suggested that Stoddard fancied himself the "Pope" of the Connecticut River Valley.[2] While their comment is seemingly loaded with hyperbole and opprobrium, others confirmed the Mathers's assessment. Writing years later about Stoddard, his maternal grandfather, Edwards commented, "Many of [the people in Northampton] looked on him almost as a sort of deity."[3] To Northampton and Solomon Stoddard's aging side, Edwards came in 1727. Little did anyone know at the time that the legend of the assistant would one day outshine that of the great river god he came to serve.

After leaving New York and turning down a call to the church in Bolton, Edwards eventually settled into the rhythms of the ministry under the watchcare of Stoddard. He settled in with his new wife, Sarah Pierrepont, the daughter of a prominent pastor in New Haven. In Sarah, Edwards found a paradigm of Christian spirituality.

---

2 Cotton Mather and Increase Mather, "A Defense of the Evangelical Churches," in *The Young Man's Claim Unto the Sacrament of the Lord's Supper* (Boston: n.p., 1700), 28–29.

3 Edwards, Letter "To the Reverend Thomas Gillespie," *Works*, 16:385. Edwards's own appraisal acknowledges the power and influence of Stoddard. "[He was] a very great man, of strong powers of mind, of great grace, and great authority, of a masterly countenance, speech, and behavior" (*Works*, 16:381).

Writing years earlier about Sarah, Edwards had waxed poetically
about her faith.

> They say there is a young lady in [New Haven] who is
> beloved of that almighty Being, who made and rules the
> world, and that there are certain seasons in which this
> great Being, in some way or other invisible, comes to her
> and fills her mind with exceeding sweet delight, and that
> she hardly cares for anything, except to meditate on
> him—that she expects after a while to be received up
> where he is, to be raised out of the world and caught up
> into heaven; being assured that he loves her too well to let
> her remain at a distance from him always. There she is to
> dwell with him, and to be ravished with his love, favor,
> and delight, forever.[4]

Sarah's communion with God, her attitude of prayer and praise,
impressed upon Edwards's mind the ideal Christian relationship
with the Father.

> She will sometimes go about, singing sweetly, from place to
> [place]; and seems to be always full of joy and pleasure; and
> no one knows for what. She loves to be alone, and to
> wander in the fields and on the mountains, and seems to
> have someone invisible always conversing with her.[5]

In Sarah, Edwards found both a helpmate and a soulmate. The
affection they shared, both matrimonial and spiritual, was obvious
to all. Fifteen years later, after having had spent a short time with
the Edwardses, George Whitefield remarked, "A sweeter couple I
have not yet seen."[6] For Edwards, Sarah was all that he wanted to

---

4 Edwards, "On Sarah Pierpont," *Works*, 16:789–790.
5 Edwards, "On Sarah Pierpont," *Works*, 16:790.
6 George Whitefield, *George Whitefield's Journals* (Edinburgh: Banner of Truth,

be and all that a soon-to-be famous pastor would need.

The next two years brought great changes in the Edwards household. The first of their many children was born in 1728. The greatest change and challenge of his young life, however, came one year later when the great Solomon Stoddard passed from the earth on February 11, 1729. Speaking of his death and his legacy, Edwards reminded the Northampton church, of the blessings they had enjoyed under Stoddard's care.

> There have [been] few places that have enjoyed such eminent powerful means of grace as you of this place have enjoyed. You have lived all your days under a most clear, convincing dispensation of God's word. The whole land is full of gospel light, but this place has been distinguishingly blessed of God with excellent means for a long time under your now deceased minister.[7]

With Stoddard gone, Edwards moved out of his grandfather's shadow and into the limelight.

The ecclesiastical spotlight of New England lit upon Edwards two years later. Called to deliver the Public Lecture in Boston on July 8, 1731, Edwards preached about the glory of God revealed in salvation and the nature of true faith, a faith that "abases men, and exalts God."[8] With his sermon, "God Glorified in Man's Dependence," Edwards sparkled in the eyes of the theological elites of his day. Recognizing his great talents and finding him a "workman that needs not be ashamed," his audience that day impressed upon Edwards the need to have the sermon published so it could be broadcast throughout the colonies. Of the young pastor from Northampton, the publishers commented, "We cannot therefore but express our joy and thankfulness that the great head of the church

---

1960), 476–477.
7 Edwards, "Living Unconverted," *Works*, 14:366.
8 Edwards, "God Glorified in Man's Dependence," *Works*, 17:213.

is pleased still to raise up from among the children of his people, for the supply of his churches, those who assert and maintain these evangelical principles."[9] With his message of the gospel proclaimed and printed, Edwards's career as a defender of the faith began.

The notoriety that "God Glorified" created for Edwards, however, would be but a spark compared to the forest fire of fame that would be lit in Northampton just four years later as the revival that began there in 1734 spread throughout the region. Appraisals of his fame and influence vary. Friend and biographer, Samuel Hopkins, held Edwards in high esteem, calling him "one of the greatest— best—and most useful of men, that have lived in this age."[10] Perry Miller, on the other hand, expressed great ambivalence toward Edwards, labelling him both a "genius" and an "enigma," a great mind hopelessly committed to a dying theological system.[11] Regardless of one's appraisal of Edwards, however, his influence was and is such that he stands, as Harry Stout rightly argued, "center stage" in the history of revival, a bright light of reason and faith who knew both intimately.[12]

Reviving souls

The years immediately following Stoddard's death were marked by spiritual degeneracy in Northampton. A "spirit of contention" divided the town with the *haves* and the *have nots* waging social war against each other. All that began to change late in 1734 as the Spirit of God began to move. The town enjoyed "a very remarkable blessing of heaven to the souls of the people in [Northampton]."[13] Over the next six months scores of people came to faith. Over the next several years fame came to Edwards.

---

9 Thomas Prince and William Cooper, "To the Reader," Appendix to "God Glorified in Man's Dependence," *Works*, 17:214–215.

10 Hopkins, *The Life and Character of the Late Reverend Mr. Jonathan Edwards*, iii.

11 Miller, *Jonathan Edwards*, xiii.

12 Harry S. Stout, "Edwards as Revivalist," in *The Cambridge Companion to Jonathan Edwards*, ed. Stephen J. Stein (Cambridge: Cambridge University Press, 2007), 141.

13 Edwards, *A Faithful Narrative of the Surprising Work of God*, *Works*, 4:149.

As Edwards recounted in his first report of the Northampton awakening, *A Faithful Narrative* (1737), several factors were in play. As he often did, Edwards had spent considerable effort trying to reform the morals of the town's youth, by which he meant teenagers and unmarried young adults. In the years leading up to the outbreak of revival, he had preached against their sinful behaviour and called upon parents to rise to the occasion and control their wayward children. Rather than offending the people, young and old, Edwards's call was answered. Of the former he noted, "The young people shewed more of a disposition to hearken to counsel, and by degrees left off their frolicking, and grew observably more decent in their attendance on the public worship, and there were more that manifested a religious concern than there used to be."[14] Even young children came to be touched by the awakening of religion in Northampton. Upwards of thirty children between the ages of four and fourteen were saved during this period. Though considered unusual in previous years, Edwards saw it as further proof of God's gracious providence and the extraordinary nature of the Northampton awakening.[15]

Edwards realized, however, that revival was about more than correcting public behaviour. It was about calling people to God in newfound exercises of faith. To that end, Edwards remarked, a faithful preaching of the gospel fueled the spiritual boom of 1734 and 1735. After preaching a sermon on the surprisingly controversial doctrine of justification by faith alone, Edwards witnessed his first harvest in Northampton: "And then it was, in the latter part of December, that the Spirit of God began extraordinarily to set in,

---

14 Edwards, *A Faithful Narrative of the Surprising Work of God, Works*, 4:147. Of their newfound spirituality, he noted, "Our young people, when they met, were wont to spend time in talking of the excellency and dying love of Jesus Christ, the gloriousness of the way of salvation, the wonderful free, and sovereign grace of God, his glorious work in the conversion of a soul, the truth and certainty of the great things of God's Word, the sweetness of the view of his perfection, etc." (*Works*, 4:151–152).

15 Edwards, *A Faithful Narrative of the Surprising Work of God, Works*, 4:158.

and wonderfully to work amongst us," he commented. "There were, very suddenly, one after another, five or six persons who were to all appearances savingly converted." Within six months hundreds of new souls were added to the church rolls.[16]

Individual testimonies proved to be vital to the spread of revival as well. The first of several mentioned in *A Faithful Narrative* was that of a young woman of questionable repute. Known more for her moral laxity, "company keeping" Edwards called it, than spiritual vitality, she came to faith in the early months of the revival. In her, Edwards saw "a glorious work of God's infinite power and sovereign grace."[17] Her salvation and ensuing transformation convinced many of the reality of her experience and their need for the same. Because of her example many others were saved, while yet more devoted themselves to Bible reading and prayer.

Two other individuals merited Edwards's special attention, as well. The first, also a young woman, was Abigail Hutchinson.[18] Her awakening began in the winter following the start of the revival. Hearing of others being saved, her heart burned with envy for the peace she did not know. Determined to experience God's grace as her peers had already done, she devoted herself to reading the Bible. Beginning in the Old Testament, she experienced a season of profound guilt for her sin before turning to the Gospels for consolation. Her studies, however, merely confirmed what she feared: her strivings could not save her from God's wrath. In less than two weeks, though, she discovered the grace of God for herself. She came to have "a sweet sense of the excellency and loveliness of Christ" and spent entire days in "a constant ravishing view of the glory of God and Christ."[19] Dwelling on those things, he wrote, she was consumed with a sense of "the glory of Christ, and of God in his

---

16 Edwards, *A Faithful Narrative of the Surprising Work of God, Works*, 4:149.

17 Edwards, *A Faithful Narrative of the Surprising Work of God, Works*, 4:149.

18 Edwards, *A Faithful Narrative of the Surprising Work of God, Works*, 4:191–199.

19 Edwards, *A Faithful Narrative of the Surprising Work of God, Works*, 4:195.

various attributes."[20] Along with her young faith came her untimely death. In the days prior "she had great longings to die," longings to meet her Saviour.[21] "Thoughts of dying were sweet to her."[22] Abigail Hutchinson's passion for all things divine, her right understanding of God and her complacence in the beauty of Christ were for Edwards evidence of true conversion.

More remarkable yet was the conversion narrative of Phebe Bartlett.[23] Barely past her fourth birthday, Phebe experienced the saving love of God. About this time, Edwards said, she listened intently to the spiritual advice given to others. Moreover, as is clear from the amount of ink he spilled on her prayer life, Edwards believed prayer played a vital role in her salvation. During this time of spiritual birth, the young girl would "retire several times in a day" for private prayer.[24] As her interest in all things religious continued to grow, so too did her attention to prayer, praying as often as five or six times per day. Nothing could distract her from this duty. Several months later, in mid-summer, she was overheard in her closet, crying to God, "Pray, blessed Lord, give me salvation! I pray, beg, pardon all my sins!"[25] Shortly thereafter she began to pray for the salvation of others, particularly children. Of a couple young friends, she remarked to her mother, "I told 'em they must pray, and prepare to die, that they had but a little while to live in this world, and they must be always ready."[26] Not surprisingly, she reduced a number of her playmates to tears with her dire warnings of death and damnation. The young girl remained faithful in her witness and her prayer up until the time of Edwards's writing two years later.[27] Thus, sharing a kindred spirit with her pastor, Phebe Bartlett also became a model

---

20 Edwards, *A Faithful Narrative of the Surprising Work of God*, *Works*, 4:195.

21 Edwards, *A Faithful Narrative of the Surprising Work of God*, *Works*, 4:196.

22 Edwards, *A Faithful Narrative of the Surprising Work of God*, *Works*, 4:196.

23 Edwards, *A Faithful Narrative of the Surprising Work of God*, *Works*, 4:199–205.

24 Edwards, *A Faithful Narrative of the Surprising Work of God*, *Works*, 4:199.

25 Edwards, *A Faithful Narrative of the Surprising Work of God*, *Works*, 4:200.

26 Edwards, *A Faithful Narrative of the Surprising Work of God*, *Works*, 4:204.

27 Edwards, *A Faithful Narrative of the Surprising Work of God*, *Works*, 4:205.

believer in his paradigm for revival with her enraptured views of heaven and her constant converse with God.

The parish in Northampton experienced a time of wondrous awakening in the mid-1730s. Of this, Edwards had no doubt. The Spirit moved; people believed. Edwards was convinced and he was encouraged. Yet, he was concerned, as well. They must be ever vigilant, he warned, if the blessing of God was to continue. They must not take the salvation of their souls for granted. Preaching just months into the revival, Edwards reminded them that this remarkable work of God's grace was, in some way, in their hands.

> God is pleased at this time, in a very remarkable manner, to pour out his Spirit amongst us (glory be to his name therefore!). You that have a mind to obtain converting grace, and to go to heaven when you die, now is your season! Now, if you have any sort of prudence for your own salvation, and have not a mind to go to hell, improve this time! Now is the accepted time! Now is the day of salvation! You that in time past have been called upon, and have turned a deaf ear to God's voice, and long stood out and resisted his commands and counsels, hear God's voice today, while it is called today! Don't harden your hearts at such a day as this is! Now you have a special and remarkable price put into your hands to get wisdom, if you have but a heart to improve it.[28]

To this he added warnings for those who already believed. Two years after the revival, when the embers of those wonderful days were already growing cool, Edwards warned that they must pray lest they turn back to their old ways, letting division and diversion reign again.

---

28 Edwards, "Pressing into the Kingdom of God," *Works*, 19:291.

The second thing I would mention, as a proper thing for us to attend that the Spirit of God may not leave us, is prayer. This will be a proper acknowledgement of God as the only author of this mercy. As [God] expects to be inquired of, and sought to, for the bestowment of such a mercy, so likewise for the continuance of it. And besides prayer for such a mercy of God in secret, and in our families, and in our ordinary public worship, I should think it would be a fit and suitable thing that, at sometimes, days of prayer should be kept by private societies and, at other times, parts of days, to beg of God the continuance of his presence amongst us. But in our prayers we should be sure not to forget to bless God for what we have received.[29]

History suggests that Edwards's concerns were well-founded, his point clear and his counsel wise. Christians, above all else, must be like Phebe Bartlett; they must always prove and improve their faith by prayer.

Reviving the revival

Edwards was justly concerned about the future of religion in Northampton. In short order, the revival fires of 1735 were damped and then finally extinguished. The "spirit of contention" that marked the town in years prior returned and with it divisions among the people. Even such a joyous occasion as the building of a new, larger church came to be divisive as the members jockeyed for the choicest seats. Edwards saw it coming, but was unable to stop it. The joy of the revival gone, the now famous pastor admitted that he had erred in his estimation of the extent of spiritual renewal. While the mouths of the people had "been filled with praises," they were also "filled with backbitings."[30] Some had not been truly reformed but merely carried along by the winds of excitement.

---

29 Edwards, "Continuing God's Presence," *Works*, 19:403.
30 Edwards, "Peaceable and Faithful Amid Division and Strife," *Works*, 19:674.

The remedy to their problem, he believed, was meek and humble prayer.[31]

Edwards knew something about the value of a healthy prayer life. Continuing habits developed in his younger years, he was observed to spend thirteen hours of every day in his study preparing his heart and mind for the duties at hand. Part of the time spent there was spent in prayer.

...there is much evidence that he was punctual, constant, and frequent in secret prayer, and often kept days of fasting and prayer in secret, and set apart time for serious, devout meditations on spiritual and eternal things, as part of his religious exercises in secret. It appears from his diary, that his stated seasons of secret prayer were, from his youth, three times a day,—in his journeys, as well as at home. He was, so far as can be known, much on his knees in secret, and in devout readings of God's word, and meditations upon it. And his constant, solemn converse with God, in these exercises of secret religion, made his face, as it were, to shine before others.[32]

Edwards expected other Christians to be equally devoted to prayer. His prayer life was to be the example, not the exception.

During the latter years of the decade, Edwards preached often on spiritual reformation. Though many sermons bear testimony to his conviction that this was much needed in Northampton, two well-known sermons serve as exemplars of Edwards's ability to turn the jeremiad into encouragement. The first of these sermons he brought to the pulpit in 1738 in a series now known as *Charity and Its Fruit*. Taking 1 Corinthians 13 as his text, Edwards spent thirteen weeks extolling the virtue of Christian love. As his doctrinal

---

31 Edwards, "Peaceable and Faithful Amid Division and Strife," *Works*, 19:679.
32 Sereno E. Dwight, "Memoirs of Jonathan Edwards," *Works* (Hendrickson), 1:ccxxv.

summary statement for the entire series explains, a loving attitude proves the reality of one's faith: "All that virtue [which] is saving, and distinguishing of true Christians from others, is summed up in Christian or divine love."[33] Those who are truly regenerated, he said, are truly loving. "They dispose to love to God as the supreme good. They unite in heart in love to Christ. They incline the heart to flow out in love to God's people."[34] Such was the message that Northampton needed at that time. Such was the message that Northampton was given.

Seeking to reform the church permanently, Edwards told his people that he was looking for changed behaviour. "Saving faith," he explained, "tends to practice."[35] The implication was clear. Many in Northampton did not possess saving faith because many in Northampton did not practice what he preached. To that end, he once more called them to trust God and hold him in high esteem. Desire God and seek him, he begged, prayer being the means by which these ideals were to be accomplished.

> You must in your meditations and holy exercises be much in conversing with heavenly persons and enjoyments. You cannot earnestly and constantly seek heaven without having your thoughts much there. Therefore turn the current of your thoughts and meditations towards that world of love, and that God of love who dwells there, and towards Christ who is ascended and sits there at the right hand of God; and towards the blessed enjoyments of that world. And be much in conversation with [God and Christ,] without which heaven is no heaven.[36]

---

33 Edwards, *Charity and Its Fruit, Works*, 8:131.
34 Edwards, *Charity and Its Fruit, Works*, 8:145.
35 Edwards, *Charity and Its Fruit, Works*, 8:299.
36 Edwards, *Charity and Its Fruit, Works*, 8:395.

If their souls were to be saved, Edwards believed, it would begin with prayer.

The second sermon of note was also a prolonged series. In 1739, Edwards led his congregation through a thirty-sermon study of *A History of the Work of Redemption*. Based upon Isaiah 51, this Christ-centred series explained all of history as it relates to God's supreme act of redemption at the cross. Here, too, prayer repeatedly came to the fore as both a means to and an evidence of salvation. Beginning with Genesis 4 and the account of Enoch, Edwards showed his congregation that this has always been the case. "Prayer is a duty of natural religion, and a duty that a spirit of piety does most naturally and manifestly lead men [into]." Prayer is, he said, "the very breath of a spirit of piety."[37] Moreover, prayer is the key to continued revival. To this, and not their personal interests, they should turn their attention.

The work of God did resume. Another remarkable season of awakening came. This time, however, the fires of revival could be found beyond the Connecticut River valley as far south as Georgia and as far east as Europe. Utilizing the efforts of men like Edwards, George Whitefield and Gilbert Tennent, the Spirit of God moved upon the face of the earth again. With great rejoicing, however, came great dissension. Just as had happened in 1735, contention came close upon the heels of the revival. Those for and those against the revivals worked against each other, some arguing that the revivals brought needed enthusiasm to religion while others argued that such enthusiasm was sinful excess unrelated to any true work of God. To this contention over the nature of revival, Edwards directed considerable attention in the first years of the 1740s.

Even Yale, Edwards's spiritual proving grounds, became an ecclesiastical battlefield in the fight for the soul of New England's churches. This time, however, Yale found itself pitted squarely against Edwards. The administration aligned itself with the anti-

---

37 Edwards, *A History of the Work of Redemption*, *Works*, 9:141.

revival party in response to the personal attacks of some of the revivalists against those on the faculty and in the community who opposed them. To this arena Edwards came in 1741, just two months after he delivered his already famous "Sinners in the Hands of an Angry God." In the sermon that Edwards preached at the Yale commencement that year, he outlined what he believed to be the "distinguishing marks of a work of the Spirit of God." This sermon, given in bold opposition to the prevailing spirit at Yale, became the foundation for Edwards's first apologetic for the validity of the revivals.

The title of Edwards's defense, *Distinguishing Marks of a Work of the Spirit of God*, in typical Puritan fashion, accurately portrays the contents of the piece. In this work, Edwards considered those signs, or marks, that distinguished a true work of God from that which is false. He began with a list of nine ambivalent signs, things which their presence alone does not prove or disprove the revival to be truly gracious. Edwards then turned his attention to five marks that do prove the revival to be an authentic work of God. First among these was an increase of esteem for Christ. The second sure sign is the presence of opposition as Satan's kingdom comes under attack, just as he warned his congregation in *A History of the Work of Redemption*. True revival also results in an increased appreciation for the Bible and a greater display of the spirit of truth. Finally, echoing his teaching in *Charity and Its Fruit*, a spirit of love to God and man prevails in times of real revival. All these, said Edwards, were present in the revival that came to be known as the Great Awakening just as they had been in the harvests experienced in the days of the "venerable Stoddard."[38]

Again, Edwards pointed to pious prayer as proof of revived souls and churches. Those who are revived, he said, the Spirit revives and draws to God. "The Spirit excites to love on these motives, and makes the attributes of God as revealed in the Gospel and manifested in Christ, delightful objects of contemplation; and makes the

---

38 Edwards, *Distinguishing Marks of a Work of the Spirit of God*, *Works*, 4:268.

soul to long after God and Christ, after their presence and communion, and acquaintance with them, and conformity to them."[39] Moreover, those truly converted could not but support the further work of God upon those who had not been so blessed. Those who oppose the revivals, on the other hand, necessarily run the risk of finding themselves guilty of the unpardonable sin. To keep themselves from falling into that egregious error, the people of New England should throw themselves wholeheartedly behind the revivals and become zealous promoters of a thing that brings such great glory to God, he said. As he had written to Deacon Lyman Moses, those who supported the revival as they should would pray for its continued success. To that end, Edwards encouraged Deacon Moses, "Let us look to God to plead his own cause, and to get to himself the victory."[40]

Edwards's most significant work to date also focused on the revival. "We in New England are at this day engaged in a more important war [than any geopolitical conflict]," he wrote in the introduction to *Some Thoughts Concerning the Present Revival of Religion in New England*.[41] He penned *Some Thoughts* in 1741 at the height of the debate. Edwards wrote expressly for the purpose of warning his readers against interfering with the "extraordinary," "glorious work of God" taking place in their midst.[42] While many complained of the variety of religious experience seen among the revived, Edwards argued that such things were perfectly in keeping with the character of God.

Indeed God has not taken that course, nor made use of those means, to begin and carry on this great work, which

39 Edwards, *Distinguishing Marks of a Work of the Spirit of God, Works*, 4:256.
40 Edwards, Letter "To Deacon Lyman Moses," *Works*, 16:98.
41 Edwards, *Some Thoughts Concerning the Present Revival of Religion in New England, Works*, 4:291.
42 Edwards, *Some Thoughts Concerning the Present Revival of Religion in New England, Works*, 4:293.

men in their wisdom would have thought most advisable, if he had asked their counsel; but quite the contrary. But it appears to me that the great God has wrought like himself, in the manner of his carrying on this work; so as very much to show his own glory, and exalt his own sovereignty, power and all-sufficiency, and pour contempt on all that human strength, wisdom, prudence and sufficiency, that men have been wont to trust, and to glory in; and so as greatly to cross, rebuke and chastise the pride and other corruptions of men.[43]

God can work in any manner he so deems, Edwards argued, because he is God. In fact, he continued, God may allow error to mingle with spiritual perfection so as to humble people. For that reason, God's work is to be respected rather than challenged, supported rather than opposed.

Among those revived in this second season of awakening, Edwards recognized many of the same signs he had seen in the first. The young people changed their ways.

There is a strange alteration almost all over New England amongst young people: by a powerful, invisible influence on their minds, they have been brought to forsake those things in a general way, as it were at once, that they were extremely fond of, and greatly addicted to, and that they seemed to place the happiness of their lives in, and that nothing before could induce them to forsake; as their frolicking, vain company-keeping, nightwalking, their mirth and jollity, their impure language, and lewd songs.[44]

---

43 Edwards, *Some Thoughts Concerning the Present Revival of Religion in New England*, *Works*, 4:294.

44 Edwards, *Some Thoughts Concerning the Present Revival of Religion in New England*, *Works*, 4:326.

Now, he said, they dedicated themselves to matters divine. Not only the youth, but great multitudes displayed the same change in character. Among these he included young and old, slave and free. As an example of such a person, Edwards included a lengthy, though veiled, description of Sarah's renewed spiritual vitality. As in the Northampton revival of the 1730s, young children were also redeemed. Like Phebe before them, groups of children, now *en masse*, devoted themselves to group prayer. In that way, this revival displayed the same signs as Edwards had recognized and promoted six years earlier.

Just as Edwards had encouraged his church to pray during and following the local revival, he now encouraged his broader audience to do so as well. Prayer for the revival, he argued, is the duty of the revived.

> It seems to me that the circumstances of the present work do loudly call God's people to abound in this; whether they consider the experience God has lately given 'em of the worth of his presence, and of the blessed fruits of the effusions of his Spirit, to excite them to pray for the continuance and increase, and greater extent of such blessings, or whether they consider the great encouragement God has lately given 'em to pray for the outpouring of his Spirit and the carrying on this work, by the great manifestations he has lately made of the freeness and riches of his grace.[45]

God's plan demands their participation, he continued.

> So [it] is God's will, through his wonderful grace, that the prayers of his saints should be one great and principal means of carrying of the designs of Christ's kingdom in the world. When God has something very great to accomplish for his

---

45 Edwards, *Some Thoughts Concerning the Present Revival of Religion in New England, Works*, 4:516.

church, 'tis his will that there should precede it the extra-ordinary prayers of his people.[46]

The prayers of God's people for this glorious work must be constant. Until they do pray, God waits in heaven, holding back the streams of his great blessing.

God seems now, at this very time, to be waiting for this from us. When God is about to bestow some great blessing on his church, it is often his manner, in the first place, so to order things in his providence as to shew his church their great need of it, and to bring 'em into distress for the want of it, and so put 'em upon crying earnestly to him for it.[47]

Such prayers, he believed, were requisite to God's sending revival because they glorified God and revealed the depths of man's great dependence upon him. If the people of God were to see the revival spread and the glory of God magnified, they must do more than stand by passively as the debates raged on. They must weigh in with their spiritual support, the great and the small, the congregation and the congregational minister. They all must go to God with their "earnest and importunate prayer."[48] They must, as it were, storm the gates of heaven "with their humble, fervent, and incessant prayers."[49] Or, they must go to him for forgiveness. There are no neutral parties in this debate, Edwards said.

Indeed, Edwards did go to God in prayer. He called the people

46 Edwards, *Some Thoughts Concerning the Present Revival of Religion in New England*, *Works*, 4:516.

47 Edwards, *Some Thoughts Concerning the Present Revival of Religion in New England*, *Works*, 4:517.

48 Edwards, *Some Thoughts Concerning the Present Revival of Religion in New England*, *Works*, 4:517.

49 Edwards, *Some Thoughts Concerning the Present Revival of Religion in New England*, *Works*, 4:518–519.

of the church to do the same, but to no avail. Again the revival fires faded into the night, smothered by incessant controversy. Edwards's hopes were once more too high and his warnings true. What he feared, spiritual apostasy, descended upon New England and Northampton as they ignored or rejected the true work of God in their midst.

Reviving prayer for revival

While revivals continued throughout 1741, signs of abatement began to appear by the summer of 1742. Evidence of spiritual declension returned. The end was at hand. To one correspondent, Edwards commented, "But in the general people's engagedness in religion and the liveliness of their affections have been on the decline: and some of the young people especially have shamefully lost their liveliness and vigor in religion, and much of the serious-ness and solemnity of their spirits."[50] By 1743, the spiritual outlook was but one of "melancholy." Edwards wrote:

> Many high professors are fallen, some into gross immorali-ties; some into the opinions of sectaries; some into a rooted, spiritual pride, enthusiasm, and an incorrigible wildness of behavior; some into a cold, carnal frame of mind, showing a great indifference to things of religion.[51]

Still Edwards hoped that God's gracious work would continue.

> But there are many—and I hope those the greater part of those that were professed converts—appear hitherto like the good ground. And notwithstanding the thick and dark clouds that so soon follow that blessed sunshine that we have had, yet I cannot but steadfastly maintain an hope and persuasion that God will revive this work, and that

---

50 Edwards, Letter "To the Reverend Thomas Prince," *Works*, 16:125.
51 Edwards, Letter "To the Reverend William McCulloch," *Works*, 16:135.

what has been so great and very extraordinary is a fore-
runner of a yet more glorious and extensive work.[52]

To that end, Edwards applied himself in the mid-1740s.

Explaining the spiritual malaise among the supposedly regenerated was Edwards's first order of business for, as he said, there is no
greater question, than "What is the nature of true religion?"[53] "In
the midst of the dust and smoke" that followed the abrupt end of
the awakenings, Edwards wrote *Religious Affections* for the purpose
of answering that question. As he acknowledged, now matured
by the conflict, false religion creeps in during times of great revival.
The task at hand was to discern the reality of the conversions that
had so quickly gone awry.

"True religion, in great part," Edwards wrote, "consists in holy
affections."[54] Holy affections prove themselves to be true in the
vigorous application of the will toward things divine. Look no
further than Jesus for an example of these affections at work.

> He whom God sent into the world, to be the Light of the
> World, and Head of the whole church, and the perfect
> example of true religion and virtue, for the imitation of all,
> the shepherd whom the whole flock should follow
> wherever he goes, even the Lord Jesus Christ, was a person
> who was remarkably of a tender and affectionate heart;
> and his virtue was expressed very much in the exercise of
> holy affections.[55]

In other words, those who are true followers of Christ *will* follow
Christ. They will do what Jesus did for his affections *will* become
theirs.

---

52 Edwards, Letter "To the Reverend William McCulloch," *Works*, 16:135.
53 Edwards, *Religious Affections*, *Works*, 2:84.
54 Edwards, *Religious Affections*, *Works*, 2:95.
55 Edwards, *Religious Affections*, *Works*, 2:111.

Edwards knew that it was easier to make such a broad statement than to prove it. So, as he had done in *Distinguishing Marks*, he gave an extensive list of signs, both ambivalent and positive, related to the validity of the revival of one's soul. Speaking negatively, Edwards said many of the excesses of the revival and so-called proofs given at the time were not necessarily sure signs. Among these he included high emotions, bodily affectations and excited talk of religion. There are, however, twelve sure signs of true religion. True religion, he said, begins with a work of God not man and will result in an interest in divine things and a complete appreciation of the things of God and Christ. The twelfth sign, Edwards wrote, proves to be the most reliable of all. "Gracious and holy affections have their exercise and fruit in Christian practice."[56] That is, those who are truly converted will not return to the sins of their past but will be ever-striding toward Christlikeness in all their actions.

Throughout the positive signs given in *Religious Affections* Edwards mentions prayer as a fruit of saving faith. Among the saints, Edwards argued, there will be a "holy boldness in prayer."[57] "True Christianity," he continued, "has as great, yea, a greater tendency to…the pouring out [of] the soul before God in secret earnest prayer and praise to him."[58] The true believer "delights at times to retire from all mankind, to converse with God in solitary places."[59] False religion, on the other hand, displays an inconsistency when it comes to prayer for nonbelievers are not disposed to "holy meditation and prayer."[60] Those who are truly the product of a supernatural work of God will remain constant in their prayers, "crying to God day and night."[61] Those who are not, do not.

---

56 Edwards, *Religious Affections*, *Works*, 2:383.
57 Edwards, *Religious Affections*, *Works*, 2:361.
58 Edwards, *Religious Affections*, *Works*, 2:371.
59 Edwards, *Religious Affections*, *Works*, 2:374.
60 Edwards, *Religious Affections*, *Works*, 2:374.
61 Edwards, *Religious Affections*, *Works*, 2:382.

The implications of Edwards's convictions are clear. Many supposed converts of the recent revivals were not converts at all for they had failed to remain committed in things of the faith, particularly prayer. For evidence, he might have argued, they had to look no further than the failed revival itself. Had they been truly converted they would have continued in prayer. Had they continued in prayer, the revival would not have ended and God would not have been denied his glory yet again. Instead, their supposed faith had failed and the revival faded away.

By 1745, the season of revival had clearly passed and many in the town remained unconverted. Extraordinary measures were needed to change the prevailing spirit of malaise that had descended on Northampton. To that end, Edwards was pleased when he learned of a prayer movement afoot in Scotland. There a group of ministers covenanted together to pray for the continuance of the revivals that were occurring on their side of the Atlantic. When Edwards heard of this endeavour, he affirmed his support and set about to promote the cause in New England. Turning to the pages of the Bible he found the encouragement and justification he needed to make his case. "There is yet remaining a great advancement of the interest of religion and the kingdom of Christ in this world, by an abundant outpouring of the Spirit of God, far greater and more extensive than ever yet has been."[62] Armed with the prophetic utterances of Scripture, Edwards penned *An Humble Attempt* in 1747 as one last attempt to revive true religion in New England.

Exegeting Zechariah 8:20–22, Edwards connected the necessity of prayer for the revival of religion with the Christian's great eschatological hope, Christ's second coming.

Such being the state of things in this future promised glorious day of the church's prosperity, surely 'tis worthy praying for. Nor is there any one thing whatsoever, if we viewed

62 Edwards, *An Humble Attempt*, *Works*, 5:329.

things aright, which a regard to the glory of God, a concern
for the kingdom and honour of our Redeemer, a love to
his people, pity to perishing sinners, love to our fellow creatures in general, compassion to mankind under its various
and sore calamities and miseries, a desire of their temporal
and spiritual prosperity, love to our country, our neighbors
and friends, yes, and to our own souls, would dispose us to
be so much in prayer for, as for the dawning of this happy
day, and the accomplishment of that glorious event.[63]

Doing so, he merely continued to articulate what he had been
arguing for all along: a prayerful commitment to the glory of God
as revealed in the salvation of lost souls. Thus, once again, he exhorted
Christians to be much in prayer for another remarkable season of
salvation for this, he said, is the teaching of the Bible and the will
of God. Moreover, God awaits their prayers before sending revival.
"God speaks of himself as standing ready to be gracious to his church,
and to appear for its restoration, and only waiting for such an
opportunity to bestow this mercy, when he shall hear the cries of
his people for it, that he may bestow it in answer to their prayers,"
Edwards warned them.[64] Yet, taking all of this into account, God's
people enjoy his promise that he will use their prayers as "instruments of pulling down the kingdom of Satan."[65] Thus, the answer
to their prayers is as sure as the God who hears them.

Edwards was not afraid to use personal motivations in his exhorta-
tions. "Those that are engaged in such prayer might expect the first
benefit," he wrote. "God will come to those that are seeking and
waiting for him."[66] The benefits to which he referred were not
earthly but spiritual gain. "For persons to be thus engaged in
extraordinarily praying for the reviving and flourishing of religion

---

63 Edwards, *An Humble Attempt, Works*, 5:340–341.
64 Edwards, *An Humble Attempt, Works*, 5:354.
65 Edwards, *An Humble Attempt, Works*, 5:355.
66 Edwards, *An Humble Attempt, Works*, 5:356.

in the world, will naturally lead each one to reflect on himself, and consider how religion flourishes in his own heart, and how far his example contributes to the thing that he is praying for."[67] Thinking of and praying for the salvation of others would drive them to consider their own spiritual estate. Even those who were already truly converted would be drawn ever closer to God in perfect communion.

A united effort such as the one to which Edwards called the church, the Concert of Prayer as it became known, would benefit the church at large as well. As interest in religion increased the church would be protected from external attack as more and more of the enemy came over to their side.[68] Plus, such a union not only displays the love of Christ in the church in a mighty way, it promotes its growth among believers.[69] Nothing but good, he said, can come of praying for the outpouring of God's Spirit. The praying church will be a stronger church, living in the abiding blessing of God.

In the end, Edwards did not care which motive served his ends. All of the various motives to subscribe to Edwards's plan outlined in *An Humble Attempt* were, in and of themselves, good and biblical. His point was not to determine the merit of any one reason but to overwhelm the callous soul of the church with the need to pray. What he was doing yet again was working to bring the church back to prayer and revival back to the colonies.

Valediction

When Edwards arrived in Northampton in 1727, little did he or the world know what would become of the young man called to the aid of the great Solomon Stoddard. As it turned out, the protégé was a prodigy and his renown quickly came to outshine that of his grandfather. As season after season of revival descended upon his

---

67 Edwards, *An Humble Attempt, Works*, 5:366.
68 Edwards, *An Humble Attempt, Works*, 5:358.
69 Edwards, *An Humble Attempt, Works*, 5:364–365.

town in the 1730s and 40s fame came to Edwards's door. With it came trials and tribulations as he sought first to propagate true revival among his people and then to protect the work of God— and finally to promote it once again. Those works for which Edwards received acclaim in his lifetime were written to those ends during this period of his life.

Due to the influence and profundity of those writings and their author, Martyn Lloyd-Jones crowned Edwards the "theologian of Revival."[70] He was right insofar as he went. But, Edwards was more than that. He was the theologian of *prayer* for revival. For, according to Edwards himself, the two cannot be separated. Prayer is one of the great God-appointed means to revival, and prayer is one of the great God-annointed fruits of revival. As such, the people of God will be a people of prayer, offering up both words of thanksgiving for blessings given and supplication for blessings of the Spirit yet to come. "Believing this," Michael Haykin correctly summarized Edwards's stance, "the church has only one posture: prayer."[71]

---

70 Lloyd-Jones, *The Puritans: Their Origins and Successors*, 361.
71 Haykin, *Jonathan Edwards: The Holy Spirit in Revival*, 146.

Chapter 5

The "*true spirit of prayer*"

The true spirit of prayer is no other than God's own Spirit
dwelling in the hearts of the saints.[1]

By 1740, the revival was over in Northampton, its
memory clouded by enthusiasm and disappointment.
The impending colony-wide Great Awakening remained
just over the spiritual horizon, an object of earnest
prayer as yet unanswered. Division and strife returned to Edwards's
church just as he had warned. All that remained to do was explain
what had happened. Serious questions confronted Edwards's mind.
Had Northampton experienced true revival at all? If so, where was
the social reformation that was expected to follow such spiritual
renewal? Was his widely acclaimed published account of the events
of 1734 and 1735 wrong? Did he misread the signs? Through it all
Edwards maintained that there had been a remarkable work of

---

1 Edwards, "Hypocrites Deficient in the Duty of Prayer," in ed. Nichols, *Seeking
God*, 359.

God in their midst. People had been saved. Others, however, had been misled, not by Edwards, but by the affections of their sinful hearts. They had been swept away in the flood of excitement, assuming they had been converted, only to find themselves unchanged when the waves of revival receded into history.

Edwards made his case for such an interpretation in "Hypocrites Deficient in the Duty of Prayer." In this sermon, he argued that many who were thought to be converted were not. Instead, they were spiritual hypocrites. They looked like Christians and talked like Christians. For a season, they even acted like Christians. But, in the end, they proved not to be Christians. What was the evidence against such supposed converts? They had left off from a faithful fulfillment of the Christian duty of prayer and returned to their old sinful ways "like the dog to his vomit."[2] Such people, he argued, had never been given the true spirit of prayer, the Holy Spirit. Had they been truly converted the Spirit of God would be dwelling in their hearts. As Edwards argued, those in whom the Spirit lives "naturally tend to God in holy breathings and pantings."[3] The Spirit-filled believer longs for God and his company. The Spirit of prayer leads him "to God, to converse with him by prayer."[4] Believing that "prayer is as natural an expression of faith as breathing is of life," Edwards contended that the so-called Christian "that lives a prayerless life, lives without God in the world."[5] That is, he is no Christian at all.

All three Persons of the Trinity play a vital role in Edwards's theology of prayer. God expects, hears and answers prayer. Christ mediates and facilitates prayer. The Holy Spirit motivates believers

---

2 Edwards, "Hypocrites Deficient in the Duty of Prayer," in ed. Nichols, *Seeking God*, 360.

3 Edwards, "Hypocrites Deficient in the Duty of Prayer," in ed. Nichols, *Seeking God*, 359.

4 Edwards, "Hypocrites Deficient in the Duty of Prayer," in ed. Nichols, *Seeking God*, 359.

5 Edwards, "Hypocrites Deficient in the Duty of Prayer," in ed. Nichols, *Seeking God*, 365.

to prayer. More than that, however, the Spirit is the answer to their prayers. The Spirit is the blessing to be sought. He is, Edwards preached, "the greatest blessing,"[6] "the choicest gift,"[7] "the fullness of good" and "the great promise of God."[8] Therefore, Christians, following the example of Christ, must make the "Spirit of God, the chief subject matter of prayer."[9] They must pray in the Spirit and they must "pray for the Spirit."[10]

Three questions follow, the answers to which illustrate the importance of the Spirit to Edwards's theology of prayer. The Person and nature of the Spirit will be found in answer to the first question, "Who is the Holy Spirit?" Following the logic of Edwards's thought, the reader must then ask, "What does the Holy Spirit do?" The answer given reveals the centrality of the Spirit in God's redemptive purposes. Then, the last question arises from the second: "What does the Holy Spirit have to do with prayer?" In his answers to these three queries, Edwards's theology of prayer stands in total dependence upon the Person and work of the Holy Spirit. For without the Spirit, there is no prayer.

Who is the Holy Spirit?

> From what has been said, it follows that the Holy Spirit is the sum of all good. 'Tis the fullness of God. The holiness and happiness of the Godhead consists in it; and in the communion or partaking of it consists all the true loveliness and happiness of the creature.[11]

Considerable ink has been spilt over Edwards's Trinitarian theology. Within that broader category, Edwards's pneumatology, his under-

---

6 Edwards, "Terms of Prayer," *Works*, 19:785.
7 Edwards, "The Dangers of Decline," *Works*, 17:97.
8 Edwards, "God Glorified in Man's Dependence," *Works*, 17:209.
9 Edwards, "Suitableness of Union in Extraordinary Prayer," *Works*, 25:203.
10 Edwards, "The Threefold Work of the Holy Spirit," *Works*, 14:436.
11 Edwards, "Treatise on Grace," *Works*, 21:188.

standing of the Holy Spirit, has caused no little amount of debate. Amy Pauw has commented, "The role of the Holy Spirit is in many respects the most original...aspect of Edwards's trinitarianism."[12] Scholars explain the originality and complexity of his pneumatology in various ways. Pauw, following others before her, argued for Augustinian influences in Edwards's thought.[13] Sang Lee believed Edwards to be exhibiting a synthesis of the pneumatological thought of Peter Lombard and Thomas Aquinas.[14] Adding to the diversity of opinions and explanation, Pauw herself noted manifold witnesses in Edwards, notably his Puritan forebears William Ames, Richard Baxter and Cotton Mather.[15] Beyond those influences, Edwards admitted a dependence upon John Owen for at least a portion of his pneumatology.[16]

That Edwards's position proves so difficult to pin down comes as no surprise. The doctrines of the Trinity and the Holy Spirit are notoriously complex topics. Edwards acknowledged as much in his "Discourse on the Trinity."

> But I don't fully pretend to explain how these things are, and I am sensible a hundred other objections may be made, and puzzling doubts and questions raised, that I can't solve. I am far from pretending to explaining the Trinity so as to render it no longer a mystery. I think it to be the highest and deepest of all divine mysteries still, notwithstanding

---

12 Amy P. Pauw, *The Supreme Harmony of All: The Trinitarian Theology of Jonathan Edwards* (Grand Rapids: Eerdmans, 2002), 14.

13 Amy P. Pauw, "The Trinity," in *The Princeton Companion to Jonathan Edwards*, 48.

14 Sang Lee, "Grace and Justification," in *The Princeton Companion to Jonathan Edwards*, 135.

15 Pauw, *The Supreme Harmony of All*, 46–47.

16 Edwards, "Miscellanies" No. 1047, *Works*, 20:389. Here Edwards quotes Owen as saying, "The Spirit is the *mutual love* of the Father and the Son" (emphasis Edwards's). Owen's quote can be found in *A Discourse Concerning the Holy Spirit*, vol. 3 of *The Works of John Owen* (Carlisle, PA: Banner of Truth, 1991), 1.3.5.

anything that I have said or conceived about it.[17]

Yet, bound by a resolution made in youthful exuberance, anything short of a solution left Edwards theologically unsatisfied.[18] Thus resolved to find a solution to any and all theological conundrums, he plunged into the doctrines of the Trinity and the Spirit with typical Edwardsean vigour, spilling much ink of his own and still causing discussion three centuries later.

While Edwards admitted that the doctrines of the Trinity and the Holy Spirit are mysteries shrouded in uncertainty that cannot be fully explained, he never shied away from attempting to describe them. Moreover, his analyses of the Persons of the Trinity and their operations go a long way toward explaining these doctrines. In these descriptions, Edwards developed a robust doctrine of the Holy Spirit. In the end, it is the oneness of the Trinity that explains who the Spirit is as an individual. The Spirit is God. The reader shall see that Edwards's pneumatology is not unique but unified, bound together by love, for love is who the Spirit is not just what the Spirit does.

THE SPIRIT IS GOD

When one prays for the Spirit, Michael Haykin understood Edwards to say, one prays for God.[19] Edwards's pneumatology logically and necessarily connects the two for the Spirit is God. All that God is, excepting his role as Father, the Spirit is.[20] Thus, while the Spirit is a Person unto himself, distinct from the Father and Son within the economy of the Trinity, all that has been said about God's attributes and Person applies to the Holy Spirit as well.

---

17 Edwards, "Discourse on the Trinity," *Works*, 21:134.

18 "Resolved, when I think of any theorem in divinity to be solved, immediately to do what I can towards solving it, if circumstances don't hinder" (Edwards, "Resolutions" No. 11, *Works*, 16:754).

19 Haykin, *Jonathan Edwards: The Holy Spirit in Revival*, 40.

20 Edwards, "Discourse on the Trinity," *Works*, 21:121.

Though the Spirit is a distinct Person within the Trinity, he remains fully God, diminished in no way.[21] That which constitutes God's being makes up the Spirit's as well. They are of the same essence.[22] Speaking of all three Persons of the Trinity, Edwards taught his congregation that "they are all the same God, and it is impossible there should be any {inferiority}. They all are the same substance, the same divine essence; and therefore whatsoever perfection, dignity or excellency belongs to the divine essence, belongs to every one of them."[23] As such, coequality reigns among the Persons of the Trinity; the Spirit is God in his all-infinite perfections.

Equality in essence brings with it equality in honour. Each, Edwards wrote, possesses "the honor which is common to 'em all," because all three are God.[24] Of the honour enjoyed within the Trinitarian context the Spirit plays a central role.

> The Father's honor is that he is as it were the author of perfect and divine wisdom. The Son's honor is that he is that perfect and divine wisdom itself, the excellency of which is that from whence arises the honor of being the author or generator of it. The honor of the Father and the Son is that they are infinitely excellent, or that from them infinite excellency proceeds. But the honor of the Holy Ghost is equal, for he is that divine excellency and beauty itself.[25]

This sharing of glory becomes most evident in the course of redemption as the Father "appoints and provides the Redeemer," the Son as Redeemer offers up himself to reconcile man's sin debt,

---

21 Edwards, "Treatise on Grace," *Works*, 21:181.

22 Edwards, "Miscellanies" No. 308, Works, 13:392, and *Charity and Its Fruits*, *Works*, 8:370.

23 Edwards, "The Threefold Work of the Holy Ghost," *Works*, 14:379.

24 Edwards, "Discourse on the Trinity," *Works*, 21:135.

25 Edwards, "Discourse on the Trinity," *Works*, 21:135.

and the Spirit "is the thing purchased." [26] As such, the Spirit "is the sum of good" and worthy of the same honour given the Father and the Son. [27]

Just as a sharing of honour arises out of a shared essence, so too does a sharing of attributes. What can be said of God's moral character can be said of the Son and Spirit. Of these attributes, Edwards's pneumatological musings focus on the "fullness of God" residing in the Spirit, notably his holiness. [28] Thus, the name given for the third Person of the Trinity comes as no accident. He is not just *the* Spirit, but the *Holy* Spirit. "God's holiness consists in him." He is the "Spirit of God's holiness." [29] The holiness of the Spirit, therefore, is equal to the holiness of God. [30] More than that, however, the Spirit's holiness arises out of the holiness of God. God's holiness, Edwards contended, arises out of God's love for himself. "'Tis in God's infinite love to himself that his holiness consists." [31] That is, because God loves himself most supremely, he will be and act such that it promotes his own good and glory. He will be holy, protecting his person and reputation, because he loves himself. Thus, the Spirit who is holy because God is holy must necessarily be love also.

THE SPIRIT IS LOVE

The profundity of the connection between the Spirit as God and the Spirit as love sits unadorned on the surface of Edwards's pneumatology. The Spirit is God. God is love. Therefore, the Spirit is love. Speaking of 1 John 4:8 in one of his "Miscellanies," Edwards argued that the love of God "is the Holy Spirit." [32] In *Charity and*

---

26 Edwards, "Discourse on the Trinity," *Works*, 21:136.
27 Edwards, "Treatise on Grace," *Works*, 21:188.
28 Edwards, "Discourse on the Trinity," *Works*, 21:187.
29 Edwards, "Miscellanies" No. 1047, *Works*, 20:389.
30 "The Father and Son are both infinitely holy, and the Holy Ghost can be no holier," Edwards commented (Edwards, "Discourse on the Trinity," *Works*, 21:122).
31 Edwards, "Discourse on the Trinity," *Works*, 21:123.
32 Edwards, "Miscellanies" No. 146, *Works*, 13:300.

Its Fruit, he wrote, "The Spirit of God is a spirit of love."[33] Using such language, Edwards meant more than that the Spirit is loving. To say that the Spirit "is love" speaks of more than action. Though the Spirit does love and communicates God's love, he does so out of the overflow of his own being. He loves because he is love. That is, the Spirit's being is one of love. Edwards had in mind an ontological state of being. Love is not just what the Spirit does but who he really is. Love arises properly out of his very nature. The Spirit does not merely act in a loving manner; he acts in such a manner because he is love.

The Spirit as love relates, first, to God's love for himself. Loving himself displays the nature of God's love and his own approval of himself and his attributes. "The sum of all God's love," that is the finest expression of it, "is love to himself," Edwards proposed. It is the highest form of love. God's goodness, his moral perfection, makes self-love on his part praiseworthy rather than sinful as it would be in the case of man. Because God is infinite and his attributes infinite in their perfections, God's self-love must be infinite in quantity and quality as well. God, Edwards wrote, "infinitely loves himself, because his being is infinite."[34] Edwards couched his Trinitarian theology in this language of divine self-love and delight with the Spirit being the product of that love.[35]

> God's love is primarily to himself, and his infinite delight
> is in himself, in the Father and the Son loving and delight-

---

33 Edwards, *Charity and Its Fruit, Works,* 8:132.

34 Edwards, "The Mind," *Works,* 6:381.

35 Brooks Holifield's explanation is helpful here. "Divine excellency required a divine plurality, and reason alone could recognize that God must have an idea of himself, since otherwise God would lack self-awareness. But God's ideas were perfect, so that God's idea of himself was also God—God the Son. And because the Son and the Father delighted in one another, the begetting of the Son issued in a perfect act of mutual love—or Spirit—which was distinct from and yet one with the Son and Father" (E. Brooks Holifield, "Edwards as Theologian," in *The Cambridge Companion to Jonathan Edwards,* 148–149).

ing in each other. We often read of the Father loving the
Son, and being well-pleased in the Son, and of the Son
loving the Father. In the infinite love and delight that is
between these two persons consists the infinite happiness
of God.... And therefore seeing the Scripture signifies that
the Spirit of God is the love of God, therefore it follows
that the Holy Spirit proceeds from, or is breathed forth
from, the Father and the Son in some way or other infinitely above all our conceptions, as the divine essence
entirely flows out and is breathed forth in infinitely
pure love and sweet delight from the Father and the Son;
and this is that pure river of water of life that proceeds out
of the throne of the Father and the Son, as we read at the
beginning of the twenty-second chapter of the Revelation:
for Christ himself tells us that by the water of life, or living
water, is meant the Holy Ghost.[36]

---

36 Edwards, "Treatise on Grace," *Works*, 21:184. In addition to the analogy of
water, Edwards used other word pictures to describe the inter-Trinitarian relationship.
A favourite analogy was that of fire and heat. "[God] is seen by his image, the Son,
and is felt by the Holy Spirit, as fire is perceived by its light and heat, seen by one
and felt by the other. Fire by its light, represents the Son of God, and by its heat, the
Holy Spirit (Edwards, *Notes on Scripture*, *Works*, 15:387).

Edwards also explained the nature of the Trinity using the sun as his illustration.
"We have a lively image of the Trinity in the sun. The Father is as the substance of
the sun; the Son is as the brightness and glory of the disk of the sun; the Holy Ghost
is as the heat and continually emitted influence, the emanation by which the world
is enlightened, warmed, enlivened, and comforted" (Edwards, "Miscellanies" No.
370, *Works*, 13:434).

Finally, building on Augustine [Augustine's use of love as an analogy for the Trinity
can be found in Book IX of *De trinitate* and *Confessions* 13.11], Edwards spoke of
the Trinity in terms of the idea and love conjointly. "And this I suppose to be that
the blessed Trinity that we read of in the holy Scriptures. The Father is the Deity
subsisting in the prime, unoriginated and most absolute manner, or the Deity in its
direct existence. The Son is the Deity generated by God's understanding, or having
an idea of himself, and subsisting in that idea. The Holy Ghost is the Deity subsisting
in act, or the divine essence flowing out and breathed forth, in God's infinite love
to and delight in himself. And I believe the whole divine essence does truly and
distinctly subsist both in the divine idea and divine love, and that therefore each of

From this love to himself arises God's love for all other things. "This love includes in it, or rather is the same as," Edwards said, "a love to everything, as they are all communications of himself."[37] The Holy Spirit is the sum and the substance of that love of God which he shows toward himself and communicates to others.

If God loves himself infinitely beyond measure, he also loves those within the Trinity infinitely. Since the Spirit is the personification of God's love, the one he loves infinitely, the primary object of his love, is the Son. Borrowing language and concepts mentioned in Augustine and Owen, Edwards described the inter-Trinitarian relationship as one of love flowing between Father and Son. God is the lover. Christ is the loved. The Spirit is the love shared. Thus, each distinct Person of the Trinity plays a vital role within the Trinity wherein divine love binds the Three into One.

Within the Trinity, the "Holy Spirit is the act of God between the Father and the Son infinitely loving and delighting in each other."[38] This is a "pure and perfect act" that vibrates with the "sweet energy" of delight as the Father and Son enjoy each other's company.[39] In this act of divine love, this inter-Trinitarian love, "an infinitely holy and sweet energy arises." "Their love and joy is mutual," flowing to and fro between God and Christ in the Person of the Spirit who is "Deity in act."[40] That is, the Holy Spirit as the "act" is the love expressed between Father and Son. Moreover, just as "the Godhead or the divine nature and essence does subsist in love," the Spirit of God, the Holy Spirit, must himself be love.[41] Thus, Edwards inseparably links divine essence, act and love, in the Person of the Spirit as seen within the inter-Trinitarian relationship.

---

them are properly distinct persons" (Edwards, "Discourse on the Trinity," *Works*, 21:131).

37 Edwards, "Outline of 'A Rational Account'," *Works*, 6:396.
38 Edwards, "Miscellanies" No. 94, *Works*, 13:260.
39 Edwards, "Miscellanies" No. 94, *Works*, 13:260.
40 Edwards, "Discourse on the Trinity," *Works*, 21:121.
41 Edwards, "Discourse on the Trinity," *Works*, 21:121.

The bond of love between the Father and Son which is the Spirit also serves to express the love of God toward the creature. God's self-love and his love for the creature are intimately related, for from the former flows the latter.

> …so the Holy Spirit does in some ineffable and inconceivable manner proceed and is breathed forth both from the Father and Son, by the divine essence being wholly poured and flowing out in that infinitely intense, holy and pure love and delight that continually and unchangeably breathes forth from the Father and the Son, primarily towards each other and secondarily towards the creature; and so flowing forth in a different subsistence or person [the Holy Spirit]: and that this is that person [the Holy Spirit] that is poured forth into the hearts of angels and saints.[42]

Without love, which is the Holy Spirit, there is no Trinity and there could be no love for man. But, because there is love in the Trinity in the Person of the Spirit, there is hope for man as can be seen in the work of the Holy Spirit.

SUMMARY

That Edwards's doctrine of the Holy Spirit, particularly in his explanation of the Spirit as love, attracts much scholarly interest and debate should come as no surprise. Edwards himself may have suspected as much. Very little of the discussion above comes from his sermons. Instead, the metaphysical discussions concerning the character and the nature of the Spirit are found almost exclusively in his "miscellanies" and his intellectual works on the Trinity and grace. These discussions alternate between attempts to deal with biblical data and attempts to fill in the gaps of that same biblical data. While his conclusions are often speculative at best, Edwards

---

42 Edwards, "Treatise on Grace," *Works*, 21:185–186.

remained true to his commitment to a Trinitarian theology that maintains that the Father, Son, and the Spirit are distinct persons who are also co-equal and co-eternal, sharing all attributes and glory, while fulfilling various roles within the Trinity and creation. More importantly, Edwards's conviction that the Spirit is the love of God personified proves to be central to his theology of prayer as it is the love of God that calls fallen men back into relationship with him through the Son that he might come and live in them in the Person of the Holy Spirit, loving them for all eternity.

What does the Holy Spirit do?

> That blessing asked for, viz. the Holy Spirit, which is the greatest blessing that can be asked. 'Tis that by which we are sanctified and quicked, by which we have spiritual life, by which we are conformed to God and have his image, and have the redemption of Christ applied to us and so are possessed of all the blessing of his purchase. In short, 'tis that by which we are actually possessed of true holiness and happiness.[43]

Edwards also connected the work of the Holy Spirit to the love of God. Everything that the Spirit does relates intimately to his loving nature. Since the Spirit is love, he must love. These acts of love flowing from the Spirit's are an intrinsic part of God's grand redemptive purposes. Every interaction between God and man, from self-revelation to conviction to salvation, hinges upon the work of the Holy Spirit.

THE REVELATION OF GOD

Edwards saw the influence of the Holy Spirit in every revelatory act of God. Without God's self-revelation, fallen man would know

---

43 Edwards, "Praying for the Spirit," *Works*, 22:214.

nothing of God nor have any hope of knowing God himself. God, however, under the impulse of love chose to reveal himself to man for the purpose of calling man back to himself that he might enjoy God's love. In this, God's self-revelation, from Scripture to creation to the incarnation, Edwards believed the Spirit played a vital role.

The basis for all that Edwards preached, however speculative it may be at points, he found in God's written revelation. In this, the Bible, God speaks through the Spirit to men. According to Edwards, and the Protestant tradition to which he belonged, the Holy Spirit stands as the one and only author of Scripture. He "indited the Scriptures."[44] That is, the Spirit wrote them. The truthfulness, consistency and completeness of God's Word depend upon such divine authorship. Yet, he knew that the Spirit had used men to speak to men. The Spirit communicated through the human authors of the Bible. He did so in such a way that his words became theirs. To hear the prophets speak was to hear the Spirit of God speak.[45]

Though Edwards's view of inspiration might sound like that of the dictation theory, and such a theory would be consistent with his view of God's sovereignty, he saw God's use of fallen men to communicate his message as a means of loving condescension. By means of immediate revelation God directed "the penmen to such a phrase and manner of speaking" as would permit his message to be communicated in a manner comprehensible to man.[46] Through verbal plenary inspiration, God gave life to the written word.[47] Due to the divine nature of the Scriptures, the power of life and of preaching resides in the written word.[48] It is the love of God, displayed in the work of the Son of God, that is revealed by the Spirit of God in the Word of God.

---

44 Edwards, "Ruth's Resolution," *Works*, 19:307.

45 Edwards, "The Mind," *Works*, 6:346.

46 Edwards, "Miscellanies" No. 229, *Works*, 13:347–348.

47 "The Word alone, however managed, explained, confirmed and applied, is nothing but a dead letter without the Spirit" (Edwards, "The Threefold Work of the Holy Ghost," *Works*, 14:433).

48 Edwards, "Miscellanies" No. 972, *Works*, 20:272.

Referring to God's first act of revelation to those outside of himself, the creation of the universe, Edwards saw in Genesis 1:2 the hand of the Spirit at work. "It was more especially the Holy Spirit's work to bring the world to its beauty and perfection out of the chaos, for the beauty of the world is a communication of God's beauty."[49] In the process of creation, the Spirit brought the "harmony," "excellency," and "beauty" of the Godhead into sight where the creature might see and savour his Creator. Without the work of the Spirit, God's self-revelatory work of creation would have been incomplete.

> God's greatest act of self-revelation also displays the fruit of the Spirit's labors. In the incarnation, God became man and dwelt among men that they might be redeemed by him and love him in return. The Spirit initiated the incarnation process. Merging "infinite condescension" and "divine dignity," Christ was "conceived by the power of the Holy Ghost."[50] Christ's purity was preserved even as he took on human flesh. Christ's earthly ministry, initiated in eternity past, arises from the loving operations of the Spirit. The name of the Son of God is Messiah and Christ, not only because there was an extraordinary pouring out of the Holy Ghost upon the man Christ Jesus, and giving the Spirit without measure unto him, as separating him to and preparing him for his work; nor are these names proper to Christ only as man, or as Mediator: but God the Son from all eternity was Christ, or anointed with the Holy Spirit without measure, strictly speaking, or with the infinite love of the Father towards him.[51]

---

49 Edwards, "Miscellanies" No. 293, *Works*, 13:384.
50 Edwards, "The Excellency of Christ," *Works*, 19:573.
51 Edwards, "Miscellanies" No. 225, *Works*, 13:346.

Furthermore, the annointing of the Spirit empowered Christ to fulfill his role as Mediator. "'Tis his anointing that qualifies and fits him for the work of mediator" and gives "value and efficacy" to "his sufferings and obedience."[52] Commenting on the role of the high priest in the Exodus and the analogy that ministry bore to Christ, Edwards said,

> When the high priest lighted and dressed the lamps, then was he to burn incense on the golden altar of incense, signifying that sweet and infinitely acceptable incense of Christ's merits as by the Holy Spirit signified by the lamps.... It was by the eternal Spirit that Christ offered up himself without spot to God. It was by the Holy Spirit many ways. It was by the Holy Spirit that the human nature of Christ was united to the divine Logos, from which union arises the infinite value of his blood and righteousness. It was by the eternal Spirit that Christ performed righteousness. It was by the Spirit of God that Christ was perfectly holy and performed perfect righteousness. It was by the Holy Spirit not only that his obedience was perfect, but performed with such transcendent love. It was by this Spirit that his sacrifice of himself was sanctified, being an offering to God in the pure and fervent flame of divine love, which burnt in his heart as well as in the flame of God's vindictive justice and wrath into which he was cast. And it was this that his obedience and sacrifice were offered with such love to his people that he died for, as implied a perfect union with them, whereby it was accepted for them.[53]

The operations of the Spirit touch upon the success of all of Christ's earthly ministry, Edwards thought. Not one aspect of the incarnation is free of the Spirit's influence. The Spirit annointed and

---

52 Edwards, "Miscellanies" No. 487, *Works*, 13:530.
53 Edwards, *Notes on Scripture*, *Works*, 15:575.

assured all that was accomplished in the God-man by and for the love of God.

COMMON GRACE

Common grace, as generally understood, refers to those gifts of God that he showers upon all men regardless of their spiritual condition out of the overflow of his loving heart. Man does not deserve these things. God gives them. Under the larger rubric of common grace fall such things as health, harvest, culture and comfort. What follows falls outside that broader definition of common grace. Instead, common grace as it relates to the operations of the Holy Spirit speaks to his interaction with all of mankind on a moral/spiritual level. Here we speak of common grace as God's extending his gracious hand to all fallen men that they might be restored to his fellowship.

"The Spirit of God was given at first, but was lost," Edwards observed.[54] Before Adam's fall from grace in the Garden, the Holy Spirit dwelled within him. But, immediately prior to Adam's transgression, God withdrew that grace which would have been common to all men apart from sin. Thereafter, all mankind finds themselves destitute of the indwelling presence of God that would have served to protect and preserve their fragile souls. From that moment on, from the first Adam to the crowning of the Second Adam (Christ), the Spirit has been operating primarily external to man, limiting the effects of the Fall upon society and calling individuals back to God.

Now external, the Spirit acts *on* not *in* man. In the aftermath of the Fall, "the Spirit of God may many ways influence natural men," Edwards noted in *Religious Affections*, "yet because it is not thus communicated to them, as an indwelling principle, they don't derive any denomination or character from it; for there being no

54 Edwards, "Miscellanies" No. 755, *Works*, 18:403. See also "The Threefold Work of the Holy Spirit," *Works*, 14:378, and *Charity and Its Fruit*, *Works*, 8:354.

union it is not their own."[55] That is to say, the Spirit's holiness is not and cannot be theirs. The Spirit, on their behalf, guides and assists them toward holiness. He "influences and operates upon" fallen men, "assisting [their] natural principles to do the same work which they do of themselves, to a greater degree."[56] The Spirit uses the remnant of the *imago Dei*, the "natural principles," tainted though it may be, to promote God's glory by restraining evil and displaying his grace. Thus, the Spirit provides and promotes moral virtue in society without indwelling and changing eternally the status of those upon whom he operates.[57] They are, if you will, the instruments of his common grace to others and themselves, not the recipients of saving grace.

In the same way, operating from the outside, the Spirit provides intellectual enlightenment, a clearer understanding of spiritual matters as explained in the Bible, by operating on those natural faculties that reside in all men.[58] Even in the preparatory work of the gospel the Spirit acts upon the fallen without indwelling them for there is "no holiness in it, and so nothing of the nature of the Holy Spirit communicated to the soul, or exerted in the soul in it."[59] The Spirit works upon the mind, giving a clear conviction of sin and guilt without giving "any new and supernatural principle," Edwards remarked.[60] Thus, fallen man remains fallen until such a time as God graciously sends his Spirit to permanently dwell within him and forever change his disposition. Until such a time, natural man should pray for that gift of God, that internal expression of his love.

---

55 Edwards, *Religious Affections*, *Works*, 2:201.

56 Edwards, "Miscellanies" No. 471, *Works*, 13:512–513.

57 "There are many in this world, who are wholly destitute of saving grace, who yet have common grace: they have no true holiness, but nevertheless, have something of that which is called 'moral virtue'; and are the subjects of some degree of the common influences of the Spirit of God" (Edwards, "True Grace," *Works*, 25:611).

58 Edwards, *Religious Affections*, *Works*, 2:270.

59 Edwards, "Miscellanies" No. 734, *Works*, 18:359.

60 Edwards, "Miscellanies" No. 626, *Works*, 18:155.

Let 'em pray that God would give them his Spirit to awak-
en them; this is proper for them, whether they have any
true grace or not. And so let ['em] pray that God would
enable to strive for salvation, and that he would help 'em
to enter in at the straight gate. Let 'em pray earnestly that
God would show 'em their own hearts; [that God would]
bring ['em] off their own righteousness, {that} God would
convert 'em; {that God would} give a true sight of Christ,
and enable 'em sincerely to close with him and trust in
him alone for salvation. Let 'em pray that God would
open their blind eye; {that God would} cause light to
shine out of darkness; and that he [would] raise their dead
souls to life.[61]

Such prayer is proper, Edwards said, for without the Spirit's
indwelling presence fallen man has no hope of enjoying God's
abiding love. So long as the Spirit remains external to his soul,
external convictions and enlightenments reveal a man's sin but
can never solve his problem.

Just as the natural man can experience the external operations
of the Spirit and pray for those workings to be internalized, he
can reject them as well. So long as the Spirit does not indwell him,
fallen man can reject him and the Spirit will leave off the preparatory work that he has begun. Worse yet, those who resist the Spirit,
said Edwards, "are in more danger of being finally left by the Holy
Ghost."[62] That is, the rejection of the Holy Spirit places the unregenerate in dangerous proximity to the "unpardonable sin," a
topic in which Edwards showed much interest. He defined the
"sin against the Holy Ghost" in this way:

---

61 Edwards, "Subjects of a First Work of Grace," *Works*, 22:201.
62 Edwards, "Living Unconverted Under an Eminent Means of Grace," *Works*,
14:366.

> In order to [commit] the sin against the Holy Ghost, persons must appear in avowed malicious opposition and contumacy against the Holy Ghost in his work and office, and as communicated to men, and acting in them, either in his ordinary or extraordinary influences and operations.[63]

Those that have felt the convicting influence of the Spirit, recognized as such, and refused to be cowed by it, find themselves guilty of rejecting the Spirit. The ugliness of this rejection is compounded by that fact that such a rebellious refusal of God's grace is no less than the outright rejection of God's gracious overture of love.

> What the Holy Ghost is, is confirmed from that sin which is called the sin against the Holy Ghost, which consists in knowing, direct, professed scorn, spite and malice against God; which is diametrically contrary to the Holy Ghost, who is God's love and the love of God.[64]

Rejecting the Spirit of God is tantamount to rejecting God and his love because the Spirit is God and his love.[65] From this point there is no return.[66]

SAVING GRACE

In contrast to common grace when defined as an external work of the Spirit on all mankind, saving grace is the application of God's Spirit and love to the hearts and souls of the elect, God's "favorites and dear children."[67] In salvation, the Spirit acts as the immediate cause. That is, only the Spirit can complete this work.

---

63 Edwards, "Miscellanies" No. 703, *Works*, 18:309.

64 Edwards, "Miscellanies" No. 310, *Works*, 13:393.

65 By logical necessity, Edwards argued, those who resisted and rejected the revivals as a work of God through the Spirit were guilty of the same sin (Edwards, *The Distinguishing Marks, Works*, 4:271).

66 Edwards, *The Distinguishing Marks, Works*, 4:275.

67 Edwards, *The Distinguishing Marks, Works*, 4:279.

Only the Spirit can overcome the hardness of hearts and "lift the soul from earth."[68] In salvation, man finds himself utterly and wholly dependent upon the Spirit. "We are dependent on the Holy Ghost," Edwards told his church, "for 'tis of him that we are in Christ Jesus; 'tis the Spirit of God that gives us faith in him, whereby we receive him, and close with him."[69] Without the Spirit, there is no salvation.

Just as the Spirit prepares the unregenerate, the Spirit prepares the elect. The crucial difference, however, is that the Spirit works *in* the elect not *upon* the elect. God applies his saving grace via the Spirit internally. He comes to them in the Person of the Spirit and takes up residence in their hearts for the purpose of changing them.

> God meets them in his mercy and gives them grace in their hearts. He gives them holiness. He cleanses them from their filth and puts his own beauty upon them. He infuses a principal of spiritual life into them. He opens their blind eyes and calls them out of their darkness and causes them to see the refreshing light of his glory, so that they no longer are in a land of darkness and the shadow of death.
>
> By his grace he reunites them to himself, fills them with his Holy Spirit.[70]

God gives them what man once had, a gift greater than mere escape from eternal punishment—he gives them *himself.*

Having inhabited the heart of man, God's Spirit begins his work upon the natural principles, the resident faculties, that were damaged but not lost in the Fall. The Spirit assists, Edwards argued, such faculties to see what they lost sight of: the beauty and glory of God.

---

68 Edwards, "A Spiritual Understanding," *Works*, 14:89.
69 Edwards, "God Glorified in Man's Dependence," *Works*, 17:201.
70 Edwards, "Honey from the Rock," *Works*, 17:127.

The Spirit of God assists to an ideal view of God's natural perfections, wherein consists his greatness, and gives a view of this as manifested in his works that he has done, and in the words that he has spoken, and so gives a sensible apprehension of the heinousness of sin and his wrath against it, and the guilt of it, and the terribleness of the sufferings denounced against it.[71]

In other words, the Spirit enables them to see God and themselves as they truly are: beings separated by an immeasurable gulf of sin that they cannot cross.

The Spirit plies his legal work upon the heart and affections. He pricks their conscience. He helps them overcome that sin which holds them back by first revealing it to them, Edwards proclaimed.[72] These legal convictions, he reasoned, "consist in conviction of sinfulness of heart and practice, and the dreadfulness of sin, as committed against a God of terrible majesty, infinite holiness and hatred of sin, and strict justice in punishing of it."[73] Under the white-hot glow of the Spirit's righteousness, the blackness of their sins breaks their heart. The Spirit, because he loves them, refuses to let them rest, "to be quiet in them" in their sin.[74] Showing them their sin that they might see it aright, as God sees it, the Spirit breaks them of their sin and their hearts over their sin.

Edwards knew that moving the heart alone was insufficient for the conversion of the soul. He believed that Spirit must operate on the mind as well. Using the rational abilities of the creature, the Spirit enables the elect to understand the things of the gospel, their excellency and their sweetness.[75] Doing so, the Spirit utilizes not immediate revelation but those things given via God's other self-

---

71 Edwards, "Miscellanies" No. 782, *Works*, 18:463.
72 Edwards, "A Divine and Supernatural Light," *Works*, 17:411.
73 Edwards, *Religious Affections*, *Works*, 2:156.
74 Edwards, "Convictions and the Uses of Order," *Works*, 19:265.
75 Edwards, "Thorough Knowledge of Divine Truth," *Works*, 22:100.

revelations, both creation and the Word. Building on rational argument and powerful preaching, the Spirit of God opens the eyes of the mind to see what fallen man overlooks. "The Holy Ghost convinces by arguments," Edwards said; "He enlightens the reason, and makes use of the gospel. The Word is the sword in the hand of the Spirit."[76] Through the work of the Spirit the individual can finally see and savour the gospel. Again, it is the blazing righteousness of the Spirit that reveals to man what he most needs to hear, in this case the truthfulness of the gospel claims.

> The Holy Spirit, when he enters, he lets in that divine light that discovers truth, and makes it appear as truth and shows the way of salvation, which appears and makes itself known by its own intrinsic evidence, which it carries with it.[77]

Applying the "divine and supernatural light," the Spirit removes the sinful scales from the mind's eye, convinces the sinner of the reality of his situation and the suitableness of the gospel, and readies the heart and soul to embrace it. Doing so, the Spirit does not force the convert to believe but necessarily readies him to do so. For without the supernatural work of the Spirit in the soul, the elect are no different than the lost. But, with the indwelling presence of the Spirit, the elect are made able to believe and they do.

Indwelled by the Spirit, convicted of sin and convinced of the gospel, the individual possesses a new disposition. He experiences a change of heart[78] and is given a new temper.[79] With the presence

---

76 Edwards, "The Threefold Work of the Holy Ghost," *Works*, 14:393.

77 Edwards, "The Threefold Work of the Holy Ghost," *Works*, 14:407.

78 "That light and knowledge has been let into his soul that has so affected him that he has a new nature, just as if a new spirit were infused into that body; of an angel of darkness has made an angel of light of him; has brought the image of God upon him; has made him of an heavenly temper and an angelical mind; has sweetened and mollified his dispositions; and of an heart of stone hath made a heart of flesh, of bitter has made sweet, and of dark has made light" (Edwards, "A Spiritual Understanding," *Works*, 14:81).

79 Edwards, *Charity and Its Fruit*, *Works*, 8:133.

of the Spirit, man's heart has been brought to the point where he might truly know and worship God.

> These things are imparted in the saving work of God's Spirit on the soul. In this work it is that God gives the soul that divine light and knowledge of the glorious and joyful things that the gospel reveals, which are the subject of [the song the saints shall sing before the throne of God].
>
> And in this work it is that the heart is put in tune, and it is put into a capacity and disposition truly and sincerely to praise God and to make that heavenly melody, which is made in singing this new song, by exercising these divine principles of divine love and divine joy.[80]

This is possible only because of the gracious saving work of God who has placed his Spirit of love into those who are entirely unlovely.

> 'Tis divine as God is the only and immediate author of it. 'Tis not a principle that is human. 'Tis not anything that man is the author of. 'Tis no natural principle but 'tis supernatural. 'Tis something that is above nature; 'tis not of the earth. 'Tis of no earthly growth but 'tis immediately from heaven.
>
> Man naturally is altogether destitute of it. He has nothing of it in his soul but is totally alienated from God and is full of enmity against God. This holy principle is from God. 'Tis not from God as other things are from God by the power and influence of a second cause. But it is immediately from God, from the immediate influence and action of the Spirit of God that descends into and dwells in the soul. The love of God is shed abroad in

---

80 Edwards, "They Sing a New Song," *Works*, 22:237.

our hearts by the Holy Ghost given to us.[81]

Thus, fallen man is brought to love God by the love of God given to him by the Spirit of God's love. God forces no one to love him, but enables the elect to do so of their own renewed desire. Moreover, this Spirit of love that draws people to the love of God produces a spirit of love in those converted such that their conversion will be proved by their love for God and man.

> The Spirit excites to love on these motives, and makes the attributes of God as revealed in the Gospel and manifested in Christ, delightful objects of contemplation; and makes the soul to long after God and Christ, after their presence and communion, and acquaintance with them, and conformity to them; and to live so as to please and honor them. And also quells contentions among men, and gives a spirit of peace and goodwill, excites to acts of outward kindness and earnest desires of the salvation of others' souls; and causes a delight in those that appear as the children of God and followers of Christ: I say when a spirit operates after this manner among a people, there is the highest kind of evidence of the influence of a true and divine spirit.[82]

Therefore, salvation is entirely the work of God in three Persons shedding the love of God abroad, bringing the redeemed into that eternal fellowship of love through the power and work of the Holy Spirit.

If conversion, as Edwards argued, is a supernatural work of God resulting from the love of God that produces a saving faith in God, revival is that love writ large. As has been argued earlier, conversion

---

81 Edwards, "The Spirit of the True Saints Is a Spirit of Divine Love," in ed. McMullen, *The Glory and Honor of God*, 304–305.

82 Edwards, *The Distinguishing Marks, Works*, 4:256.

brings great glory to God. By the sheer magnitude of the events associated with revival and the number of souls savingly wrought upon by the Holy Spirit, revival brings glory in abundance to all three Persons in the Trinity for "all is *of* the Father, all *through* the Son, and all *in* the Holy Ghost (emphasis his)."[83]

Due to the glory reflected upon God in the salvation of souls and revival, Christians should desire God's greater glory, dedicating themselves to its pursuit, said Edwards. They should commit themselves to prayer for the conversion of others. "If the salvation of men's souls is so precious," he reasoned, "let us be exhorted to pray for the accomplishment of those times wherein there will be such plentiful effusions of God's spirit to the conversion of men's souls."[84] Such prayers, he said in another sermon, should be "earnest and constant."[85] Moreover, the correct subject matter of these petitions must be the Spirit of God who effects such a wonderful application of the gospel.[86] Consistent with his belief that God is a prayer-hearing God, Edwards taught his people that "God is much more ready to bestow spiritual showers [such as revival]; he is more ready to shower down of his Holy Spirit than he is rain."[87] In other words, God demands prayer unto his glory and answers prayers that appeal to that glory.

To that end, Edwards lobbied famously for a North American counterpart to the Scottish concert of prayer that his correspondents so frequently extolled in their letters. Summarizing the intent of their prayer efforts, Edwards wrote,

> In October, A.D. 1744, a number of ministers in Scotland, taking into consideration the state of God's church, and of the world of mankind, judged that the providence of God,

---

83 Edwards, "God Glorified in Man's Dependence," *Works*, 17:212.
84 Edwards, "Value of Salvation," *Works*, 10:335.
85 Edwards, "Suitableness of Union in Extraordinary Prayer," *Works*, 25:202.
86 Edwards, "Suitableness of Union in Extraordinary Prayer," *Works*, 25:203.
87 Edwards, "Praying for the Spirit," *Works*, 22:220.

at such a day, did loudly call such as were concerned for the welfare of Zion, to united extraordinary applications to the God of all grace, suitably acknowledging him as the fountain of all spiritual benefits and blessings of his church, and earnestly praying to him, that he would appear in his glory, and favor Zion, and manifest his compassion to the world of mankind, by an abundant effusion of his Holy Spirit on all the churches, and the whole habitable earth, to revive true religion in all parts of Christendom, and to deliver all nations from their great and manifold spiritual calamities and miseries, and bless them with the unspeakable benefits of the kingdom of our glorious Redeemer, and fill the whole earth with his glory.[88]

Since God has appointed prayer as a means to his glorious ends,[89] Edwards appealed, ministers should be much in prayer for revival and much in support of a similar concert of prayer in the colonies. Moreover, such is the duty of all Christians to dedicate themselves to this cause in their prayers. As if God's glory provided an insufficient motive to prayer for revival, Edwards also reminded the Christians of New England that revival would be profitable for the reformation of the church and society as well.[90] Finally, a prayer-fed revival will mark "the church's latter-day glory" and expedite the glorious return of her Christ.[91]

As with conversion itself, God's requirement of prayer prior to revival is answered by God himself. He stirs the hearts of Christians and "gives them a spirit of prayer."[92] This, too, is the work of the Spirit.

---

88 Edwards, *An Humble Attempt*, in *Apocalyptic Writings*, *Works*, 5:321.

89 Edwards, "Value of Salvation," *Works*, 10:336.

90 Edwards, *An Humble Attempt*, *Works*, 5:366.

91 Edwards, *An Humble Attempt*, *Works*, 5:426.

92 Edwards, "To Prepare Men's Hearts and Then to Answer Their Prayers," in ed. McMullen, *The Glory and Honor of God*, 79.

If it was now first that men were stirred to get together in assemblies to help and assist one another in seeking God so as they never had done before, it argues something extraordinary as the cause, and could be from nothing but uncommon influences of God's Spirit. We see by experience that a remarkable pouring out of the Spirit of God is always attended with such an effect, viz. a great increase of the performance of the duty of prayer. When the Spirit of God begins or works on men's hearts, it immediately sets them to calling on the {name of the Lord}.[93]

In a seeming theological paradox, God expects prayer, demands prayer and provides the Spirit of prayer. He leaves nothing that he ordains to chance. Instead, God provides all. "[God's] Spirit shall be gloriously poured out for the wonderful revival and propagation of religion." More than that, he continued,

God, by pouring out his Holy Spirit, shall furnish men to be glorious instruments of carrying on his work; shall fill them with knowledge and wisdom and fervent zeal for the promoting of the kingdom of Christ and the salvation of souls and propagating the gospel in the world.[94]

God equips man to do that which God requires. Thus equipped, Christians should storm the gates of heaven and "pray for the times when this light shall enlighten the whole world."[95] Until then, Christians, guided by the Spirit, will and should "give God no rest."[96]

---

93 Edwards, *A History of the Work of Redemption, Works*, 9:142.
94 Edwards, *A History of the Work of Redemption, Works*, 9:460.
95 Edwards, "Light in a Dark World, a Dark Heart," *Works*, 19:722.
96 Edwards, "Importunate Prayer for Millennial Glory" *Works*, 22:369.

SANCTIFYING GRACE

Having applied the completed work of the gospel, the Spirit's work remains yet unfinished. The Spirit's work of love continues in the life of the believer, Edwards explained. The Spirit is, he believed, "the sum of salvation and of those saving benefits that are purchased by Christ."[97] The Spirit represents the totality of God's grace in the lives of those he saves. Moreover, the Spirit continues to apply that grace throughout their earthly existence.

God purchased the redemption of man with the blood of Christ, Edwards said, for the purpose of restoring man to his proper place and character. To that end, the Spirit of God's love proves invaluable. Through the work of the Spirit the saint once more draws near to his God in a sweet relationship. "Hence our communion with God the Father and God the Son consists in our partaking of the Holy Ghost, which is their Spirit: for to have communion or fellowship with another, is to partake with them of their good in their fullness, in union and society with them," he stated.[98] In this renewed relationship, the believer's life continues to change becoming ever more like his Saviour. This, too, constitutes the work of the Spirit.

> The Holy Spirit by which Christians are led, and guided to heaven, is the Spirit of Christ: he dwells with them and in them by his Spirit. That power by which they, when they have believed, are brought on in the way to eternal life, through all obstacles and oppositions in spite of all the powers of darkness, is the power of Christ.[99]

Thus, in salvation and the ensuing sanctification of the Spirit, the believer enjoys a new disposition, becomes a new person, and delights in the love of God in a way that was previously impossible. The task of reuniting fallen man with his holy God stands as the

---

97 Edwards, "Miscellanies" No. 1164, *Works*, 23:86.
98 Edwards, "Treatise on Grace," *Works*, 21:188.
99 Edwards, "Life through Christ Alone," *Works*, 10:526.

summa of the Spirit's work. This process begins in conversion, is enjoyed in sanctification and is completed in heaven. Following Edwards's *ordo salutis* the Spirit inhabits man as his permanent dwelling place, regenerates the heart of the lost, disposes him to love toward God, and dispenses faith. In so doing, the Spirit brings the individual into the holy family by way of adoption. Newly saved, the believer experiences a sweet "fellowship with the Father and the Son" and "communion [with] the Holy Ghost."[100] This fellowship, Edwards wrote, allows the believer to "partake of" the good that is in the Father and Son, not simply observe and appreciate it.[101] What belongs to the Trinity becomes the believer's by way of association, a relationship consummated by the Spirit. In this relationship, the Spirit unites the believer to the Divine and permanently etches the love of Christ upon their soul.[102] The love that existed from all eternity within the Trinity, the Spirit pours upon and shares with the convert.

Whereas Adam enjoyed the fruits of a similar relationship prior to his fall and lost it, the new believer entertains no such worries, Edwards was convinced. Once the Spirit has taken up residence in the believer's soul, Edwards asserted, he will never leave. "The saint always has the Spirit of God dwelling in his heart to sanctify him."[103] The Spirit claims the soul as his "lasting abode."[104] Doing so, he seals "his favorites," guaranteeing his abiding presence and sanctifying work.[105] The permanent indwelling of the Spirit, Edwards contended, proves the depths and eternal nature of God's love for his people. Because love is the essence of God and his Spirit, they are assured of his continued grace from now into eternity.

Because God loves them and has filled their souls with that love

---

100 Edwards, "Of God the Father," *Works*, 25:147.

101 Edwards, "Treatise on Grace," *Works*, 21:188.

102 Edwards, "Treatise on Grace," *Works*, 21:195.

103 Edwards, "God Is Everywhere Present," in ed. McMullen, *The Blessing of God*, 112.

104 Edwards, *Religious Affections*, *Works*, 2:200.

105 Edwards, *Religious Affections*, *Works*, 2:236.

in the Person of the Spirit, he will no more leave them in their incomplete state than he would their sinful state. He will complete that which he began in salvation, the process of complete renewal and restoration. In other words, he will sanctify them, bringing them ever closer to the perfect image of his Son. This, too, is the work of the Holy Spirit, said Edwards. Speaking from personal experience, Edwards noted this in his "Personal Narrative":

> I have many times had a sense of the glory of the third person in the Trinity, in his office of Sanctifier; in his holy operations communicating divine light and life to the soul. God in the communications of his Holy Spirit, has appeared as an infinite fountain of divine glory and sweetness; being full and sufficient to fill and satisfy the soul: pouring forth itself in sweet communications, like the sun in its glory, sweetly and pleasantly diffusing light and life.[106]

That which God communicates—disperses—through the Spirit in sanctification is his holiness. God gives the Spirit that the Spirit might produce holiness. Partaking of the Godhead in this way, the believer imbibes of the holiness of God and becomes progressively more and more holy.[107] The holiness of the Spirit becomes a "vital principle" in the soul.

> Rightly to understand the nature of the habit of grace, it must be observed that the Spirit of God in the heart of a saint acts both as a natural vital principle, and also as a voluntary agent manifesting care of that heart that it is in, lest it should be overcome by temptations, and lest it should fall away.[108]

---

106 Edwards, "Personal Narrative," *Works*, 16:801.

107 Edwards, "Participation in the Divine Nature," *Works*, 8:638. See also Edwards's "Treatise on Grace," *Works*, 21:192.

108 Edwards, "Miscellanies" No. 818, *Works*, 18:528.

The active presence of the Spirit becomes both a liberating and securing force. Operating from within, the Spirit frees the soul from the chains of sin to do that which it was created to do—love God. Moreover, the presence of the Spirit keeps the saint from returning to his life of sin and undermining God's redemptive purposes. Thus, in sanctification, the soul is not made holy but is remade, remodelled if you will, so that it might become holy in the eschaton. For the time being, however, the saint must be satisfied with the incomplete nature of his present condition and continue to strive toward that holiness, living out that which is now most appealing to his will.

Renewed in his own spirit by the Spirit, the believer's disposition turns from evil to good. While the process is truly a process and remains incomplete in this lifetime, the inclination of the soul now leans toward holiness and the things of God. The Spirit leads, not drives, the believer to righteousness, Edwards said. The gracious instruction of the Holy Spirit teaches the soul to see and savour the beauty of the things of God.

> Thus a holy person is led by the Spirit, as he is instructed and led by his holy taste, and disposition of heart; whereby, in the lively exercise of grace, he easily distinguishes good and evil, and knows at once, what is a suitable amiable behavior towards God, and towards man, in this case and the other; and judges what is right, as it were spontaneously, and of himself, without a particular deduction, by any other arguments than the beauty that is seen, and goodness that is tasted.[109]

Thus enlightened, the soul now recognizes and relishes what it once abhorred.

The Spirit also guides by means of influence, "exerting his own proper nature [holiness], in the exercise of [man's] faculties."[110] In

---

109 Edwards, *Religious Affections, Works*, 2:282.
110 Edwards, *Religious Affections, Works*, 2:392.

so doing, by shedding his holiness upon the soul of the believer, the Holy Spirit gives the soul the necessary ability to choose and do what is in accord with God's holiness. When the believer acts, choosing to do what is most appealing at the present according to Edwards's theology of the will, he does so out of a holy disposition.[111] His mind and affections, those faculties that drive the will, are now drawn toward holy things because what is holy has become most appealing in his new state.

> And what has been observed of that divine teaching and leading of the Spirit of God, which there is in gracious affections, shows the reason of this tendency of such affections to an universally holy practice. For as has been observed [elsewhere in *Religious Affections*], the Spirit of God in this his divine teaching and leading, gives the soul a natural relish of the sweetness of that which is holy, and of everything that is holy, so far as it comes in view, and excites a disrelish and disgust of everything that is unholy.[112]

Filled by the Spirit and informed by his holiness, the believer no longer desires evil. Having tasted of the greater good of God, he hates the lesser evil of the world. Moreover, he does not do this because the Spirit forces him to do so but because he now wants to. The believer now loves what God loves and longs to live his life in accordance with this new affection. Such affections in the true believer, Edwards said, arising from the internal leading of the Spirit, will produce the fruits of righteousness. The holiness within will bubble forth without. That external exhibition of internal saving grace, he said, proves the reality of the saving presence of the Spirit.[113]

---

111 Of the will, Edwards said, "The soul always wills or chooses that which, in the present view of the mind, considered in the whole of that view, and all that belongs to it, appears most agreeable" (Edwards, *Freedom of the Will, Works*, 1:217).

112 Edwards, *Religious Affections, Works*, 2:394.

113 Edwards, *Religious Affections, Works*, 2:383f.

The ongoing grace of God in the presence of the Holy Spirit serves to sustain the saints as well. The Spirit provides spiritual sustenance, feeding the saints, leading them on toward glory.[114] Speaking of the hidden manna mentioned in Revelation 2:17, Edwards noted,

> By this hidden manna is doubtless meant that spiritual heavenly food with which God feeds the saints, that spiritual heavenly good that the souls of the saints are refreshed, and comforted, and satisfied with, that is reserved and laid up for them, and appropriated to them as to his dear children and peculiar favorites. This excellent bread is no other than the Holy Spirit in his sweet, soul-strengthening, and satisfying communications.[115]

God feeds the Spirit to his people for *he* is what they most need.

The Spirit offers consolation as well. His sustaining grace and kind presence bring great comfort to God's elect while they are separated from his eternal glory in their temporal state.[116] The love of God, through the ministrations of the Spirit, flows over his people like a river without fail "in times of the greatest public calamity and trouble," Edwards exclaimed.[117] God will not abandon them as they once did him. He will bless them and keep them for they are his and he has staked his claim. He has taken up permanent residence, and his presence is the greatest blessing they could ever ask.

Christ purchased for the elect the benefit of the Spirit, Edwards believed. "The Holy Ghost is the good purchased," "the sum of all

---

114 Edwards, "Images of Divine Things," in *Typological Writings*, ed. Wallace E. Anderson and Mason I. Lowance, Jr., *Works*, 11 (1993):97.

115 Edwards, *Notes on Scripture*, *Works*, 15:208.

116 Edwards, "Like Rain upon Mown Grass," *Works*, 22:303.

117 Edwards, "God's Care in Time of Public Commotions," *Works*, 22:350.

that Christ purchased for men."[118] To the elect, God has given his love. To the elect, God has given his Spirit.

> Now man at his first conversion is justified and adopted. He is received as a child and an heir, as joint heir with Christ. His fellowship is with the Father and with his Son Jesus Christ. God is theirs, and Christ is theirs, and the Holy Ghost is theirs and all things are theirs. The Holy Spirit, who is the sum of all good, is their inheritance; and that little of it that they have in this life, is the earnest of their future inheritance, till the redemption of the purchased possession.[119]

SUMMARY

According to Edwards, the Holy Spirit is the personification of God's love. He is the expression of the infinite love within the Trinity and the outward expression of that love to humanity. In love, God provides grace through the Spirit to all men. God's love is further proven in the ultimate expression of love at the cross. Through the work of the Spirit, God applies that love in a special measure to the elect. With the Spirit, God woos his blessed children into the fold. By the Spirit, he kindles their love for him. Through the Spirit, God's love abounds in the souls of his people and in the life of his church.

What does the Holy Spirit have to do with prayer?

> The Spirit of God, the chief subject matter of prayer, [is] the great purchase and promise of Christ. [We have] more encouragement to pray for this than any other [thing].[120]

---

118 Edwards, "Treatise on Grace," *Works*, 21:189.
119 Edwards, "Miscellanies" No. 755, *Works*, 18:403–404.
120 Edwards, "Suitableness of Union in Extraordinary Prayer," *Works*, 25:203.

Christians, Edwards reminded his hearers, have every reason to dedicate themselves to prayer. Illness, drought, political intrigue, the revivals and the wiles of Satan all point to the ongoing need for constant communication with God. The Christian life depends upon God for its initiation and its continuation. "Keep close to God. Forsake [him] not. Be continually with him, near to him in the duty of prayer, that he would be your guard and your counselor," Edwards implored.[121] The Bible, he commented, contains ample reason for and encouragement to the duty of prayer. Moreover, the faithful prayer of the saints for God's glory is the express will of God.[122]

The Spirit, who as the active agent of God working within the creation on a daily basis and serves to bring souls into a loving relationship with God, also takes centre stage in the drama of prayer. Just as he leads and guides believers to righteousness, the Spirit leads them in prayer as well, Edwards said. The Spirit's role in prayer, however, does not end with mere guidance. He is to be the centre of that prayer—the very object of the Christian's spiritual desires. When Christians desire such a great gift, Edwards preached, God is sure to answer, for he is "ready to bestow spiritual showers" of divine blessings.[123] Thus, the Spirit of God is the alpha and omega of prayer, the totality of all that duty entails.

THE SOURCE OF PRAYER

Given the overtures of God's grace, it is quite clear that God desires an intimate relationship with man. Through the redemptive work of Christ and the application of salvation by the Spirit, God blesses humans with the pleasure of fellowship with himself.[124] The believer needs that relationship. The indwelling

121 Edwards, "False Light and True," *Works*, 19:131.
122 Edwards, *An Humble Attempt*, *Works*, 5:348.
123 Edwards, "Praying for the Spirit," *Works*, 22:220.
124 In "Christian Happiness," Edwards explained that there are two kinds of pleasures that man might seek and enjoy, those that are ultimately "hateful and abominable lusts" and those "that are worthy of so noble a creature as man is." Loving and obeying God, seeing and savouring the beauty of Christ and communing with

presence of the Spirit facilitates that relationship. He leads the saints to the throne room so they can enjoy intimate conversations with their God.

For the natural man, in his fallen condition, immediate conversation with God proves impossible. His sin stands in the way, forever blocking access to the Father's ear. The regenerate man, saved by God's grace, must break the habits of his old ways and develop new ones. At first, prayer seems to be a foreign concept to one who has not known the sound of God's voice personally. Prayer must become something of an acquired taste. It is a learned habit that must be encouraged and promoted.

By the grace of God, Edwards taught, believers have at their disposal three ways that they can learn of this duty and its pleasures. First, God in his providence ordains events to turn the thoughts and hearts of his people to himself—as their only help, to correct their ways and to promote his glory among men.

"Great outward calamities" such as the incursion of the Catholic French and the Indian invaders into Protestant lands, and "spiritual calamities" like those experienced in Northampton over matters of theological subtlety and church discipline, are best answered by turning to God.[125] Speaking more specifically to the uproar caused by the revivals of the mid-1730s and early 1740s and its fallout, Edwards told his flock that only faithful prayer to God would restore peace in their valley.

> The more disorders, extravagancies and delusions of the devil have lately prevailed, the more need have we to pray earnestly to God, for his Holy Spirit, to promote true religion, in opposition to the grand deceiver, and all his works; and the more such prayer as is proposed, is

---

God through the power of the Holy Spirit, these Edwards said, are the pleasures that man should seek (Edwards, "Christian Happiness," *Works*, 10:305–306).

125   Edwards, *An Humble Attempt*, *Works*, 5:357.

answered, the more effectually will all that is contrary to sober and pure religion, be extirpated and exploded.[126]

Providence, both the good and the bad, draws men to their knees and to their God, Edwards proffered. Yet, rather than blaming God for circumstances that seem contrary to their worldly desires, Christians should find great hope in the midst of these struggles. God causes these events for their good—and that good is God himself. "God," Edwards argued, "will come to those that are seeking him and waiting for him."[127] Dark providence and glorious prayer bring the saint what he needs—a closer relationship with God.

In addition to the external motivations to prayer brought about by providence, the Bible provides many examples that ought to bring Christians to prayer. Christ stands as the greatest of these examples, Edwards repeatedly said. Again speaking of the revivals and attempting to renew the prayers of the saints for them, Edwards lifted Christ up as the model prayer.

The encouragement to explicit agreement in prayer is great from such instances as these; but it is yet greater from those wonderful words of our blessed Redeemer, "I say unto you, that if any two of you shall agree on earth touching anything that they shall ask, it shall be done for them of my Father which is in heaven." Christ is pleased to give this great encouragement to the union of his followers in this excellent and holy exercise of seeking and serving God; an holy union and communion of his people being that which he greatly desires and delights in, that which he came into the world to bring to pass, that which he especially prayed for with his dying breath, that

---

126 Edwards, *An Humble Attempt, Works*, 5:434.
127 Edwards, *An Humble Attempt, Works*, 5:356.

which he died for, and which was one chief end of the whole affair of our redemption by him.[128]

Christ, he pointed out, displayed the model prayer in the so-called "Lord's Prayer." And, as it relates to the present topic, Christ prayed for the Spirit.[129] To that end, Edwards counselled others to follow their exemplar in praying for what they need the most: the Holy Spirit. "Christ himself," he observed in Luke 3:21–22, "though the eternal Son of God, obtained the Holy Spirit for himself in a way of prayer."[130] In prayer, Christ is our "Great Example."

As good as the example of Christ may be, believers have yet another motive to develop a greater prayer life. They possess the Holy Spirit. He is not outside waiting to come in. He is on the inside working his way out, influencing every area of the believer's being. The Spirit indwells them so that the Godhead might communicate itself to them. Through this internal communication believers "have an intercourse with heaven by meditation, and prayer, and other duties of religion."[131] God has communicated his love to man in the Person of the Spirit so that man might communicate with God. He makes them holy that they might pray. He shows them why they should pray. And, he teaches them how to pray.

They have the same language to God in prayer and praise: expressing the same humility and repentance in confessing their sins, expressing the same adoration and admiring sense of God's glory and excellency, expressing the same humble submission and resignation, the same thankfulness, in like manner showing forth God's praises, expressing the same faith and humble dependence on the mercy and all-

128 Edwards, *An Humble Attempt, Works*, 5:367.
129 Edwards, "Of God the Father," *Works*, 25:150.
130 Edwards, "Christ the Great Example of Gospel Ministers," *Works*, 25:346.
131 Edwards, "Youth and the Pleasures of Piety," *Works*, 19:85.

sufficiency of God, expressing the same love and longing desires after God. The saints in all ages speak the same language, that [of] David and the saints of old, which we have an account of in the Word of God. The Spirit of God teaches the saints the same language in their prayers; their prayers are the breathings of the same Spirit.[132]

The same Spirit who wrote the Bible so that they might know of Christ, and who brought them to Christ, continues to work within them so that his words become theirs in prayer.

THE OBJECT OF PRAYER

In prayer, as in salvation, God graciously gives all that man needs, the Spirit, so that man might be able to come to the God who can fulfill all that he needs, the Spirit. In other words, according to Edwards's theology of prayer, the Spirit is more than the source of the believer's prayer. The Spirit ought to be the object of that prayer as well, "the sum of the blessings that Christians have to pray for."[133]

One of Edwards's favourite descriptions for the Spirit of God was the "sum of all blessings." The "Spirit" becomes shorthand for all the blessings of God, for it is through the Spirit that God delivers these blessings. He used such language in reference to the Spirit in many venues, from theological writings to sermons. He noted the priority of the Spirit among the things accomplished at Calvary.

The sum of all that Christ purchased is the Holy Ghost. God is he of whom the purchase is made, God is the purchase and the price, and God is the thing purchased: God is the Alpha and Omega in this work. The great thing purchased by Jesus Christ for us is communion with God, which is only in having the Spirit; 'tis partici-

---

132 Edwards, "Christians a Chosen Generation," *Works*, 17:303.
133 Edwards, *An Humble Attempt*, *Works*, 5:347.

pation of Christ's fullness, and having grace for grace, which is only in having of that Spirit which he has without measure; this is the promise of the Father, Luke 24:49. He purchased God's love, favor and delight, which is still the Holy Ghost, for us.[134]

In salvation, Christ purchased for the saints access to, and the promise of, the Spirit. Proving the consistency of Edwards's theological thought and his sermons, he made the same observations in his famous sermon, "God Glorified":

> Herein consists the fullness of good, which the saints receive of Christ. 'Tis by partaking of the Holy Spirit that they have communion with Christ in his fullness. God hath given the Spirit, not by measure unto him; and they do receive of his fullness, and grace for grace. This is the sum of the saints' inheritance: …. The Holy Spirit and good things are spoken of in Scripture as the same, as if the Spirit of God communicated to the soul comprised all good things.[135]

Salvation, then, culminates not only in the forgiveness of sin and the imputation of Christ's righteousness. The abiding presence of God's Spirit and the intimacy with the Creator that ensues is the end of Christ's work and God's plan.

Just as Christ had prayed for the Spirit during his humiliation, believers ought to seek the Spirit as the ultimate object of their prayers. All other desires fall short of that which represents the gift of God's love. For this, above all things, Edwards said, they should pray. "Therefore, you must every day, all of you, go alone and pray to the great God that he will enlighten your minds and give you

---

134 Edwards, "Miscellanies" No. 402, *Works*, 13:467.
135 Edwards, "God Glorified in Man's Dependence," *Works*, 17:209.

new hearts, that you may have true religion."[136] In other words, they must pray for the Spirit to be an ever-present reality in their lives. Prayer for this great blessing should be "continuing" and "instant," "crying to God day and night."[137]

The Christian's desires for God's holiness, Edwards continued, arise naturally from within. "There is a holy breathing and panting after the Spirit of God, to increase holiness, as natural to a holy nature, as breathing is to a living body. And holiness or sanctification is more directly the object of it, than any manifestation of God's love and favor."[138] In other words, the Spirit and all that he embodies—love, holiness and God's blessing—arise from within the very being of the believer. Having tasted of the goodness of God, he wants more. He needs more. He cannot live without it. He depends on God for his very being. For this, Edwards said, the Christian needs to pray without ceasing.

Seeking the Spirit as the object of his prayer, the believer concedes his dependence upon God. The blessing sought—the Spirit—brings further blessings. By the strong presence of the Spirit, the Christian gains wisdom.[139] The Spirit blesses by keeping the saint from sin.[140] This is a constant need of the people of God and should be a constant matter of prayer.

> Let God be sought frequently and carefully by prayer. The business of religion, a business that immediately respects God and religion, is vain without some communication between God and our own souls. God has appointed prayer for the maintaining of this intercourse. Let us seek to God for his grace, his pardon, and his acceptance, if ever we hope for it. A course of sin makes the least course into

136 Edwards, "The Things That Belong to True Religion," *Works*, 25:574.
137 Edwards, *Religious Affections*, *Works*, 2:382.
138 Edwards, *Religious Affections*, *Works*, 2:382–383.
139 Edwards, "A Spiritual Understanding," *Works*, 14:95.
140 Edwards, *Religious Affections*, *Works*, 2:187.

prayer. And a diligent and constant attendance on prayer
will keep us from avowed sinning.[141]

Prayer protects the saint. It keeps him in constant contact with the
Father. This communication affects the soul of man because it is
more than the exchange of simple words. It is communication with
God himself, and it is God himself that keeps the saint secure. Moreover, the Spirit of God draws out the believer's prayers and forces
them to focus on the holy rather than the profane. Prayer, Edwards
reasoned, is the principal tool in spiritual warfare because prayer
maintains the line of communication that supplies the soul and
guarantees the final victory.

"If you would keep alive a comfortable sense of the presence of
God, you must often converse with God in prayer," Edwards
remarked.[142] The subject of that conversation needs to be the Spirit,
for the Spirit is the presence and the comfort sought. Christians
depend upon God by his Spirit for all things in this life. Therefore,
the Spirit is the blessing to be sought and should be the chief
object of the prayers of the faithful. "The good that shall be
sought by prayer is God himself." Edwards continued,

> But certainly that expression of "seeking the Lord," is very
> commonly used to signify something more than merely, in
> general, to seek some mercy of God: it implies, that God
> himself is the great good desired and sought after; that the
> blessings pursued are God's gracious presence, the blessed
> manifestations of him, union and intercourse with him; or,
> in short, God's manifestations and communications of
> himself by his Holy Spirit.[143]

---

141   Edwards, "Our Present and Immediate Business," in ed. McMullen, *The Blessing of God*, 105.

142   Edwards, "God Is Everywhere Present," in ed. McMullen, *The Blessing of God*, 119.

143   Edwards, *An Humble Attempt, Works*, 5:315.

And, blessing of all blessings, Edwards affirmed, God answers such prayers liberally.

THE ANSWER TO PRAYER

God not only hears the prayers of the redeemed, Edwards contended, he longs to answer them when the proper blessing is sought. God never "bregrutches his people" anything good.[144] Because they are the objects of his love, he rejoices in the liberal giving of himself. "God's declared design is to communicate of his own fullness, and to bring men to a conformity to himself in happiness, in such a manner as to show that his goodness or willingness to communicate of his fullness has no bounds."[145] Thus, "God stands ready" to answer their prayers. "God is as ready, and more ready, to bestow than we are to ask, and more ready to open than we are to knock."[146]

The key, Edwards said, to having one's prayers answered is to ask for the right blessing, the better blessing. The more excellent the blessing sought, the more likely God will answer in the affirmative. "Of the more excellent nature any blessing is that we stand in need of," Edwards concluded, "the more ready God is to bestow it in answer to prayer."[147] Those blessings God holds to be most excellent are those intimately related to his greatness and man's desires for it. And, the Spirit is the greatest blessing God has to give. All the great spiritual blessings available to man, from salvation to glorification, are wrapped up in the indwelling presence of God, the Person and work of the Spirit. If man would but desire the Spirit of God, his every prayer would be answered. He is the "choicest gift" and the one "that God delights to bestow in answer to prayer."[148] If his people would ask for him, God would hear their cries and answer

---

144   Edwards, "The Terms of Prayer," *Works*, 19:772.
145   Edwards, "The Terms of Prayer," *Works*, 19:776.
146   Edwards, "The Terms of Prayer," *Works*, 19:783. God's readiness to answer prayer is the theme of this sermon, "The Terms of Prayer," and can be found throughout his writings on prayer and the Holy Spirit. See also, *An Humble Attempt, Works*, 5:348.
147   Edwards, "Praying for the Spirit," *Works*, 22:215.
148   Edwards, "The Dangers of Decline," *Works*, 17:97.

their prayers in abundance. Even while they yet pray, God answers this kind of prayer, giving men "refreshing discoveries of himself."[149] Take heart, Christians, Edwards preached. "God is more ready to bestow this than any other blessing."[150]

Edwards was quick to qualify the promise of God's blessings, however. The prayer of faith that God answers is one that expresses true, heartfelt desire. Prayers that arise not of the heart but selfish desire, that have no sincerity, are not true prayers at all.[151] Such prayers are prayer in word only. In these prayers there is no "spirit of prayer." The prayer that pleases God is the prayer that he himself stirs up within the believer, applying the sanctifying work of the Spirit to their soul. When God works in this manner, the believer yearns for the things of God to an even greater extent.

> Then especially it is that they want to get near to God. Then they long after the full enjoyment of God. Then they want to know more of God, and to know as much of God, and have as much of him in their hearts, and enjoy as much of God as their natures are capable.[152]

He is pleased with nothing short of the glory of God. "When God stirs up in his people the lively exercises of God, and gives them a great sense of the excellency and glory of spiritual things, this stirs up large desires in them."[153] How does God stir up these desires and bring the believer to pray for them? His Spirit.

> The true spirit of prayer is no other than God's own Spirit dwelling in the hearts of the saints. And as this spirit

---

149 Edwards, "The Most High a Prayer-Hearing God," *Works* (Hendrickson), 2:114.

150 Edwards, "The Terms of Prayer," *Works*, 19:785.

151 Edwards, "Praying for the Spirit," *Works*, 22:221.

152 Edwards, "Praying for the Spirit," *Works*, 22:784.

153 Edwards, "The Terms of Prayer," *Works*, 19:785.

comes from God, so doth it naturally tend to God in holy breathings and pantings. It naturally leads to God, to converse with him by prayer.[154]

Their appetite for God stirred by the grace of God, believers pray to God for God. God answers by giving himself in ever greater portions.

> God is not the more backward to hear the prayer of his people, because the blessings they ask are very excellent, but the more forward. Such is God's goodness, that 'tis with more delight that God bestows great blessings than small ones. The Holy Spirit is the greatest blessing that ever {God bestows}, but God is more ready to bestow this than any other blessing.[155]

SUMMARY

The rhetorical question asked of Edwards has been, "What does the Holy Spirit have to do with prayer?" His answer was anything but rhetorical. The Spirit, Edwards said, has everything to do with prayer. His theology of prayer stands or falls with the Person and work of the Spirit. The Spirit enables men to pray through his regenerating work. He leads men to pray by his abiding presence. He stirs men to pray for those things that God longs to give through his sanctifying grace. He is the source, the object and the answer to all God-centred prayer. When Christians speak of prayer, Edwards believed, they speak of, by, and about the Holy Spirit for the "Spirit of God [is] the chief subject matter of prayer."[156]

---

154 Edwards, "Hypocrites Deficient in the Duty of Prayer," in ed. Nichols, *Seeking God*, 359.

155 Edwards, "The Terms of Prayer," *Works*, 19:785.

156 Edwards, "Suitableness of Union in Extraordinary Prayer," *Works*, 25:203.

Conclusion

> So prayer (which is the expression of faith) for a particular
> mercy needed, is especially the way to obtain that mercy.[157]

Amy Pauw has argued that Edwards's pneumatology embodies his
most original thinking concerning the Trinity. As has been illus-
trated, his theology of the Spirit proves important as well. The
Spirit is the tie that binds much of Edwards's thought together.
He personifies the love that unites the Three into One in the
Trinity. He applies the work of Christ to the creature. He draws
the believer into the Trinitarian love relationship. Without the
Spirit there would be no Trinity, no incarnation, no regeneration
and no supplication. The Spirit, as Edwards conceived him, is
nothing if he is not vital to everything.

The Spirit, fully God in every attribute, plays a central part at
every point of Edwards's theology of prayer. Through the work
of the Spirit, man can know the love of God in revelation. He
can know peace with God through the Son in regeneration. He
can know God himself through his indwelling presence. He can,
in the Spirit and through Spirit, commune with God in prayer.
All of this is possible because God sought to glorify himself in the
redemption of fallen man, a work that was completed by the Son
at the cross.

> The Spirit of Christ is given to his church and people
> forever, everlastingly to influence them and dwell in them.
> The Holy Spirit is the great purchase of Christ. God the
> Father is the person of whom the purchase is made; God
> the Son is the person who makes the purchase, and the
> Holy Spirit is the gift purchased. The sum of all those

---

157 Edwards, "Justification by Faith Alone," *Works*, 19:230.

good things in this life, and the life to come, which are
purchased for the church is the Holy Spirit.[158]

The Spirit, as Edwards often said, is the "sum of all blessings." He
is the fruit of man's salvific encounter with his Creator. Moreover,
the Spirit does not rest after conversion but continues to work,
drawing man ever closer to God, shaping him into the image of
the Son, and filling him with himself.

The ongoing ministry of the Spirit forms the core of Edwards's
theology of prayer. All true prayer arises from internal leading of
the Spirit. The Spirit teaches all things, giving the believer new
tastes and "holy appetites." Having tasted of the things of God,
nothing satisfies the believer short of God and his holiness. The Spirit
then draws the believer to pray for those things that God holds most
dear. As such, the Spirit becomes the object of their desires and
prayers for he encompasses those very things.

> From what has been said, it follows that the Holy Spirit is
> the sum of all good. 'Tis the fullness of God. The holiness
> and happiness of the Godhead consists in it; and in the
> communion or partaking of it consists all the true loveliness
> and happiness of the creature. All the grace and comfort
> persons have here, and all their holiness and happiness
> hereafter, consists in the love of the Spirit.[159]

Since the Spirit knows the heart and mind of God, the prayers that
he inspires God answers. "God stands ready to give 'em their hearts'
desires."[160] Thus, from beginning to end, Edwards's theology of
prayer is God-centred, Christ-dependent and Spirit-driven.

All that remains, Edwards argued, all that stands between God
and the answers to their every need, is the honest, heartfelt prayers

---

158 Edwards, *Charity and Its Fruit, Works*, 8:353–354.
159 Edwards, "Treatise on Grace," *Works*, 21:188.
160 Edwards, "The Terms of Prayer," *Works*, 19:784.

of God's people. Therefore, he pleaded, "Let us do what in us lies to be filled with the Spirit." "Let us strive for greater and greater degrees of it." And, finally, "Let us long and thirst for it. Let [us] cherish and yield to and follow all his motions. Let us pray for the Spirit."[161]

---

161   Edwards, "The Threefold Work of the Holy Ghost," *Works*, 14:436.

Chapter 6

EXTERNAL BIOGRAPHY III
Controversy and dismissal

I need the prayers of my fathers and brethren who are
friendly to me, that I may have wisdom given me by my
great master, and that I may be enabled to conduct with a
steady faithfulness to him, under all trials and whatever may
be the issue of this affair.[1]

The enthusiasm of the Great Awakening of the 1730s and
40s was long forgotten by 1750, the intervening years
marked by disappointment and strife. The preceding
decade marked the deaths of many dear friends, among
them David Brainerd and Colonel John Stoddard, as well as
Edwards's own beloved daughter, Jerusha, "the flower of the
family."[2] Problems arose in the church with alarming frequency.
Edwards had to endure the ramifications of the Bad Book Controversy, the renewal of the Church Covenant, a long overdue

1 Edwards, Letter "To the Reverend Thomas Foxcroft," *Works*, 16:284.
2 Edwards, Letter "To the Reverend John Erskine," *Works*, 16:249.

increase in salary and a long season in which no one applied for membership to the church. Out of the latter arose the greatest challenge Edwards ever faced in Northampton. Revisiting the requirements for church membership, he arrived at a startling and socially unacceptable conclusion—the benefits of church membership are to be reserved for those who possess a valid profession of saving faith.

The events surrounding Edwards's rejection of the prevailing notions concerning admission to the church and the Lord's Supper took eighteen months to run their course. In the end, the church in Northampton submitted to the recommendation of a council of local clergymen and demanded the removal of their pastor of twenty-one years.[3] Because Edwards challenged their way of thinking, their traditions, their very right to the benefits of church membership, his congregation sent him on his way. "I am now as it were thrown upon the wide ocean of the world," he would remark weeks later.[4]

Scholarly interpretations of the so-called "Communion Controversy" are legion and vary widely. Philip Gura understood the situation as one in which Edwards sought to reestablish his authority over a rebellious congregation.[5] Perry Miller wrote of an arrogant Edwards who unwisely outwitted his opponents with "ruthless diplomacy."[6] David Hall argued that Edwards's problems arose from "long-standing tensions" present in New England, tensions between an understanding of the church as a gathering

---

3 Edwards saw a certain biblical irony in the fact that he had actually been serving in Northampton for twenty-three years, including his time as Stoddard's associate. This, he pointed out, was the exact length of time that the prophet Jeremiah had served before he was rejected by the people of Israel (Edwards, "A Farewell Sermon," *Works*, 25:475).

4 Edwards, Letter "To the Reverend John Erskine," *Works*, 16:355.

5 Edwards "did not so much reject Stoddard's ecclesiology as refine it so that ministers might regain the kind of power over their flocks that Stoddard never relinquished over his" (Gura, *Jonathan Edwards: America's Evangelical*, 155).

6 Miller, *Jonathan Edwards*, 220.

of the saints and the church as an arm of the state.[7]

While each of the interpretations may contain an element of truth, none comes close to that which touched Edwards's heart. Jonathan Edwards was concerned for the salvation of his people and the vitality of his church, both of which were intimately connected to an affective, experiential faith. He was not merely breaking ranks with his grandfather, Solomon Stoddard. He was attempting to reestablish the high standard of membership that his Puritan forebears once held, an ecclesiology marked by the centrality of a regenerate church membership.

Edwards's dismissal from his famed pulpit has been described as "one of the most painful and most surprising events in the Ecclesiastical history of New England."[8] These events, and their meaning, continue to fascinate scholars. Yet, the circumstances and Edwards's response are instructive in regards to the present study as well. For, in the midst of the communion controversy, Edwards revealed himself to be more than simply a worthy theological adversary and honourable churchman. He proved himself to be a man of great faith who, even when things seemed to be unravelling about him and his prayers seemed to fall on deaf ears, remained steadfast in his humble dependence upon God for his strength.

To understand how the controversy unfolded and served to increase Edwards's faith, we must first consider the nature of the debate. To do so, the long-held position of the Northampton church on the Lord's Supper, that of Solomon Stoddard, will be outlined first. Then, Edwards's own convictions will be considered as they stood in stark contrast to those of his grandfather. Finally, his steadfast belief in the value of prayer will be seen as the abiding proof of his faith in God even in the face of apparent defeat.

---

7   David D. Hall, "Introduction," in *Ecclesiastical Writings, Works*, 12:1. Marsden would have agreed, at least in principle, with this observation. He argued, "the effect of Stoddardeansim was that the church and the town were more or less coextensive" (Marsden, *Jonathan Edwards: A Life*, 351).

8   Dwight, *Life of Edwards*, 298.

Mr. Stoddard's way

By the end of the seventeenth century, the problems that the Half-Way Covenant sought to rectify—declining numbers of baptisms and Christian influence—had worsened. Solomon Stoddard remarked to his congregation that "to this day, there be Four to One that do neglect the Lord's Supper."[9] He further complained, "We are a people that pretend high in Religion, but indeed we fall short of other people in the very Form of it, and don't come up in our practice in their particular to many other Churches."[10] Something had to change. Stoddard saw to it that something did.

Though stationed in the western wilderness of Massachusetts, Stoddard exerted great influence from his pulpit in Northampton. When Solomon Stoddard spoke, everyone listened. In Stoddard's sermon, "The Tryal of Assurance," he outlined his case for opening the doors to communion even wider than the Half-Way Covenant allowed. He argued that it is with much difficulty that one can be completely assured of his conversion. Some Christians suffer unreasonable seasons of doubt; others wrongly assume the presence of grace in their lives. For that reason, Stoddard suggested that the church is populated by two "sorts" of Christians:

> Some are persons of great understanding and knowledge; they have a deep insight into those ways of deceit and hypocrisy that the heart is subject to…. Others are weak and ignorant and can't give many signs of true Grace nor distinctly take them up, when they are laid down.[11]

---

9 Solomon Stoddard, "The Inexcusableness of Neglecting the Worship of God, under a Pretence of Being in an Unconverted Condition" (Boston: B. Green, 1708), 26.

10 Stoddard, "The Inexcusableness of Neglecting the Worship of God," 26.

11 Solomon Stoddard, "The Tryal of Assurance Set Forth in a Sermon" (Boston: B. Green and F. Allen, 1698), 18–19.

Since Stoddard believed that no one can know for sure the status of his soul, he argued that all should have equal access to the communion table that they may fulfill their duty.

Two years later Stoddard published his new understanding of church membership in *The Doctrine of Instituted Churches Explained and Proved from the Word of God*. Believing that the "Word of God gives us sufficient Light, to direct Instituted Churches and all Administration therein," Stoddard contended that the church was "appointed for Communion with God."[12] He defined the church in typical Puritan terms. "A Church is a Society of Saints joyned together," Stoddard wrote, "according to the appointment of Christ for the constant carrying on of his publick Worship."[13] However, Stoddard departed from the standard Congregational view of the church when he described its inhabitants. Though he believed the church to be populated by "visible saints," those that can "make a serious profession of the true Religion,"[14] Stoddard redefined this profession. Stoddard admitted to the benefits of full membership all who lived lives of reasonable uprightness and desired fellowship with the saints.[15]

Qualifications for admission to the Lord's Supper, Stoddard held, paralleled those for admission to the church.

> They may and ought to come, tho they know themselves to
> be in a Natural Condition; this Ordinance is instituted for
> all Adult Members of the Church who are not scandalous,
> and therefore must be attended by them; as no Man may
> neglect Prayer, or hearing the Word, because he cannot do
> it in Faith, so he may not neglect the Lord's Supper.[16]

---

12 Solomon Stoddard, *The Doctrine of Instituted Churches Explained and Proved from the Word of God* (London: R. Smith, 1700), 1–2.

13 Stoddard, *The Doctrine of Instituted Churches*, 5.

14 Stoddard, *The Doctrine of Instituted Churches*, 6.

15 Stoddard, *The Doctrine of Instituted Churches*, 18–19.

16 Stoddard, *The Doctrine of Instituted Churches*, 21.

For Stoddard the Lord's Supper was no longer a duty for the regenerate but for all who claimed the right of church membership.[17] The theological reason for this shift, though not noticed immediately, was clear: "[I]t is not only the strengthening of the Saints, but a means also to work saving Regeneration" because it has "a proper tendency to draw sinners to Christ."[18]

Stoddard explained his understanding of the Lord's Supper as a "converting ordinance" most clearly in his sermon, "The Inexcusableness of Neglecting the Worship of God, under a Pretence of Being in an Uncoverted Condition." "Sanctifying Grace is not necessary to the lawful attending of any duty of Worship," he announced.[19] For such persons, the Lord's Supper was "a great incouragement & comfort unto them."[20] The Lord's Supper, he maintained, "is very useful that men may obtain Sanctifying Grace" since participation placed the unbeliever in the "way [for salvation] to be gained."[21]

As word of the Stoddard's proclamation spread, Increase Mather and others responded vociferously. To rebut Mather's objections and clarify his own position, Stoddard penned *An Appeal to the Learned*. This treatise, nearly 100 pages long, contained the most detailed explanation of Stoddard's new way.

"This Ordinance has a proper tendency in its own nature to

---

17 Stoddard saw many practical reasons for permitting the unregenerate to enjoy the benefits of church membership. "For hypocrites so long as they carry well, are not destructive to the State of the Church: but on the contrary do great Service to the Church, they help to maintain the Church and Ordinances of God, they do defend the Church, they are serviceable by their gifts, by their authority, by their prudence & zeal, by their Estates; and it would be exceeding difficult for the Church to subsist without them" (Solomon Stoddard, *An Appeal to the Learned Being a Vindication of the Right of Visible Saints to the Lord's Supper, Though They Be Destitute of a Saving Work of God's Spirit on their Hearts: Against the Exceptions of Mr. Increase Mather* [Boston: B. Green, 1709], 18–19).

18 Stoddard, *The Doctrine of Instituted Churches*, 22.

19 Stoddard, "The Inexcusableness of Neglecting the Worship of God," 3.

20 Stoddard, "The Inexcusableness of Neglecting the Worship of God," 11.

21 Stoddard, "The Inexcusableness of Neglecting the Worship of God," 16.

Convert men," Stoddard wrote.[22] Stoddard understood taking the Lord's Supper to be a preparatory work, one that might lead to conversion as it worked in the heart of the unbeliever. Taking the Supper, sinners would be open to the convicting work of the Spirit as they were reminded of their own sinfulness. Seeing this sinfulness, the sinner could then be brought from a confidence in his own righteousness to an evangelical humility before God. Finally, as Christ is offered to the participant in the Lord's Supper, the recipient may respond in faith to the grace proffered.[23] "The Lord's Supper," he argued, "is for the Spiritual good of all that are regularly to be admitted thereunto."[24] Thus, none but the most profligate sinner should be barred from the table.

Increase Mather rightly recognized the nature of the changes being proposed. He pronounced these "New, and Singular Notions... Contradictory not only to the Doctrine taught by the Former Ministers in New England (Prophets if ever there were among us) but also by the whole Body of Protestant Divines in the most Reformed Churches."[25] Moreover, Mather proclaimed Stoddard's teaching on this matter a "sin" against the established teaching of

---

22 Stoddard, *An Appeal to the Learned*, 25.

23 Stoddard, *An Appeal to the Learned*, 25.

24 Stoddard, *An Appeal to the Learned*, 73.

25 Increase Mather, *A Dissertation, wherein the Strange Doctrine Lately Published in a Sermon, the Tendency of which, is, to Encourage Unsanctified Persons (while such) to Approach the Holy Table of the Lord, is Examined and Confuted* (Boston: B. Green, 1708), iii. Stoddard knew that Mather would appeal to the Reformers and their Puritan descendants. Therefore, Stoddard had already determined that "those that have been Eminent Reformers in the Church of God, have seldom or never been so happy, as to Effect a perfect Reformation" (Stoddard, "The Inexcusableness of Neglecting the Worship of God," i). Stoddard continued, "We may see cause to alter some practices of our Fathers, without despising them, without priding ourselves in our own Wisdom, without Apostacy, without abusing the advantages that God has give us, without a spirit of compliance with corrupt men, without inclinations to Superstition, without making disturbance in the Church of God: And there is no reason that it should be turned as a reproach upon us.... If we be forbidden to Examine their practices, that will cut off all hopes of Reformation" (Stoddard, "The Inexcusableness of Neglecting the Worship of God," iii).

the church. These "notions" Jonathan Edwards inherited when his grandfather passed and left him the sole heir of the church in Northampton.

Edwards's way

Edwards had been called to serve alongside his grandfather, Solomon Stoddard, in 1726. By then, Stoddard was an old man, declining in health and in need of an associate with whom he could share his pastoral duties. With Stoddard's blessing the church in Northampton ordained Edwards the heir apparent of that influential pulpit. Honoured by the appointment, Edwards came under the shadow of Stoddard's reputation only to find himself a reluctant disciple. Writing from the crucible of controversy years later, Edwards remarked to a Scottish correspondent,

> My honored grandfather Stoddard, my predecessor in the ministry over this church, strenuously maintained the Lord's Supper to be a converting ordinance; and urged all to come who were not of scandalous life, though they knew themselves to be unconverted. I formerly conformed to his practice, but I have had difficulties with respect to it, which have long been increasing; till I dared no longer to proceed in the former way; which has occasioned great uneasiness among my people, and has filled all the country with noise; which has obliged me to write something on the subject, which is now in the press.[26]

The communion controversy that proved to be Edwards's undoing did not germinate in a vacuum. This controversy was bred in a decade of pastoral turmoil. The years following the Great Awakening were filled with spiritual highs and lows. Edwards enjoyed glorious successes and published several notable works,

---

26 Edwards, Letter "To the Reverend John Erskine," *Works*, 16:271.

including *Religious Affections* and *The Life of David Brainerd*. However, he also endured years of frustrating failure, moving from one conflict to another, from salary disputes to the contentious issue of disciplining the church's youth. In light of all this, Edwards began to make strategic moves to ensure more of the highs and less of the lows.

The first thing Edwards did was propose a strict church covenant, one in which the people would agree to "present [them] selves before the Lord, to renounce [their] evil ways, and put away [their] abominations from before God's eyes, and with one accord to renew [their] engagements to seek and serve God."[27] The congregation embraced this covenant. His second move was not so successful. After a spiritual drought of nearly six years, a young man presented himself to the church for membership. Edwards, going against forty years of established church tradition, asked the applicant to present a valid profession of faith prior to his admission into the church. Edwards explained the reason for this in his "Narrative of Communion Controversy."

> I have had difficulties in my mind for many years, with regard to admission of members into the church who made no pretense to real godliness. These gradually increased, and at length to such a degree, that I found I could not with easy conscience be active in admitting any more members in our former manner without better satisfaction. In consequence of this, I determined more closely to apply myself to an inquiry into the matter, and search the Scriptures, and read and examine such books as were written to defend the admission of persons to the sacraments without a profession of saving faith. And by reading and study, I found myself the more strengthened in my reasons to the contrary.[28]

27 Edwards, Letter "To the Reverend Thomas Prince," *Works*, 16:121.
28 These remarks come from Edwards's private "Narrative of Communion

Though the young man agreed to Edwards's conditions, the church balked at the violation of precedent. They saw in it a rejection of the venerable Solomon Stoddard, who, "though dead, yet speaketh" by way of his reputation.[29] When Edwards asked for the opportunity to present his case from the pulpit, the church balked, forcing Edwards to publish his thoughts instead.

In *An Humble Inquiry*, Edwards does not so much reject Stoddard as reaffirm the ways of New England's Reformed ancestors and peers. Like others before him, Edwards grounded his sacramental theology in the nature of the church itself. "[T]he visible Christian church ought to consist of such as make a visible and credible profession of faith and holiness."[30] Such a profession of faith, he contended, "ought to be attended with an honest and sober character, and with evidences of good doctrinal knowledge, and

Controversy" (Edwards, "Narrative of Communion Controversy," *Works*, 12:507). Edwards shared essentially these same thoughts in the preface to *An Humble Inquiry.* "I have formerly been of his [Stoddard's] opinion, which I imbibed from his books, even from my childhood, and have in my proceedings conformed to his practice; though never without some difficulties in my view, which I could not solve: yet, however, a distrust of my own understanding, and deference to authority of so venerable a man, the seeming strength of some of his arguments, together with the success he had in ministry, and his great reputation and influence, prevailed for a long time to bear down my scruples. But the difficulties and uneasiness on my mind increasing, as I became more studied in divinity, and as I improved in experience; this brought me to closer examine and weigh the arguments of my grandfather, and such other authors as I could get on his side of the question. By which means, after long searching, pondering, viewing and reviewing, I gained satisfaction, became fully settled in the opinion I now maintain, as in the discourse here offered to public view; and dared to proceed no further in a practice and administration inconsistent therewith: which brought me into peculiar circumstances, laying me under an inevitable necessity publicly to declare and maintain the opinion I was thus established in" (Edwards, *An Humble Inquiry, Works*, 12:169–170).

29 Edwards, *An Humble Inquiry, Works*, 12:168. Knowing that some would accuse him of attacking Stoddard personally by opposing his theology publicly, Edwards reminded his readers that Stoddard himself had perpetrated such an assault on the established thought of his own era. In fact, Edwards used Stoddard's remarks from "The Inexcusableness of Neglecting the Worship of God" to defend his own actions (Edwards, *An Humble Inquiry, Works*, 12:167–168).

30 Edwards, *An Humble Inquiry, Works*, 12:341.

with all proper, careful and diligent instructions of a prudent pastor."[31] Thus, pastors, concerned for their souls, were to examine prospective members, to "instruct and advise them, to apply the teachings and rules of God's Word unto them, ... [to be] promoters of their salvation."[32]

Edwards's concern for the sanctity of the church extended to the sacraments. "These sacramental actions all allow to be significant actions," he acknowledged in *Misrepresentations Corrected, and Truth Vindicated.* "They are not actions without meaning."[33] That meaning Edwards had expounded earlier in *An Humble Inquiry.* He described the Lord's Supper as "a mutual solemn profession of the two parties transacting the covenant of grace, and visibly united in that covenant."[34] That transaction signified the giving of Christ's life and blood for the communicant and the communicant's acceptance of the same. Through the outward signs of the sacrament, Christ "confirms and seals," applying the benefit of his work to the account of the recipient.[35] Partaking of the Lord's Supper, the human participants profess to "embrace the promises and lay hold of the hope set before them, to receive the atonement, to receive Christ as spiritual food, and to feed upon him in their hearts by faith."[36] Continuing, he wrote,

> Thus the Lord's Supper is plainly a mutual renovation, confirmation, and seal of the covenant of grace: both the covenanting parties profess their consent to their respective parts in the covenant, and each affixes his seal to his profession. And there is in this ordinance the very same thing acted over in profession and sensible signs, which is

---

31 Edwards, *An Humble Inquiry, Works,* 12:312.
32 Edwards, *An Humble Inquiry, Works,* 12:312.
33 Edwards, *Misrepresentations Corrected, and Truth Vindicated, Works,* 12:452.
34 Edwards, *An Humble Inquiry, Works,* 12:256.
35 Edwards, *An Humble Inquiry, Works,* 12:256.
36 Edwards, *An Humble Inquiry, Works,* 12:256.

spiritually transacted between Christ and his spouse in the covenant that unites them.[37]

Given the deep significance that Edwards attached to the meaning of the Lord's Supper, he could not allow just anyone to partake of the elements.

> The actions at the Lord's Supper thus implying in their nature and signification, a renewing and confirming of the covenant, there is a declarative explicit covenanting supposed to precede it; which is the profession of religion, before spoken of, that qualifies a person for admission to the Lord's Supper.[38]

Professing believers only, members of the covenant of grace not the national covenant, were permitted to attend the Lord's Supper. In this way, Edwards effectively closed the doors to the church, barring many from the way of salvation offered by Stoddard. Moreover, he implied that many of his flock were not true sheep at all. For this, he was fired.

Edwards's way of prayer

Convinced of the error of Stoddard's way, Edwards rejected it and was rejected by his people. What would motivate this man to risk fiscal security and the international fame now associated with the Northampton pulpit? Edwards saw the issue of church membership in the light of eternal rather than temporal consequences. "His conviction that the life or death of eternal souls was at stake made him willing to risk his own welfare," George Marsden observed.[39] Rather than allowing the unconverted to assume they are children of the covenant, Edwards chose to limit their access to the benefits

---

37 Edwards, *An Humble Inquiry, Works*, 12:256–257.
38 Edwards, *An Humble Inquiry, Works*, 12:257.
39 Marsden, *Jonathan Edwards: A Life*, 349.

of the covenant that they might recognize their greatest need: the Lord's salvation not the Lord's Supper. Ultimately, Edwards feared God more than man. As Dwight surmised,

> The fear of God had a controlling influence, also, in regulating his intercourse with mankind. The basis of that intercourse, in all the relations of life, and indeed of his whole character, was evangelical integrity,—a settled unbending resolution to do what he thought right, whatever self-denial or sacrifices it might cost him.[40]

Edwards was more than a theologian committed to an abstract ecclesial concept, crucial as it may have been. He was more than a "man of principle."[41] He was a man of faith, a man convinced that his God was bigger than his problems.

Just as he had believed from his earliest days as a Christian and pastor, just as he had taught the very same congregation that fired him, Edwards turned to God in prayer for the spiritual sustenance necessary to survive the challenge to his leadership and faith. While Edwards left no written account of his own prayers, the evidence suggests that throughout the protracted debate and painful events associated with the communion controversy, Edwards repeatedly turned to prayer and sought the same from both friends and foes. Moreover, when it was all over and his head was the figurative spoil of this theological war, Edwards continued to pray for his shepherdless flock. In the end, the communion controversy does more than prove Edwards's humanity. It proved his faith in the God who hears prayer.

In the midst of the controversy, Edwards preached a sermon about the value of and need for prayer in such circumstances. When he preached this sermon, his dismissal was but weeks away.[42] Preaching

---

40 Dwight, *The Life of President Edwards*, 593.
41 Marsden, *Jonathan Edwards: A Life*, 349.
42 Edwards referenced the present situation in this sermon, speaking directly to

from Nehemiah 1, Edwards encouraged his congregation to seek
God in prayer. His advice, however, spoke to his spiritual needs as
well. "It becomes saints to be praying persons," he reminded the
church and himself. Such prayer, he explained, is a "suitable
acknowledgement of God's perfection" and a "proper expression
of a sense of our emptiness, insufficiency," so that man might not
"neglect [his] dependence on God." While such prayer is always the
duty of all mankind, it is especially so in times of "calamity." In such
times, he continued, God's "help and mercy" are needed. Those who
humble themselves in prayer, himself included, should seek God's
wisdom and pray for his "light." Given the tense nature of the
moment, Edwards also added, people should "beg of God that he
would revive true religion" and "pour out a Spirit of humility and
love." Christians in times of trouble, like himself, should "come
humbly before God...as beggars to the throne of grace."[43]

Edwards frequently sought the prayerful support of his friends as
well. Realizing that he would likely end up "wholly cast out of the
ministry," Edwards pleaded with his friend Thomas Foxcroft of
Boston to plead his case before God:

> I have many enemies abroad in the country, who hate me
> for my stingy principles, enthusiasm, rigid proceedings
> and that now are expecting full triumph over me. I need
> the prayers of my fathers and brethren who are friendly to
> me, that I may have wisdom given me by my great master,

---

those he felt might still be influenced. "But I am now speaking to such as are sensible
that 'tis a time of great calamity to this church on account of its difficult broken
circumstances by reason of the controversy here respecting the qualifications of
communicants. And in a more special manner I would now address myself to such
among us as in the midst of this time of tumult and contention [who have] maintained
a calm and quiet spirit" (Edwards, "It Becomes Saints in Cases of Special Difficulty
and Calamity of God's Church, to Betake Themselves in an Extraordinary Manner
to Prayer to God" [1750], manuscript).

43 Edwards, "It Becomes Saints in Cases of Special Difficulty and Calamity of
God's Church, to Betake Themselves in an Extraordinary Manner to Prayer to God"
(1750), manuscript.

and that I may be enabled to conduct with a steady faithfulness to him, under all trials and whatever may be the
issue of this affair. I seem as it were to be casting myself
off from a precipice; and have no other way, but to go on,
as it were blindfold[ed], i.e. shutting my eyes to everything else but the evidences of the mind and will of God,
and the path of duty; which I would observe with the
utmost care.[44]

Edwards made the same prayer request nearly a year later to
Thomas Gillespie as well. "I need the prayers of my friends, that
God would be with me, and direct and assist me in such times of
trial, and mercifully order the issue."[45] To his friend, Edwards admit-
ted the spiritual battle within that so many other observers overlook.
To this letter, begun in April 1750 and completed in July of that year,
Edwards appended a heart cry for divine grace.

I desire your prayers that I may take notice of the frowns
of heaven on me and this people (between whom was
once so great an union), in the bringing to pass such a
separation between us; and that these troubles may be
sanctified to me; that God would overrule this event for his
own glory (which doubtless many adversaries will rejoice
and triumph in), that God would open a door for my
future usefulness, and provide for me and my numerous
family, and take a fatherly care of us in our present unsettled,
uncertain circumstances, being cast on the wide world.[46]

To William McCulloch, the ministerial force used of God in the
Scottish Cambuslang Revival, Edwards would admit the same
concerns and desire for prayer. After his dismissal, Edwards wrote,

---

44 Edwards, Letter "To the Reverend Thomas Foxcroft," *Works*, 16:284.
45 Edwards, Letter "To the Reverend Thomas Gillespie," *Works*, 16:327.
46 Edwards, Letter "To the Reverend Thomas Gillespie," *Works*, 16:350.

I am now separated from the people, between whom and me there was once the greatest union. Remarkable is the providence of God in this matter. In this event, we have a great instance of the instability and uncertainty of all things here below. The dispensation is indeed awful in many respects, calling for serious reflection, and deep humiliation, in me and my people. The enemy far and near will now triumph; but God can overrule all for his own glory. I have now nothing visible to depend upon for my future usefulness, or the subsistence of my numerous family. But I hope we have an all-sufficient, faithful, covenant God to depend upon. I desire that I may ever submit to him, walk humbly before him, and put my trust wholly in him.

I desire, dear Sir, your prayers for us under our present circumstances.[47]

From his friend and former disciple Joseph Bellamy, Edwards asked for prayer for discernment. "I ask a constant remembrance in your prayers," he wrote, "that I may have the presence of God under my unusual trials, and that I may make a good improvement of all God's dealings with me."[48] Through it all, Edwards never lost faith in his friends, prayer, or God.

As a pastor, Edwards understood the role of prayer in his ministry as well. "The ministers of Christ should be persons of the same spirit that their Lord was of," he told the church.[49] Preaching a year before his dismissal, Edwards believed that the spirit of Christ was one of prayer, particularly for the flock. "Ministers should imitate their great Master in his fervent prayers for the good of the souls of men."[50] While the communion controversy had begun, it was

---

47 Edwards, Letter "To the Reverend William McCulloch," *Works*, 16:358.
48 Edwards, Letter "To the Reverend Joseph Bellamy," *Works*, 16:367.
49 Edwards, "Christ the Great Example of Gospel Ministers," *Works*, 25:336.
50 Edwards, "Christ the Great Example of Gospel Ministers," *Works*, 25:337.

not yet heated. Edwards would, however, soon follow his own advice and would do so until the end.

The most pointed example of Edwards's prayers for his people came in his most pointed sermon. After being defeated before both the synod of local ministers who heard the case against him and the final vote of the church in favour of his removal, Edwards preached what he thought would be his last sermon before the church in Northampton.[51] In his "Farewell Sermon," Edwards reminded the church of the culpability of both parties in the recent affair. His tone was neither self-righteous nor vindictive. He did not, as Henry Bamford Parkes so blithely argued, simply bid "his people *au revoir* to the Day of Judgment."[52] He offered them pastoral counsel. More than that, he offered them prayer.

"But now I must bid you farewell," he said. "I must leave you in the hands of God: I can do no more for you than to pray for you."[53] He prayed for their eternal souls, and he hoped that they would pray for themselves as well. "Don't neglect to pray for yourselves," he cautioned them. "Take heed you ben't of the number of those, who cast off fear, and restrain prayer before God." Instead, they should "constantly pray to God in secret."[54] This duty, he said, applies to the "little church," the family, as well.[55] More, as a church, they should give themselves over completely to prayer, if they have any hope to return to God's favour as in times past.

> Another thing which I would advise to, that you may hereafter be a prosperous people, is that you would give yourselves much to prayer.
> God is the fountain of all blessing and prosperity, and he

---

51 As it turns out, Edwards was reluctantly asked to fill his own former pulpit repeatedly in the months after his firing as the church sought his eventual replacement.

52 Parkes, *Jonathan Edwards*, 207.

53 Edwards, "A Farewell Sermon," *Works*, 25:483.

54 Edwards, "A Farewell Sermon," *Works*, 25:484.

55 Edwards, "A Farewell Sermon," *Works*, 25:484.

will be sought to for his blessing. I would therefore advise you not only to be constant in secret and family prayer, and in the public worship or God in his house, but also often to assemble yourselves in private praying societies. I would advise all such as are grieved for the afflictions of Joseph, and sensibly affected with the calamities of this town, of whatever opinion they be with relation to the subject of our late controversy, often to meet together for prayer, and to cry to God for his mercy to themselves, and mercy to this town, and mercy to Zion and the people of God in general through the world.[56]

Edwards closed his fond adieu with a promise to pray fervently for them and his desire that they do likewise even as they went their separate ways.[57] Throughout the course of the communion controversy, Edwards stood firm in his convictions. As he first reported to a correspondent, Edwards recognized the severity of the situation. "I have nothing very comfortable to inform of concerning the present state of religion in this place. A very great difficulty has arisen between me and my people, relating to the qualifications for communion at the Lord's table."[58] Yet, he firmly believed that "'tis the mind and will of God that none should be admitted to full communion in the church of Christ but such as in profession, and in the eye of reasonable judgment, are truly saints or godly persons."[59] And, he firmly believed to the end that God's gracious answer to prayer was his only hope: "God can overrule all for his own glory."[60]

---

56 Edwards, "A Farewell Sermon," *Works*, 25:487.
57 Edwards, "A Farewell Sermon," *Works*, 25:488.
58 Edwards, Letter "To the Reverend John Erskine," *Works*, 16:271.
59 Edwards, "Qualifications for Full Communion," *Works*, 25:354.
60 Edwards, Letter "To the Reverend William McCulloch," *Works*, 16:358.

Final observations

The observations of David Hall, an eyewitness to the synod that recommended Edwards's dismissal from Northampton, speaks volumes about the strength of Edwards's faith and his wholehearted dependence upon God. "I never saw the least symptoms of displeasure in his countenance the whole week, but he appeared like a man of God, whose happiness was out of reach of his enemies."[61] While his confidence in his own abilities and the grace of the townspeople wavered, Edwards's faith did not. He prayed and he prayed. When God did not answer according to his requests, he prayed again.

In the end, Edwards lost his job but not his faith. He was driven from his pulpit and to his knees. He had tempted the powers that be and wrestled with God and lost. His loss, however, was the church's gain. By not answering Edwards's prayers as asked, God answered a greater need. He moved Edwards from the troubled and busy pulpit in Northampton to the quiet wilds of the missionary post in Stockbridge. There he would write his most influential works, works like *Freedom of the Will*, *Original Sin*, and the two treatises, *The Nature of True Virtue* and *The End for Which God Created the World*. At the time, however, Edwards could only rely upon the perfect wisdom of God and prayer. He knew that "in times of greatest difficulty and when the case has looked most dark" God "brings light out of darkness [and] turned the shadow of death into morning."[62]

---

61 David Hall, *The Diary of David Hall* (MS in Massachusetts Historical Society, Boston), cited in Marsden, *Jonathan Edwards: A Life*, 353.

62 Edwards, "It Becomes Saints in Cases of Special Difficulty and Calamity of God's Church, to Betake Themselves in an Extraordinary Manner to Prayer to God" (1750), manuscript.

Chapter 7

"His people" and their happiness

It will appear that there [is] no happiness that God is unwilling to bestow on {his people} as too good, if it be considered that [he] has thought nothing too much as the means of procuring their happiness.[1]

In the years that separated the local awakening in Northampton from the broader awakening throughout New England and the mid-Atlantic colonies, Jonathan Edwards had much to say about prayer. He called on his people to pray for revival. He also called on them to pray for themselves. He never had more to say on that topic than he did in the sermon "The Terms of Prayer." Edwards interrupted a more famous sermon series, the thirteen-part *Charity and Its Fruit*, to bring an exposition of Psalm 24:1 to his congregation. In this sermon, he explained his theology of prayer from the human point of view.

---

1 Edwards, "The Terms of Prayer," *Works*, 19:777.

Desiring to drive his people to their knees, Edwards encouraged them to seek and find their happiness not in the things of this world but in God.[2] For Edwards, the key to this concept is found in the preposition "in."[3] The happiness they seek, he told them, does not come *through* or *from* God but is found *in* God.

> The good that is promised them is of the highest kind. 'Tis a mansion, an inheritance in heaven, the highest and most glorious part of the creation, {the most glorious} palace {in heaven} that God hath built. And then the happiness that is promised them is the full enjoyment of God, without restraint, in the boldness and nearness of access, in the cold draughts they take....If the greatest good that God gives them even in himself, what can God give more than himself? He gives himself with all his attributes, power, {glory, dominion, and majesty}. And he gives himself in the highest possible enjoyment {to his people}, as much as they can desire, or are capable of. {And he gives himself to} fully satisfy {their happiness}.[4]

God's goodness, he promised them, knows no bound.[5]

---

2 Interestingly, Edwards's earliest extant sermon addressed this very topic (Edwards, "Christian Happiness," *Works*, 10:296–307).

3 Edwards made the same argument in "God Glorified in Man's Dependence." "The redeemed have all their good in God," he said. "We not only have it of him and through him, but it consists in him; he is all our good." He continued, "The redeemed have all their objective good in God. God himself is the great good which they are brought to the possession and enjoyment of by redemption. He is their highest good, and the sum of all that good which Christ purchased. God is the inheritance of the saints; he is the portion of their souls. God is their wealth and treasure, their food, their life, their dwelling place, their ornament and diadem, and their everlasting honor and glory" (Edwards, "God Glorified in Man's Dependence," *Works*, 17:207–208).

4 Edwards, "The Terms of Prayer," *Works*, 19:780.

5 Edwards, "The Terms of Prayer," *Works*, 19:780.

Those that God is pleased to make the objects of his love, let them be who they will, or what they will—never so mean, never so great sinners—they are the objects of a love that is infinitely full and sufficient.

And therefore nothing that they need, nothing that they ask of God, nothing that their desires can extend themselves to, nothing that their capacity can contain, no good that can be enjoyed by them, is so great, so excellent that God begrutches it to them.[6]

Thus, for Edwards, God is the good to be sought and the blessing to be desired. He is both the source and the subject of all true happiness.

Faith, Edwards reasoned, serves as the introit to that blessed relationship, both in salvation and prayer. "There is no other way that the heart can look to God," he said, "but only looking by faith, by faith seeking the blessing of God, and by faith depending on God for the mercy sought." Prayer, he reiterated throughout this sermon, and over the span of his preaching career, is "the voice of faith." God, and the happiness that he brings, will be found and enjoyed by his people when they pray. And, if they are his people, pray they will.[7]

To appreciate the richness of Edwards's theology of prayer one needs not only a right understanding of the persons and work of the Trinity but an equally profound view of the human condition. For Edwards, the doctrine of man consisted of man's purpose, his problem and his potential. These things, he maintained, are best understood in regard to man's relationship with God as revealed in his communion with God whether in person or in prayer—or the lack thereof. To that end, Edwards's responses to the following questions flesh out the human factor in his theology of prayer. First, he must be asked, "What did man have?" Knowing that man no longer exists in his innocency, one must then ask of Edwards, "What did man

---

6 Edwards, "The Terms of Prayer," *Works*, 19:781.
7 Edwards, "The Terms of Prayer," *Works*, 19:787.

214 THE VOICE OF FAITH

lose?" Finally, given the hopeful bent of his theology, he must be asked, "What can man have again?" In his answers to those questions, Edwards always kept God and man's ability to communicate with him central.

What man had: a relationship with God

Man enjoyed the favor of God and smiles of heaven; there were smiles without any frowns. He had communion with God; God was wont to come to him and converse as a friend and father. How sweet was it thus to have the smiles and fellowship of the glorious Creator![8]

While Edwards failed to produce a single sermon or treatise on the nature of man, he never failed to recognize its importance, repeatedly addressing this theological category in his sermons and writings alike. For Edwards the doctrine of man served as the foundation upon which other pillars of the faith were to be constructed. This doctrine impacted his understanding of the will, original sin, the nature of true religion and his theology of prayer.

CREATED IN THE IMAGE OF GOD

God did not create out of a lack of anything within himself as he was perfectly fulfilled and revealed in the Trinity. Nor did God create that he might receive anything back from the creation for God lacks nothing. No, Edwards reasoned, God created that he might be glorified forever.[9] To that end, God created man in his own image so that he might reflect God's glory and communicate with God to extol that glory.

When it comes to the doctrine of the *imago Dei*, the image of God in man, Edwards was something of an innovator. Rather than casting the *imago Dei* in the narrow categories of the past, which

---

8 Edwards, "East of Eden," *Works*, 17:334.
9 See, for example, "Importance of a Future State," *Works*, 10:359.

defined man solely according to either his function or his composition, Edwards forged a theocentric, unified approach. He couched this approach in bipartite language that reflects his theology proper.

> As there are two kinds of attributes in God, according to our way of conceiving of him, his moral attributes, which are summed up in his holiness, and his natural attributes, of strength, knowledge, etc. that constitute the greatness of God; so there is a twofold image of God in man, his moral or spiritual image, which is his holiness, that is the image of God's moral excellency (which image was lost by the Fall); and God's natural image, consisting in men's reason and understanding, his natural ability, and dominion over the creatures, which is the image of God's natural attributes.[10]

In his own way, Edwards constructed a comprehensive and holistic doctrine of the *imago Dei*, one that is truly reflective of moral and natural attributes of God.

For Edwards the moral image of God in man, that which he referred to as the supernatural image, does not consist of "extraordinary gifts," "the power to work miracles," nor the ability to "foretell future events," but in holiness.[11] He recognized Adam's original righteousness to be a principal part of the *imago Dei*. Possessing this holiness Adam reflected God's own moral excellency. "Holiness," Edwards remarked in a sermon, "is the image of God."[12] In that same sermon, Edwards commented that "holiness is a conformity of the heart and life unto God," a willing and doing as God wills and does.[13] Holiness disposes one to delight in the very things that delight God. God endowed man with the ability to do so, bestowing on him a moral excellency reflective of his own that

---

10 Edwards, *Religious Affections, Works*, 2:256.
11 Edwards, *Charity and Its Fruit, Works*, 8:159.
12 Edwards, "Way of Holiness," *Works*, 10:472.
13 Edwards, "Way of Holiness," *Works*, 10:471–472.

enabled man to recognize and embrace the good, to be "holy as God is holy," and to lead "gracious and heavenly [lives]."[14] Man, in his federal head Adam, possessed such holiness.

Edwards took the concept of holiness, however, one step further. He sought to explain not only the source but also the enduring power of that principle of holiness in the *imago Dei*. He argued that this holiness came as a special gift of God, one that elevated the soul to greater heights.

> And even in the first creation of man, when his body was formed immediately by God not in a course of nature, or in the way of natural propagation, yet the soul is represented as being in a higher, more direct and immediate manner from God, and so communicated that God did therein communicate something of himself, something of his own Spirit or life or divine vital fullness.[15]

That something which was communicated in the creation was God's holiness. In Edwards's construct, holiness is not *a* gift of the Holy Spirit but the gift *of* the Holy Spirit. Holiness results from the indwelling of the Spirit.[16] Presumably for Adam this indwelling occurred at the moment of the in-breathing of the "breath of life" (Genesis 2:7). Drawing a parallel between creation and re-creation, Edwards announced, "The Holy Spirit becoming an inhabitant is a vital principle in the soul. He acting in, upon, and with the soul, becomes a fountain of true holiness and joy, as a spring of water, by the exertion and diffusion of itself."[17] Thus, for Edwards, holiness is not only proof of the image of God in man, it is also the result of the Spirit of God in man.

---

14 Edwards, *Charity and Its Fruit*, *Works*, 8:159.

15 Edwards, "Miscellanies" No. 1003, *Works*, 20:328.

16 Edwards, "The Threefold Work of the Holy Ghost," *Works*, 14:378 and *Charity and Its Fruit*, *Works*, 8:354.

17 Edwards, "God Glorified in Man's Dependence," *Works*, 17:208.

In keeping with others in his branch of the Reformed tradition, Edwards maintained that the *imago Dei* also involved an element that reflected the natural image of God as well. "God's natural image," he acknowledged in *Religious Affections*, consists of "man's reason and understanding, his natural ability, and dominion over the creatures."[18] This element, he posited, is both substantive and functional. That is, the natural image of God in man bears upon his faculties as well as how he is to utilize those faculties.

Whereas the supernatural image of God, the moral excellency with which man was endowed at creation, was mutable, the natural image is immutable. The supernatural was alien to man, the natural inalienable. That Edwards believed this to be true can be seen most clearly in his understanding of the substantive nature of the *imago Dei*. As the soul serves as the image-bearing component of man's constitution, it reflects the natural image of God in two faculties, the understanding and reason. At the moment of creation, these faculties were the jewels of Adam's being.

> And man then had excellent endowments. His mind shone with the perfect spiritual image of God, being without any defect in its holiness and righteousness, or any spot or wrinkle to mar its spiritual beauty. God had put his own beauty upon it; it shone with the communication of his glory. And man enjoyed uninterrupted spiritual peace and joy that hence arose. His mind was full of spiritual light and peace as the atmosphere in a clear and calm day.[19]

The presence of these traits guaranteed man's position as a voluntary agent, like God, capable of obedience, wise choices, and rationally, freely determining his own course of action according to the predominant inclinations of his will.[20] The ability to think, to choose

---

18 Edwards, *Religious Affections*, *Works*, 2:256.
19 Edwards, "East of Eden," *Works*, 17:334.
20 In the period before the Fall, man was more free than at any time since. In

rationally, to act as a moral agent separates the human creature from the rest of the created order, placing him in a position to exercise dominion.

> The only thing wherein man differs from the inferior creation is in intelligent perception and action. This is that in which the Creator has made men to differ from the rest of creation, and by which he has set him over it, and by which he governs the inferior creatures and uses them for himself.[21]

Mankind was the highest and greatest of God's creation.

Like many of his Reformed predecessors, Edwards reflected little on the functional element of the *imago Dei*. However, quotes like the one immediately above from "Miscellanies" No. 864 reveal a concern about this element, at least insofar as it related to man's intellect. The first man, Adam, "was crowned with glory and honor" and was "set over the works of God's hand, made to have dominion over all brute creatures."[22] Dominion, Edwards believed, extended beyond man's oversight of lower animals to his fellow man. God "has made it natural and necessary," he wrote, "that they should be concerned with one another, and linked together in

---

"Miscellanies" No. 174, Edwards wrote, "And probably before the fall, when our bodies were not such dull sluggish things, the affections of the mind had a more quick, easy and notable influence upon the whole body, as it has on the face now" (Edwards, "Miscellanies" No. 174, *Works*, 13:325).

A short time later, he added in another of his "Miscellanies," "Man has not so much freedom now as he had before the fall, in this respect: now he has a will against a will, an inclination contrary to his reason and judgment, which begets a contrary inclination; and this latter inclination is often overcome and suppressed by the former. But before the fall, the inclination that arose from reason and judgment never was held down by the inferior inclination; so that in that sense he was more free, or as they speak, had more freedom of the will" (Edwards, "Miscellanies" No. 291, *Works*, 13:383).

21 Edwards, "Miscellanies" No. 864, *Works*, 20:97.
22 Edwards, "Miscellanies" No. 702, *Works*, 18:288.

society."²³ Of societal government, he said, "'Tis doubtless the original design of the Creator that there should be such a kind of thing as moral subordination amongst men."²⁴ This dominion over man and creation must operate on those principles instilled at creation, "reason and understanding." Moreover, given that these abilities are the direct result of God's natural image residing in man, the use of this sovereignty must be benevolent, clearly reflecting God's own "disposing power," his gracious sovereignty over creation.²⁵

Thus, man in his primal state possessed the image of God. In so arguing, Edwards believed that man was created capable of reflecting God's own nature as revealed in his moral and natural attributes. God is holy. Man was created holy. God is all-knowing. Man was created capable of learning. God is sovereign. Man was created to be sovereign over his domain. God so created man for a purpose distinct from that of the rest of creation.

> The special end for which God made mankind, is something very diverse and very superior to those ends for which he made any parts of the inferior creation. Because God has made man very different from them; he has vastly distinguished him, in the nature that he has given him, and faculties with which he has endowed him, and the place he has set him in the creation.²⁶

That special end "respects the Creator."²⁷ That is, God communicated his perfections to condescend to his creation so that the creation might know its Creator.

23 Edwards, "Miscellanies" No. 864, *Works*, 20:98.
24 Edwards, "Miscellanies" No. 864, *Works*, 20:99.
25 Edwards, "Miscellanies" No. 864, *Works*, 20:99.
26 Edwards, "Miscellanies" No. 864, *Works*, 20:103.
27 Edwards, "Miscellanies" No. 864, *Works*, 20:104.

CREATED FOR A RELATIONSHIP WITH GOD

As Edwards understood the *imago Dei*, man was no longer just *what* one is or does, but *who* one is—a creature, created by God in his own image, endowed with holiness, wisdom and dominion, all driven by an overarching need to know and love God. For Edwards a direct link exists between the presence of God in the image and man's relationship with God. Because man has been created in the image of God he has been created with that divine relationship in mind both as the beginning and the end of creation.

The moral image of God in man serves to introduce and keep man in a fitting relationship with his Creator. "God's own holiness," he wrote, "must primarily consist in the love of himself."[28] If that is true, he continued, "Holiness in the creature must chiefly consist in love to him."[29] Thus arguing, Edwards added nothing new to the Reformed conception of the chief end of man: the glory of God and the enjoyment of the same. Yet, he applied that end to the *imago Dei* itself ontologically.

> Man in his first state before the fall had a disposition to praise his Creator, for he was then perfectly holy. And therefore the love of God reigned in his heart, which will necessarily dispose to the praises of God. His heart was not only full of love but full of joy. Man was then in an happy state, without anything to trouble him, and everything smiling upon [him]; his heart was full of bliss so that then he could joyfully praise God in a paradise of delights.[30]

Man was created not only to glorify God but also to enjoy the relationship that brings about that glorification, a relationship of love that arises naturally out of his being created holy. Finally, "man is perfectly holy, when his love to God bears a just proportion to

28 Edwards, *The End for Which God Created the World*, *Works*, 8:455.
29 Edwards, *The End for Which God Created the World*, *Works*, 8:456.
30 Edwards, "They Sing a New Song," *Works*, 22:229.

the capacities of his nature."[31] That is, even after the Fall had so marred the *imago Dei*, the measure of a man's holiness is still to be found in the depth of his love for God.

The natural image of God in man manifests itself in a relational manner.

> 'Tis evident, that man was made to behold and be delighted with the excellency of God in his works, or in short, to be made happy by beholding God's excellency; as it has been shown that intelligent beings, the consciousness of the creation, must be. But if man was made to delight in God's excellency, he was made to love God; and God being infinitely excellent, he ought to love [him] incomparably more than any man is capable of loving a fellow creature; and every power, and all that is in man, ought to be exercised as attendants on this love.[32]

Using the mind for meditation on and the worship of God is man's chief end, his highest purpose. "He has made us capable of understanding so much of him here as is necessary in order to our acceptable worshipping and praising him," proclaimed Edwards.[33]

Moreover, the natural image of God consists of intelligence in that God has communicated divine knowledge of himself to man that man might love God as God loves himself: "The motive of God's creating the world must be his inclination to communicate his own happiness to something else."[34] This knowledge renders the creature not only capable of worshipping his Creator but also of knowing him, loving him and enjoying that relationship.

Thus, Edwards saw the fullness of the *imago Dei* in both God's

---

31 Edwards, "Miscellanies" No. 894, *Works*, 20:153.
32 Edwards, "Miscellanies" No. 99, *Works*, 13:265–266.
33 Edwards, "God's Excellencies," *Works*, 10:417.
34 Edwards, "Nothing Upon Earth Can Represent the Glories of Heaven," *Works*, 14:146.

supernatural image—man's holiness—and God's natural image—man's reason and understanding. In the relational component, Edwards married the two.

> Thus 'tis easy to conceive how God should seek the good of the creature, consisting in the creature's knowledge and holiness, and even his happiness, from a supreme regard to himself; as his happiness arises from that which is an image and participation of God's own beauty; and consists in the creature's exercising a supreme regard to God and complacence in him; in beholding God's glory, in esteeming and loving it, and rejoicing in it, and in his exercising and testifying love and supreme respect to God: which is the same thing with the creature's exalting God as his chief good, and making him his supreme end.[35]

As such, the creature perfectly reflects his Creator, knowing him and loving him, glorifying him by reflecting his perfect nature back to himself.

SUMMARY

God created man for the purpose of glorifying himself eternally, Edwards taught. To accomplish this end, God created man perfectly in his image, possessing the created equivalents of his own divine attributes. So long as man, in Adam, fulfilled his end, God was glorified in the very nature of his creation. God desired more than a simple reflection of his own perfections, however. He created man for the purpose of knowing him. More than that, man was created for personal, unmediated communion with his Creator. The first man enjoyed a firsthand, face-to-face relationship with God. Of Adam, Edwards noted,

---

35 Edwards, *The End for Which God Created the World*, *Works*, 8:533.

Here is described the sum of the blessedness that man had in his first estate. Here is first his inherent spiritual good, which lay in the favor of God; his blessing of him is a testimony of it. Here is the happiness he had in intercourse with God, for his thus talking with him in this friendly manner.[36]

That intercourse, that pleasant conversation that Adam enjoyed with God in the Garden, was both miraculous,[37] dependant upon God's grace and frequent.[38] Created in God's image and able to commune with God because of that image, man was to "glorify God forever, and to enjoy him to all eternity."[39]

What man lost: his relationship with God

And his communion with God was lost; he lost God's favor and smiles. God ascended and forsook the earth, and instead of smiling and blessing, as he was wont to, now pronounces a curse on man. Instead of delighting in God's love and friendship, he had now the anger of the great God to think of, and his own folly in procuring it.[40]

The first man was, according to Edwards, "in a state of complete *manhood* (emphasis his)."[41] That is, Adam was all he had been created to be, the perfect man created for God's perfect glory. In such a position, he stood as the federal head of all mankind, their representative in intent and deed.[42] As such, Adam enjoyed great blessings; first and foremost was that of free intercourse and

36 Edwards, *Notes on Scripture, Works*, 15:395.
37 Edwards, "Miscellanies" No. 1263, *Works*, 23:208.
38 Edwards, "Value of Salvation," *Works*, 10:327.
39 Edwards, "Importance of a Future State," *Works*, 10:359.
40 Edwards, "East of Eden," *Works*, 17:335.
41 Edwards, *Original Sin, Works*, 3:396.
42 Edwards, "All God's Methods Are Most Reasonable," *Works*, 14:177.

unhindered communion with his Creator. Moreover, just as his happiness was unquestionably connected to God, that of his heirs would be undeniably connected to him. Had Adam remained covenantally faithful, God's fellowship and blessings would have continued to flow through Adam to the whole of the human race.

Tragically, however, the news from the Garden was not all good. Adam failed the covenant and he failed his children. He fell from grace and they fell with him.[43] Adam's descendents now inherit not the wealth of God's grace but the debt of Adam's disgrace. With him paradise was lost and true happiness discarded in favour of something far inferior. When Adam broke the covenant, he broke all lines of communication with the Creator for himself and all who would follow.

For Edwards, the doctrines of man and prayer intertwined, tightly knit together both in the creation and in the Fall. God created man in his image and shared fellowship with him in his innocence. Now, post-Fall, that image is ruined and that fellowship lost. The spiritual scar left by Adam's sin proves to be a frequent theme in Edwards's sermons and writings as he explored the consequences of Adam's folly. To fathom the heights from which man has fallen, the reader must consider the nature of man's Fall, the totality of man's depravity and the desperation of man's broken relationship with God.

THE FALL OF MAN

The doctrine of the Fall of man presents theologians with a particularly thorny problem. Edwards himself acknowledged this challenge in "Miscellanies" No. 290. "It has been a matter attended with much difficulty and perplexity, how sin came into the world, which way

---

43 Edwards, true to his theological roots, attributed the guilt of Adam's sin, the original sin, to all of mankind through his federal representation. "All men are guilty of Adam's first sin. Adam was our common father and representative who stood in our room: we were all in his loins. The covenant which he broke was made with us all, and for us all in him" (Edwards, "True Repentance Required," *Works*, 10:512).

came it into a creation that God created very good."[44] Yet, Edwards was bound by a youthful resolution to assault any and all theological quandaries he might encounter. "Resolved," he had written, "when I think of any theorem in divinity to be solved, immediately to do what I can towards solving it, if circumstances don't hinder."[45] Thus, aware of the difficulty and energized by the challenge, Edwards waded into the murky waters of the Fall determined to answer the question that humbled so many before him: How could that good man do such a bad thing?

For Edwards the question was not *if* man fell—that was an accepted theological fact—but *why* man fell. As difficult as the problem of the Fall may be, Edwards did not fall short on potential solutions. In fact, he offered several explanations for the seemingly contradictory facts of the goodness of the creation, including man, and the badness of that man's decision. First, from a theological perspective, Edwards appealed to God's decree to permit such a Fall. Second, from a more soteriological standpoint, Edwards reasoned that Adam fell because he failed to look to God for his salvation. Finally, from an anthropological point of view, Edwards argued that Adam fell because he ultimately loved himself more than he loved God.

The primary reason that Adam could and did fall, Edwards commented, was God's decision to permit this tragedy. Note the caution with which Edwards proceeded in *Freedom of the Will*, ever aware of the danger of making God guilty of evil himself.

> But if by "the author of sin," is meant the permitter, or not
> a hinderer of sin; and at the same time, a disposer of the
> state of events, in such a manner, for wise, holy and most
> excellent ends and purposes, that sin, if it be permitted or
> not hindered, will most certainly and infallibly follow: I say,
> if this be all that is meant, by being the author of sin, I
> don't deny that God is the author of sin (though I dislike

---

44 Edwards, "Miscellanies" No. 290, *Works*, 13:382.
45 Edwards, "Resolutions" No. 11, *Works*, 16:754.

and reject the phrase, as that which by use and custom is apt to carry another sense), it is no reproach for the most High to be thus the author of sin.[46]

However, God did not permit the Fall without reason. Edwards offers two such reasons. The first reason, Edwards maintained, was to reveal the beauty of God's own nature. "This is not to be the actor of sin, but on the contrary, of holiness," he reasoned. "What God doth herein, is holy; and a glorious exercise of the infinite excellency of his nature."[47] Edwards explained this more fully in "Miscellanies" No. 553:

> There are many of the divine attributes that, if God had not created the world, never would have had any exercise: the power of God, the wisdom and prudence and contrivance of God, and the goodness and mercy and grace of God, and the justice of God. It is fit that the divine attributes should have exercise. Indeed God knew as perfectly, that there were these attributes fundamentally in himself before they were in exercise, as since; but God, as he delights in his own excellency and glorious perfections, so he delights in the exercise of those perfections.[48]

God created that he might be known and glorified. God decreed the Fall that his holiness, justice and grace might be magnified and experienced. Thus, for Edwards, the Fall actually fulfills part of God's grand creative purposes.

Edwards further suggested that God's reason for permitting the Fall relates directly to God's redemptive purposes. Here one can clearly recognize the supralapsarian construct in which Edwards conceived God's decrees. In a note on John 16:8–11, Edwards com-

---

46 Edwards, *Freedom of the Will*, *Works*, 1:399.
47 Edwards, *Freedom of the Will*, *Works*, 1:399.
48 Edwards, "Miscellanies" No. 553, *Works*, 18:97.

mented, "God permitted the Fall that his elect people might know good and evil."[49] "Miscellanies" No. 702, a lengthy one in which Edwards sought to explain the "works of creation, providence, and redemption," offers this interpretation of God's purposes: "[the] world [was] made for the work of redemption."[50] If there had been no Fall for which man might be found guilty, there would be no need for salvation and God's ultimate plans would have been thwarted from the very beginning.

While God may be the "author of sin" as Edwards cautiously defined it, all blame for Adam's Fall falls on Adam. The burden of guilt belongs to him alone. "Miscellanies" No. 290, serves as a focal text in his doctrine of the Fall of man.

> If it be inquired how man came to sin, seeing he had no sinful inclinations in him, except God took away his grace from him that he had been wont to give him and so let him fall, I answer, there was no need of that; there was no need of taking away any that had been given him, but he sinned under that temptation because God did not give him more. He did not take away that grace from him while he was perfectly innocent, which grace was his original righteousness; but he only withheld his confirming grace, that grace which is given now in heaven, such grace as shall fit the soul to surmount every temptation. This was the grace Adam was to have had if he had stood, when he came to receive his reward.[51]

Several key concepts stand out in this passage. First of all, Adam possessed "no sinful inclinations," nothing that predisposed him to choose the evil rather than the good. Therefore, as Edwards proclaimed in "East of Eden," "It was in man's own power perfectly

49 Edwards, *Notes on Scripture, Works*, 15:592.
50 Edwards, "Miscellanies" No. 702, *Works*, 18:307.
51 Edwards, "Miscellanies" No. 290, *Works*, 13:382.

to obey the law of God" because "he had no sin then that he was under the power and dominion of."[52] In other words, there was nothing in Adam's nature that predisposed him to moral failure.

Second, Adam's difficulty arose not from what was within but what he was without. Careful to protect God's impeccable image, Edwards argued that God had given Adam "sufficient grace" for all contingencies. Here Edwards posited,

> I say, this must be meant by his having sufficient grace, viz. that he had grace sufficient to render him a free agent, not only with respect to [his] whole will, but with respect to his rational, or the will that arose from a rational judgment of what was indeed best for himself.[53]

Moreover, "Adam had a sufficient assistance of God always present with him, to have enabled him to obey, if he had used his natural abilities in endeavoring it."[54] Adam fell because he failed to use that "sufficient assistance" in the time of his trial. That is, God had given Adam all of the necessary grace, faculties and abilities needed for success but did not force him to use them.

What Adam lacked, however, was "confirming grace," that grace which would have guaranteed his preservation. God sovereignly "withheld" this grace from Adam for God was under no obligation to provide it.

> God is no way obliged to afford to his creature such grace and influence as shall render it impossible for him to sin. God is not obliged to make the creature unchangeable and at first to be in a confirmed state of holiness, so that it should be impossible for him to be otherwise....God created man in a state of innocency, and gave him such

---

52 Edwards, "East of Eden," *Works*, 17:338.
53 Edwards, "Miscellanies" No. 436, *Works*, 13:485.
54 Edwards, "Miscellanies" No. 501, *Works*, 18:51.

grace that he was perfectly free from any corruptions or sinful inclinations; nor did he take away that grace from him. But neither did he oblige himself to give him more, so as certainly to prevent him from giving way to any temptation: that was to be given to him when his time of probation was over, if he had continued innocent during that probation....God gave man sufficient warning, and He had no sinful inclinations to hurry him on to sin; he did it of his own free and mere choice. Only God did not prevent him by his confirming grace. Thus God was not obliged to prevent man's sin by his grace in a state of innocency....[55]

It was Adam's mutability that made "confirming grace" so necessary.

Again from "Miscellanies" No. 436, Edwards described "confirming grace" as "an efficacious grace," "a grace that should certainly uphold him in all temptations he could meet with."[56] Such "confirming grace" Edwards believed to be reserved for the saints in heaven to prevent any further apostasy by making the soul fit "to surmount every temptation." Such a grace was to be the reward for those who persevere.

Adam's perseverance would have guaranteed his reception of this "confirming grace." As Edwards said, "This was the grace Adam was to have had if he had stood."[57] Or, "[confirming grace] was to be given to him when his time of probation was over, if he had continued innocent during that probation."[58] Echoing the language of the Genesis account, Edwards remarked in his sermon "East of Eden," "Adam had a glorious opportunity of obtaining eternal life if he would persist in perfectly obeying the law and performed righteousness, which he had the power to do. He was then to be

---

55 Edwards, "All God's Methods Are Most Reasonable," *Works*, 14:167–168.
56 Edwards, "Miscellanies" No. 436, *Works*, 13:485.
57 Edwards, "Miscellanies" No. 290, *Works*, 13:382.
58 Edwards, "Miscellanies" No. 436, *Works*, 13:484.

invited by God to eat of the tree of life and to live forever."[59] "Confirming grace," withheld from Adam, dependent upon the keeping of his covenantal obligation, would have guaranteed success and promised eternal life.

Edwards's attempts to explain the Fall examined thus far seem reasonable enough. His commitment to a theology proper that readily accepted the sovereignty of God concurred with his belief that God had in some way and for some reason decreed the Fall. Likewise, his theological presuppositions easily lined up with the idea that Adam alone must bear the guilt for his sin and that he had failed to depend upon the divine grace available to him. Great difficulty arises, however, when one considers Edwards's understanding of the Fall in light of his theology of the will.

As Edwards pointed out, Adam's nature prior to the Fall was that of one free of sin, in action or disposition. Of Adam's will, Edwards noted, "he was more free, or, as they speak, had more freedom of will."[60] Elsewhere he claimed, "Adam's will was free in a respect that ours since the fall is not."[61] In other words, Adam was free to choose exactly as he willed, free of corrupt and untrustworthy inclinations that would lead him to choose evil. It is at this very point, however, that the clarity of Edwards's own thinking further complicated the situation. He reasoned in *Freedom of the Will*,

> ...because every act of the will is some way connected with the understanding, and is as the greatest apparent good is, in the manner which has already been explained; namely, the soul always wills or chooses that which, in the present view of the mind, considered in the whole of that view, and all that belongs to it, appears most agreeable. Because as was observed before, nothing is more evident than that, when men act voluntarily, and do what they

---

59 Edwards, "East of Eden," *Works*, 17:343–344.
60 Edwards, "Miscellanies" No. 291, *Works*, 13:383.
61 Edwards, "Miscellanies" No. 436, *Works*, 13:484.

please, then they do what appears most agreeable to them; and to say otherwise, would be as much as to affirm, that men don't choose what appears to suit them best, or what seems most pleasing to them; or that they don't choose what they prefer.[62]

The human will is inclined to choose the "greatest apparent good" as it appears to its present state. Adam, devoid of sin and an appetite for it, appeared to have no logical reason to choose to sin. The "greatest apparent good" in the Garden was that of God and his covenantal promise of life in exchange for man's obedience.

In light of this internal tension in Edwards's theology, Sam Storms admitted Edwards's apparent theological defeat: "Edwards's scheme is capable only of explaining how Adam might continue to sin but not how he might begin to sin."[63] Edwards, however, saw the predicament and had an answer, an answer that he first learned from his aged grandfather Stoddard before his death. "The best philosophy that I have met with of original sin and all sinful inclinations, habits and principles," he wrote, "is undoubtedly that of Mr. Stoddard's, of this town of Northampton: that is, that it is self-love in conjunction with the absence of the image and love of God, that natural and necessary inclination that man has to his own benefit together with the absence of original righteousness."[64]

According to Edwards's estimation, Adam before the Fall possessed a pure form of self-love, one undefiled by sin and bent toward the maintenance of the happiness which he found in God alone. In light of this understanding of self-love, the covenantal language of God's prohibition against eating of the tree of the knowledge of good and evil can be seen as appealing to Adam's innate desire to propagate pleasure and avoid misery. As such,

---

62 Edwards, *Freedom of the Will, Works*, 1:217.

63 Sam Storms, "The Will: Fettered Yet Free," in *A God-Entranced Vision of All Things*, eds. John Piper and Justin Taylor (Wheaton: Crossway, 2005), 214.

64 Edwards, "Miscellanies" No. 301, *Works*, 13:387.

"Self-love is a good principle, if well-regulated."⁶⁵ Adam's primitive self-love was "directed and regulated by the will and word of God," guiding him to do good, to be obedient to his Creator.⁶⁶ Obedience, motivated by self-love, resulted in man's happiness and God's great pleasure. True to his theological heritage, Edwards understood that the proper end of such self-love was "to love God (read: glorify) and enjoy him [forever]."⁶⁷

Thus, in his doctrine of self-love, Edwards offered a third, and final, reason for the Fall. When Adam chose to eat of the forbidden fruit, he was acting upon his native principle of self-love. Adam had been endued with the principles of God-love and self-love, both of which were good and proper, free of any evil. So long as Adam's God-love reigned, his otherwise good self-love remained in check. In the Garden, Adam enjoyed regular fellowship with God and readily recognized God as the "greatest apparent good" and responded with God-love that manifested itself in obedience and self-love. According to Genesis 3, however, God sovereignly permitted the circumstances to be changed; he denied Adam the pleasure and security of his presence. Adam found himself alone. Apart from God's guiding presence, Adam was left to determine his course using the faculties that God had provided. He had to choose between continued obedience to an unseen God and its incumbent blessings or the possibility of increasing his immediate pleasure by eating of the fruit that was then pleasant to the eyes and was, at that moment, the "greatest *apparent* good" (emphasis mine).

Seen in this light, Adam was presented with two options, both of which could appear to be good and both of which appealed to his innate loves. Therein lies the temptation or test. Adam had to persevere in obedience by choosing the truly greater good, one that is motivated by his concern for God's glory. However, "self-love

65 Edwards, "Degrees of Mercy," *Works*, 19:622.
66 Edwards, "Degrees of Mercy," *Works*, 19:622.
67 Edwards, "Born Again," *Works*, 17:190.

became the absolute master of his soul."[68] "By reason of the weakness or absence of other-love [love for God] which should restrain and regulate its influence, …[self-love's] influence [became] inordinate," Edwards argued.[69] Thus, Adam succumbed to neither deceit nor feminine wiles. He chose to disregard God's command by responding to the urgings of his self-love and pursued what appeared to be in his immediate best interest, that which would bring him the greatest happiness.

In the beginning, Adam succumbed to temptation and fell. In the end, Edwards succumbed to temptation and rose to the theological occasion. He offered several related solutions to the conundrum of how a good man could choose to do otherwise. He argued that the Fall could occur not contrary to God's will but as one part of it. He added that God's sovereignty does not mitigate Adam's responsibility. Adam freely chose to rebel and he must suffer the consequences of his choices. Those choices, Edwards continued, were freely made because Adam succumbed to a lesser principle, albeit good in and of itself—self-love. The outcome of Adam's choices and the Fall, Edwards believed, is beyond doubt.

> The great depravity of man's nature appears, not only in that they universally commit sin, who spend any long time in the world, but in that men are naturally so prone to sin, that none ever fail of immediately transgressing God's law, and of so bringing infinite guilt on themselves, and exposing themselves to eternal perdition, as soon as they are capable of it.[70]

Adam's fall became humanity's failure.

---

68 Edwards, *Charity and Its Fruits*, *Works*, 8:253.
69 Edwards, *Charity and Its Fruits*, *Works*, 8:256.
70 Edwards, *Original Sin*, *Works*, 3:134.

THE FALLEN MAN

Speaking of Adam's descendents, Edwards wrote, "their nature is corrupt and depraved with a moral depravity, that amounts to and implies their utter undoing."[71] As Edwards further explained the effects of the total depravity of man in one sermon,

> They are naturally, totally blind, wholly without any light... deprived of spiritual light....They never understand the meanings of the things that are [crucial] concerning Christ and the vital religion. They have many clear and plain instructions, an abundance of them, but they are never plain to them....They never understand the way of salvation by Christ tho' they have it so often described.... They are like dull scholars that go to school many years but never learn to read.[72]

By reason of the totality of his corruption, man has been catastrophically affected by the Fall. Sin now infects every fibre of man's being. "They are totally corrupt, in every part, in all their faculties; and all the principles of their nature, their understandings, and wills; and in all their dispositions and affections, their heads, their hearts, are totally depraved."[73] Fallen man, following the dictates of his fallen nature, Edwards said, cannot please God in any way because he will not try. Sin cripples the individual in heart, mind and will.

The themes of the nature of the sinful human heart appear throughout Edwards's theological writings and sermons, across the span of his ministerial career. Writing in his diary at a very early date,

---

71 Edwards, *Original Sin*, *Works*, 3:113.

72 Edwards, "Tho a People That Live Under Means Are Wont in General to Seek and Hope for Salvation, Yet 'Tis the Elect Only That Obtains It and the Rest Are Blinded" (1740), Beinecke Rare Book and Manuscript Library, Yale University, New Haven. See also, "We Are All in Ourselves Utterly Without Any Strength or Power to Help Ourselves" (1735), Beinecke Rare Book and Manuscript Library, Yale University, New Haven.

73 Edwards, "The Justice of God in the Damnation of Sinners," *Works*, 19:344.

Edwards observed, "[I am] very much convinced of the extraordinary deceitfulness of the heart, and how exceedingly affection or appetite blinds the mind, and brings it into entire subjection."[74] In his defense of the doctrine of human depravity, *Original Sin*, Edwards argued that "the heart of man is naturally of a corrupt and evil disposition."[75] His sermons echo the strokes of his pen. Just as he had argued in *Original Sin*, Edwards declared from his pulpit, "Nothing in man is either good or bad any other wise than as arising some way from the heart."[76] The heart of the natural man, stained by sin, is not right. That heart is "possessed by corruption" and "filthiness."[77]

In his sermon, "The Justice of God in the Damnation of Sinners," Edwards explained the extent to which sin has damaged the human heart.

> However, sinful men are not only thus, but they are full of sin; full of principles of sin, and full of acts of sin: their guilt is like great mountains, heaped one upon another, till the pile is grown up to heaven. They are totally corrupt, in every part, in all their faculties; and all the principles of their nature, their understandings, and wills; and in all their dispositions and affections, their heads, their hearts, are totally depraved; all the members of their bodies are only instruments of sin; and all their senses, seeing, hearing, tasting, etc. are only inlets and outlets of sin, channels of corruption. There is nothing but sin, no good at all. …the heart is under the power of [all manner of evil], is sold under sin, and is a perfect slave to it.[78]

---

74 Edwards, "Diary," *Works*, 16:777.

75 Edwards, *Original Sin*, *Works*, 3:107.

76 Edwards, "All That Natural Men Do Is Wrong," *Works*, 19:523.

77 Edwards, "The Pure in Heart Blessed," *Works*, 17:79.

78 Edwards, "The Justice of God in the Damnation of Sinners," *Works*, 19:344–345.

As such, the sin-stained heart is "dull and stupid to any sense or taste of those things wherein the moral glory of the divine perfections consists."[79] Sin bankrupts man's spiritual estate, Edwards would argue, by permanently staining the heart with all manners of evil. The longer one remains in his sinful state, Edwards preached, the harder his heart grows, becoming ever more like a "rock."[80] Eventually this rock will obstruct the pathway to heaven as it blocks the sinner's view of his sinfulness. Over time, the nature of the sinner comes to resemble that of a pig. "They see no filthiness in sin," Edwards said. "They don't nauseate it; it is no way uncomfortable to them amongst it, to have it hanging about them. They can wallow themselves in it without any reluctance; yea, they take pleasure in it."[81] Sinners, he argued, grow accustomed to hearing the power of the gospel proclaimed. As they resist its message, their heart grows calloused. In the process, they become "sermon proof."[82]

Self-love, that once good principle now gone bad, also reflects the darkness of the sinful heart. "Natural men may seek the good of their souls, for they are influenced by self-love," Edwards preached. Self-love, he continued, "may make them desire and seek their eternal happiness, as well as their temporal."[83] Such motives, he noted in "Ruth's Resolution," are driven by his sinful nature.

A natural man may choose deliverance from hell; but no man doth ever heartily choose God, and Christ, and the spiritual benefits that Christ has purchased, and happiness of God's people, till he is converted. On the contrary, he is averse to them; he has no relish in them and is wholly ignorant of the inestimable worth and value of them.[84]

79 Edwards, *Religious Affections*, *Works*, 2:301.
80 Edwards, "The Justice of God in the Damnation of Sinners," *Works*, 19:345.
81 Edwards, "The Pure in Heart Blessed," *Works*, 17:79.
82 Edwards, "Living Unconverted Under an Eminent Means of Grace," *Works*, 14:365.
83 Edwards, "All That Natural Men Do Is Wrong," *Works*, 19:521.
84 Edwards, "Ruth's Resolution," *Works*, 19:313–314.

Elsewhere Edwards cautioned that some "men may have a sort of respect to God that is not true respect because the spring of which is altogether self-love." That is, they are motivated only by a sinful self-interest. The attitudes of such sinners betray their true motives.

> They never did anything out of respect to him....They never had the least true gratitude for any of the [blessings] they have received from him...they never so much as one time gave him any hearty thanks for it....They have sought themselves in all that they have done....They made a show as tho' they would glorify God but never cared a farthing what became of the glory of God.... They never desired to be like God....They never had any mind to enjoy God.
>
> [Yet] they expect that God should love them only for their doing something from self-love. They expect that God should look upon himself much obliged to them for their doing a small matter that they might not go to hell.[85]

Such people, motivated solely by self-love, are hopelessly deluded and devoid of the new heart requisite for communion with God and true happiness.

The ability of the mind to function as God had designed, Edwards held, has been horribly scarred by the Fall as well. While sin has rendered the human mind darkened, the mind nonetheless retains its ability to reason. Its ability to function accurately, however, has been tarnished. Fallen man, he argued in a sermon on Romans 5:6, is a "sickly creature."[86] He no longer can think as he should.

---

85 Edwards, "That No Religion Is Acceptable to God but that Which Is Done from a True Respect to Him" (n.d.), Beinecke Rare Book and Manuscript Library, Yale University, New Haven.

86 Edwards, "Our Weakness, Christ's Strength," *Works*, 19:382.

A person may have a strong reason, and yet not a good reason. He may have a strength of mind to drive an argument, and yet not have even balances. It is not so much from a defect of the reasoning powers, as from a fault of the disposition.[87]

Sin, its affections and its appetites, jaundices the mind's eye and blinds the intellect.

...learning is at a great height at this day in the world.... And now the world by their learning and wisdom don't know God. They seem to wander in the dark, are miserably deluded, stumble and fall in matters of religion as in midnight darkness. Trusting to their learning, they grope in the daytime as in the night.... They scorn to submit their reason to divine revelation, to believe anything that is above their comprehension, and so being wise in their own eyes, they become fools....[88]

Sin renders fallen man mentally incapacitated.

Because of the damage to his mind caused by the Fall, the natural man cannot rightly understand matters of a spiritual nature. The mind of man and the things of God are now incompatible. This tension arises not because of a natural deficit in man but the presence of sin. Sin, Edwards said, "fatally prevents spiritual knowledge."[89]

The dreadfulness of their depravity appears in that they are so sottishly blind and ignorant. God gave man a faculty of reason and understanding, which is a noble faculty....[He] is made capable to know God, and to know spiritual and eternal things. And God gave him heavenly things, and

87 Edwards, "The Mind," *Works*, 6:384.
88 Edwards, *A History of the Work of Redemption*, *Works*, 9:440–441.
89 Edwards, "A Spiritual Understanding," *Works*, 14:87.

made him as capable to know these things as any others. But man has debased himself, and has lost his glory in this respect. He has become as ignorant of the excellency of God as the very beasts. His understanding is full of darkness; his mind is blind, is altogether blind to spiritual things.[90]

Moreover, fallen man finds the things of God above his ability to rightly comprehend.

It is not rational to suppose, if there be any such excellency in divine things, that wicked men should see it. 'Tis not rational to suppose, that those whose minds are full of spiritual pollution, and under the power of filthy lusts, should have any relish or sense of divine beauty, or excellency; or that their minds should be susceptive of that light that is in its own nature so pure and heavenly.[91]

He finds himself ignorant of spiritual things due to the damnable flaw in his nature.

They are naturally, totally blind, wholly without any light.... They never understand the meanings of the things that are [crucial] concerning Christ and the vital religion. They have many clear and plain instructions, an abundance of them, but they are never plain to them.... They never understand the way of salvation by Christ tho' they have it so often described.... They are like dull scholars that go to school many years but never learn to read.[92]

---

90 Edwards, "A Natural Condition Is a Dreadful Condition," in ed. Nichols, *Seeking God*, 74.

91 Edwards, "A Divine and Supernatural Light," in *The Sermons of Jonathan Edwards: A Reader*, eds. Wilson H. Kimnach, Kenneth P. Minkema, and Douglas A. Sweeney (New Haven: Yale University Press, 1999), 136.

92 Edwards, "Tho a People That Live Under Means Are Wont in General to Seek and Hope for Salvation, Yet 'Tis the Elect Only That Obtains It and the Rest Are

The Fall has not removed man's capacity to think, but it has marred his ability to think *clearly*. Man so handicapped, aware of the world around him but unable to comprehend it fully, lives for all intents and purposes as a practical atheist, unable to understand the reality of God and his need for him.

The nature of the human will also plays a central role in Edwards's understanding of fallen man. Edwards defined the will as "that by which the soul chooses." By this he meant "in every act of will whatsoever, the mind chooses one thing rather than another; it chooses something rather than the contrary, or rather than the want or nonexistence of that thing." He continued,

> So that whatever names we call the act of the will by—
> choosing, refusing, approving, disapproving, liking, disliking,
> embracing, rejecting, determining, directing, commanding,
> forbidding, inclining or being averse, a being pleased or
> displeased with—all may be reduced to this of choosing.[93]

The exercise of the will is the outworking of inclinations, informed by the response of the heart and mind, leading man to choose one way and not another.

The problem, however, is that the will of the fallen man is flawed as well. According to Edwards, there still resides in fallen humanity the natural ability to choose as he pleases, even for the good. This ability to choose arises out of the very basic nature of man. "A man may be said properly," Edwards noted, "to have it in his power to do that which he surely will not."[94] Therein, however, lies man's difficulty. While he possesses the ability to choose good, he is no longer willing to do so.

Mankind, after the Fall, finds himself held captive by his depraved

---

Blinded" (1740), Andover Newton Theological School, Newton Centre.
93 Edwards, *Freedom of the Will, Works*, 1:137.
94 Edwards, "Miscellanies" No. 573, *Works*, 18:112.

nature. "Sin … is a thing seated in the will itself."[95] For that reason, "Man has not so much freedom now as he had before the fall," Edwards reasoned. "Now he has a will against a will, an inclination contrary to his reason and judgment, which begets a contrary inclination."[96] The Fall has not altered what he can and cannot do but what he will and will not do. That is, his sinful nature, which flows from man like bitter water from a poisonous stream in the form of sinful acts and thoughts, Edwards contended, leaves him morally unable to choose what is right.

> A great degree of habitual wickedness may lay a man under an inability to love and choose holiness; and render him utterly unable to love an infinitely holy Being, or to choose and cleave to him as his chief good.[97]

As Edwards wrote to one of his frequent correspondents, "The very notion of hardness of heart [which would be evidenced by ongoing sin] implies moral inability."[98]

In the grasp of sin, his will firmly bound by his own depravity, fallen man cannot do for himself what he most needs and what would bring him the most true happiness, because he no longer truly desires that happiness. "You have not only neglected your salvation," he warned his congregation, "but you have willfully taken direct courses to undo yourself.… You have destroyed yourself, and destroyed yourself willfully."[99] The reason for this, Edwards believed, is that the sinner cannot see that which is to his eternal benefit because of his fallen condition. "How exceedingly are men blinded by their own interest."[100] These interests, informed by his fallen

95 Edwards, "Persons Ought to Do What They Can for Their Salvation" (1733), Beinecke Rare Book and Manuscript Library, Yale University, New Haven.
96 Edwards, "Miscellanies" No. 291, *Works*, 13:383.
97 Edwards, *Freedom of the Will*, *Works*, 1:160.
98 Edwards, Letter "To Mr. Erskine," *Works*, 1:468.
99 Edwards, "The Justice of God in the Damnation of Sinners," *Works*, 19:371.
100 Edwards, "A Spiritual Understanding," *Works*, 14:87.

condition, affect every decision he makes and leave him wholly opposed to the things of religion.

> And men's wills are opposite to the gospel. The gospel, the Savior, and his way of salvation don't suit with their natural inclination. The way to salvation is too holy for 'em; it ascribes too much to God and not enough to themselves. They can see no beauty in Christ wherefore they should desire, and it is impossible they should be persuaded to love Christ if they see no beauty in him. They see no excellency, no fitness in the way of salvation, but, on the contrary, 'tis a way contrary to the strongest bent and inclination of their souls.[101]

These inclinations direct the choices men make and the actions they take. Edwards could proclaim with confidence, "Many neglect [the concerns of their soul] because of their contrarity to their lust and sinful inclinations."[102] Such is the strength of these inclinations that man is left impotent to choose anything other than what pleases his sinful biases. Bound by sin, fallen man prefers his present condition; evil has become the greatest apparent good. Fallen man is lost and he loves it.

Humanity has fallen, Edwards knew, and that fall is complete. All are guilty of Adam's sin and are the inheritors of his rotten legacy. The dread effects of that sinful legacy touch upon every area of man's being. Man loves the flesh more than the spirit. He possesses no spiritual knowledge. He enjoys no spiritual beauty. With Adam,

> [man] wholly lost his spiritual life and became dead in sin. He wholly lost the favor of God. He lost his honor and

---

101 Edwards, "Stupid as Stones," *Works*, 17:177.

102 Edwards, "If We Would Be in the Way of God's Grace and Blessing We Must Wait upon Him in His Own Way and in the Use of His Appointed Means" (1729), Beinecke Rare Book and Manuscript Library, Yale University, New Haven.

dignity and sank into an exceeding vile state. He lost his happiness. The union was cut off between heaven and earth. He lost communion with God.[103]

Man was, as a race, excommunicated and cut off from the glory of God.[104]

For Edwards, the Fall bears directly upon his theology of prayer at this point. Bereft of his communion with God, the prayer life of the common man lies in waste. He enjoys no access to God. He finds himself wholly unfit "to go into the presence of God by prayer."[105] Unlike the saint who has been given the Spirit of prayer, the natural man has "no prayer-hearing God to whom [he] may go."[106]

Edwards did not believe that God could not hear the prayers of the lost as if God was incapable of such a feat. The issue is not one of cognition but recognition. God knows that they are praying but refuses to acknowledge their petitions. While fallen men may attempt to approach the throne of grace with much supposed piety and cries for mercy, God sees their hearts and finds no faith.[107] "Their prayer is not the voice of the heart, but only of the mouth," he said.[108] Those who approach God in such a manner do so not out of respect for who God is but what God can do.

---

103 Edwards, "Like Rain upon Mown Grass," *Works*, 22:304.

104 Edwards, "The Means and Ends of Excommunication," *Works*, 22:76.

105 Edwards, "It Becomes Saints in Cases of Special Difficulty and Calamity of God's Church, to Betake Themselves in an Extraordinary Manner to Prayer to God" (1750), manuscript.

106 Edwards, "The Most High a Prayer-Hearing God," *Works* (Hendrickson), 2:116.

107 Edwards, "The Most High a Prayer-Hearing God," *Works* (Hendrickson), 2:117.

108 Edwards, "The Terms of Prayer," *Works*, 19:787. Edwards picked up much of the same language and this exact line of thought in another sermon. "At the same time that we pretend to ask this mercy we may, in effect, ask a denial…[by] a cold, indifferent asking without any engagedness of spirit, only asking in a formal manner. Such an asking is an asking of the mouth but not of the heart," he said. "'Tis no prayer in the sight of God" (Edwards, "Praying for the Spirit," *Works*, 22:221).

244 THE VOICE OF FAITH

> 'Tis no real prayer in the sight of God, because it is not
> made with a humble sense of their unworthiness of what
> is prayed for, and a submissive sense of its being something
> that is in God's free disposal. If a prayer ben't made with
> such a frame as this, 'tis no real prayer.[109]

People who pray in this faithless manner are not praying to God
but for themselves. God does not hear such prayers for prayer lifted
up without true faith is no prayer at all.

Edwards made the same argument, sometimes using the same
words, in his signal sermon on prayer, "The Most High a Prayer-
Hearing God." "God looketh not at words, but at the heart," he said
then. Fallen man prays for what pleases his flesh not his soul. His
prayers are the acts of a hypocrite who neither loves nor trusts the
God to whom he supposedly prays. Instead, he comes to God as a
creditor expecting his due rather than as a beggar acknowledging
that he is due nothing. God sees through this deception, Edwards
warned. The natural man's lack of faith bears testimony against
himself. "That prayer which is not of faith, is insincere; for prayer
is a show or manifestation of dependence on God, and trust in his
sufficiency and mercy. Therefore, where this trust or faith is wanting,
there is no prayer in the sight of God."[110]

Regardless of whether or not God "hears" the prayers of fallen
men, prayer is no less a duty for them than for the community of
saints. The reason for this, Edwards held, is that prayer, for the
faithful and the unfaithful alike, functions as an admission of God's
superiority and a preparation of the heart for the reception of his
mercies. By praying to God, man recognizes God for who he is and
what man is not. Moreover, doing so, he argued, would render them
guilty of a lesser evil. While they would be praying out of sinful
self-love, they would still be honouring God's command to pray

---

109 Edwards, "Terms of Prayer," *Works*, 19:787.
110 Edwards, "The Most High a Prayer-Hearing God," *Works* (Hendrickson),
2:117.

and, therefore, lessening their guilt before God. "There is a great difference," Edwards taught. "For in praying they do that that is materially good, though it may be formally evil, or evil as to the principle, and of the action. But in neglecting prayer they do that that is materially evil and formally evil too." To pray for the wrong reason is better than not praying at all.

Neglecting prayer, on the other hand, brings guilt upon the one who refuses to honour God or his commands and increases the likelihood that he will fall even further into sin. The duty of prayer faithfully kept acts as an antidote to the sinful proclivities of fallen man. Edwards offered one further reason for the natural man to pray. By praying, man puts himself in the way of God's mercy. God will never save him until he comes to recognize the greatness of God and his sin. Praying forces him to do just that.[111]

While God does not hear the prayers of fallen man, Edwards admitted that God does occasionally answer the prayers of the wicked. "God is pleased sometimes to answer the prayers of unbelievers," he announced. Such answers come not in response to the worthiness of the petitioner but "of [God's] sovereign mercy." He continued, "Though there be no regard to God in their prayers, yet he, of his infinite grace, is pleased to have respect to their desires of their own happiness, and to grant their requests." When God answers the requests of the unbeliever he does so not for the purpose of satisfying man's fleshly lusts but revealing his grace and magnifying his glory.[112] And, again, with his pastoral eye ever toward the application of the gospel, Edwards reminded his hearers that God moves in such a way as to prepare the sinner for mercy.[113]

---

111 Edwards, "There Is No Goodness in Praying, Though It Be Never So Earnestly, Merely Out of Fear of Misery" (1728), manuscript.

112 Edwards, "The Most High a Prayer-Hearing God," *Works* (Hendrickson), 2:117.

113 Edwards, "The Most High a Prayer-Hearing God," *Works* (Hendrickson), 2:118.

His heart hard, his mind cloudy and his will bound, fallen man seeks the happiness he has forsaken. Unfortunately, he cannot find what he seeks because he fails to recognize the true nature of his dilemma. Even when he turns to the God he has spurned, he does so with his own happiness as the highest of goals, seeing God as the lowest of means. In such a frame of mind, he knows not who God really is and cares not what God really wants. God rejects that self-centred, demanding form of speech that fallen man calls prayer. In his fallen condition, devoid of the Spirit of prayer and saving faith, man cannot enjoy the sweet fellowship with God that he so desperately needs.

SUMMARY

Though the doctrine of the Fall proves notoriously difficult for theologians to explain, fraught with dangers on both sides of the very narrow trail of orthodoxy, the effects of the Fall are clear. After the Fall, man is not only spiritually lost, he has lost all of the spiritual benefits of Adam's original state as well. Guilty of the federal head's sin, "[man] has destroyed and undone himself; he has deprived and confounded his whole nature." In this state of despair his soul is "clogged," "darkened," and "exceedingly hindered" by his ever present sin.[114] As such, "They are in a state," Edwards said, "wherein they are destitute of all true comfort." That true comfort, Edwards knew, relates directly to the intimacy of one's relationship with God for true happiness is found in God alone. Adam and his children have abandoned that relationship. They have lost the friendship of God that was enjoyed in the Garden. They no longer walk with him or talk with him. Rather than relishing God's smile, Edwards lamented, they must fear God's frown.[115]

---

114 Edwards, "Our Weakness, Christ's Strength," *Works*, 19:382.
115 Edwards, "East of Eden," *Works*, 17:335.

What man can have again: a relationship with God

Hence we may undoubtedly conclude that the redeemed of Jesus Christ will be advanced to a great honor and happiness, and a more intimate union and communion with God.[116]

Seeing the great depravity of their souls and the greatness of the gospel, Edwards longed to shepherd his hearers through God's door of mercy and see them embrace their Saviour. The gospel, he knew, offered man both forgiveness of sin and restoration of fellowship with God. Reconciled to their Creator, they would know him, love him, commune with him and enjoy him just as they had been created to do.

Edwards realized, however, that sin corrupts the individual—the heart, mind and will are wholly ruined. "They are totally corrupt, in every part, in all their faculties; and all the principles of their nature, their understandings, and wills; and in all their dispositions and affections, their heads, their hearts, are totally depraved."[117] Fallen man, following the dictates of his fallen nature, cannot please God in any way, nor does he try. The gospel, though freely offered, is freely rejected. If there is to be any hope at all, this depravity and its resultant destruction demand that man be changed. When the change is completed, regeneration accomplished, faith instilled and justification applied, the new man of God can truly pray and once again enjoy "intimate union and communion with God."

A NEW MAN

Man cannot proceed as he has and legitimately hope for the happiness that salvation brings. The change needed, Edwards

---

116 Edwards, "Miscellanies" No. 702, *Works*, 18:298.
117 Edwards, "The Justice of God in the Damnation of Sinners," *Works*, 19:344.

believed, necessitates intervention. God produces the alteration of character required that, in turn, produces the faith of man. In this Edwards counted on God to do everything within his power to convert the fallen man. He called on man to do the only thing within his power: trust God to do what is right.

> In efficacious grace (read: salvation) we are not merely passive, nor yet does God do some, and we do the rest. But God does all, and we do all. God produces all, and we act all. For that is what he produces, viz. our acts. God is the only proper author and fountain; we only are the proper actors. We are, in different respects, wholly passive and wholly active.[118]

In this way, Edwards joined the doctrines of God's sovereignty and man's responsibility.

The work of salvation depends upon the grace of God at several levels according to Edwards. First, in necessity and order, God determines to save some from the doom and destruction that all so rightly deserve. Salvation is, however, more than a spiritual rescue from eternal damnation—it is a restoration. In election, God calls out and separates some for the purpose of showering his favour upon them in a way known only by Adam in the long history of mankind. These he elects "to the highest happiness."[119] Unlike the temporal happiness that Adam sought in the Garden, the happiness God provides in salvation is of the greatest eternal value. When God elects men to salvation, he chooses them so that he might communicate his happiness to them by communicating himself to them through his Spirit.[120] Doing so brings the fallen back to God.

---

118   Edwards, "Remarks on Important Theological Controversies," *Works* (Hendrickson), 2:557.

119   Edwards, "Miscellanies" No. 702, *Works*, 18:299.

120   Edwards, "The Terms of Prayer," *Works*, 19:776.

The work of God in salvation does not end with election, Edwards contended. Those who are saved are saved entirely of God. They are "born of God" by "God's power."[121] Having elected some to salvation, God intervenes directly through the work of his Spirit, remodelling the soul, changing the elect's heart, mind and will. For salvation to take place, there must be a turning of the heart, a "change of nature" of supernatural proportions.[122] The heart must be properly disposed to the things of God. Adults and children, equally deserving of God's wrath, were encouraged to give their hearts to him, freely and willingly.

> Your heart does not go out after Christ of itself; but you are forced and driven to seek an interest in him. Christ has no share at all in your heart; there is no manner of closing of the heart with him. This forced compliance is not what Christ seeks of you; he seeks a free and willing acceptance.[123]

The first manifestation of such a willingness, Edwards taught, is a recognition of the depth and despair of one's sinful nature. The sinner who has experienced this sense of heartfelt conviction has reason for hope. Once they had been brought to see their sin as God sees it, Edwards told sinners, "you will be prepared for Christ, and you may rationally hope that a conviction of righteousness will follow."[124]

In the renewal of the heart, legal humility follows upon the heels of conviction. "The effect of this contrition," Edwards argued, "is

---

121 Edwards, "How True Believers Receive Christ" (1755), Beinecke Rare Book and Manuscript Library, Yale University, New Haven.

122 Edwards, "There Is Such a Thing as Conversion" (1740), Beinecke Rare Book and Manuscript Library, Yale University, New Haven.

123 Edwards, "The Justice of God in the Damnation of Sinners," *Works*, 19:361.

124 Edwards, "Persons Ought to Endeavor to Be Convinced of Sin," in ed. Nichols, *Seeking God*, 303.

a deep humiliation."[125] Seeing the sinfulness of his heart, a person has every reason to humble himself and lie low before God: "Such thoughts as these make the proud heart…come down low before the throne of grace."[126] Humility, he said, "prepares the heart for God's grace and makes it better."[127] Humility leads to repentance. Edwards continued, "When once the heart has been thus broken for sin, it shall be forsaken; when once the sinner hath thus seen the vileness of it, he takes his leave of [it]—bids it an eternal adieu, desires to have no more to do with it."[128] That is, the heart is turned and the life is changed. The change of heart that God expects, God exacts. This he does through the threefold work of the Holy Spirit.

There must also be, however, as Perry Miller understood Edwards to say, "a union of the hot heart and the cool head."[129] Man's mind must be changed as well because mentally, Edwards knew, natural man finds himself dazed and confused. There is good news, however. "Persons, with but an ordinary degree of knowledge, are capable, without a long and subtile [sic] train of reasoning, to see the divine excellency of the things of religion: they are capable of being taught by the Spirit of God, as well as learned men," Edwards offered.[130] Alluding to Proverbs 4:7, he exhorted "all that desire ever to be savingly profited by the Word to get the understanding of it. With all your gettings, get this understanding."[131]

The understanding required also comes from God, Edwards said. God has determined to impart the spiritual light of his Spirit according to his gracious purposes. In this, the Spirit unites with

125   Edwards, "True Repentance Required," *Works*, 10:514.

126   Edwards, "True Repentance Required," *Works*, 10:515.

127   Edwards, "If We Would Be in the Way of God's Grace and Blessing We Must Wait upon Him in His Own Way and in the Use of His Appointed Means" (1729), manuscript.

128   Edwards, "True Repentance Required," *Works*, 10:515.

129   Miller, *Jonathan Edwards*, 139.

130   Edwards, "A Divine and Supernatural Light," in eds. Kimnach, Minkema and Sweeney, *The Sermons of Jonathan Edwards: A Reader*, 138.

131   Edwards, "Profitable Hearers of the Word," *Works*, 14:264.

the mind of man and makes use of those resident faculties that sin had rendered useless. Spiritual light shed by the Spirit, Edwards argued in both "False Light and True" and "A Divine and Supernatural Light," "reveals no new thing to men, but only gives a due understanding of them."[132] Spiritual knowledge, aided by the Spirit, consists in a "clear apprehension and a lively infixed sensibleness" of divine things. In this way, the elect receives a new and "real sense and apprehension of the divine excellency of things revealed in the Word of God."[133]

All men operating under the influence of the Spirit will discover a new taste for divine things in a similar fashion. Spiritual knowledge, Edwards contended, will be found to be "above all others sweet and joyful."[134] Whereas, the sinner sees no manner of excellency in divine things, the regenerate discovers a "holy joy."[135] He relishes the things of God. He has a new taste for things of the Spirit. This new taste, or sense, is what Edwards spoke of in *Religious Affections* as he attempted to describe the traits of a true believer. There Edwards wrote that the awakened man experiences

> [a] new sense of mind, in spiritual and divine things, as entirely diverse from anything that is perceived in them, by natural men, as the sweet taste of honey is diverse from the ideas men get of honey by only looking on it, and feeling of it. So that the spiritual perceptions which a sanctified and spiritual person has, are not only diverse from all that natural men have, after the manner that the ideas or perceptions of the same sense may differ one from another,

132 Edwards, "False Light and True," *Works*, 19:138 "A Divine and Supernatural Light," in eds. Kimnach, Minkema and Sweeney, *The Sermons of Jonathan Edwards: A Reader*, 125–126.

133 Edwards, "A Divine and Supernatural Light," in eds. Kimnach, Minkema and Sweeney, *The Sermons of Jonathan Edwards: A Reader*, 127.

134 Edwards, "A Divine and Supernatural Light," in eds. Kimnach, Minkema and Sweeney, *The Sermons of Jonathan Edwards: A Reader*, 139.

135 Edwards, "A Spiritual Understanding," *Works*, 14:82.

but rather as the ideas and sensations of different senses do differ. Hence the work of the Spirit of God in regeneration is often in Scripture compared to the giving a new sense, giving eyes to see, and ears to hear, unstopping the ears of the deaf, and opening the eyes of them that were born blind, and turning from darkness unto light.[136]

That which once made no sense, he now knows and loves. God has changed man's mind.

Once the heart has been touched and the mind changed, the will follows. This, too, requires divine intervention. The state of the man's fallen will necessitates God's sovereign gift of that "divine and supernatural light" of his Holy Spirit as well. "[Sinners] are not willing to come to Christ" and "can't make [themselves] willing."[137] God sends his light and influences the inclinations of the will. "This light is such as effectually influences the inclination," Edwards preached, "and changes the nature of the soul."[138]

This change that God affects does not require the implantation of new principles or faculties. Rather, the Spirit alters those faculties resident within the fallen individual.

'Tis not intended that the natural faculties are not made use of in it. The natural faculties are the subject of this light: and they are the subject in such a manner, that they are not merely passive, but active in it; the acts and exercises of man's understanding are concerned and made use of in it.[139]

---

136 Edwards, *Religious Affections*, *Works*, 2:206.

137 Edwards, "The Justice of God in the Damnation of Sinners," *Works*, 19:365.

138 Edwards, "A Divine and Supernatural Light," in eds. Kimnach, Minkema and Sweeney, *The Sermons of Jonathan Edwards: A Reader*, 139.

139 Edwards, "A Divine and Supernatural Light," in eds. Kimnach, Minkema and Sweeney, *The Sermons of Jonathan Edwards: A Reader*, 130.

Those revived human faculties, once damaged by the Fall, now figure prominently in the salvation drama. The transfigured man sees the wisdom of the gospel and the beauty of God's sovereignty. These things draw the individual to the things of religion.

The proof of the Spirit's operation on the will lies in the will's working. "The will," Edwards said, "always necessarily approves of, and rests in its own acts."[140] That is, the actions of the person reveal the character of their will. As one will only choose that to which they are predisposed, a person in whom sin is the predominant motivator chooses to do only those actions that fulfill his sinful appetite. They are self-centred and sin-motivated. On the other hand, the person whose will has been altered by God will be henceforth inclined to do those things that are God-honouring and God-seeking. With his will freed from the bondage of sin, man is now free to recognize the beauty of the gospel and choose that which is not just the "greatest *apparent* good," but that which truly *is* the greatest good.

What, then, is man's role in the salvation process? Faith, said Edwards.

> As there is nobody but what will allow that there is a peculiar relation between Christ and his true disciples, by which they are in some sense in Scripture said to be one; so I suppose there is nobody but what will allow, that there may be something that the true Christian does on his part, whereby he is active in coming into this relation or union, some act of the soul of the Christian, that is the Christian's uniting act, or that by which is done towards this union or relation (or whatever any please to call it), on the Christian's part: now faith I suppose to be this act.[141]

---

140 Edwards, "The Justice of God in the Damnation of Sinners," *Works*, 19:365.

141 Edwards, "Justification by Faith Alone," *Works*, 19:157.

It is by faith that man rejoices in God's sovereignty, accepts Christ's excellency and yields to the Spirit's conviction whereby he does the only thing that man can do: trust God. Edwards spoke often of the nature of faith. His thoughts on the topic can be found throughout his sermons and writings. Defined negatively, faith, he wrote, "is not the same things as a course of obedience, or righteousness."[142] If it were so, faith would be a work for which God would reward salvation. Faith, however, is not something to be accomplished, according to Edwards, but something to be had. Put positively, then, faith is a "coming to," or a "receiving of" Christ.[143]

Simple definitions, however, did not satisfy Edwards. He searched for and found many ways to communicate the meaning and the beauty of faith. Faith is, he said, "a looking to God" in humble dependence.[144] As he mused in one of his many miscellanies, "Faith in its very nature and essence consists in nothing else but a direct according, suiting or closing of the soul with the Savior and his salvation."[145]

In Edwards's notebook on faith one would expect to find a clear definition of faith. Instead, the entire work reveals the difficulty with which Edwards met as he struggled to find a sufficient manner to explain this vital concept. The very first entry succinctly defines faith as "belief."[146] The rest of the work reads like the manic concatenation of a man who cannot say exactly what he means. Faith

---

142 Edwards, "Justification by Faith Alone," *Works*, 19:148.

143 Edwards, "Justification by Faith Alone," *Works*, 19:160. Before his examiners at Yale, he commented, "[Faith is] that motion of the entire soul towards Christ that is described in various ways in Scripture as coming, believing, trusting, receiving, submitting, etc." (Edwards, "A Sinner Is Not Justified in the Sight of God Except Through the Righteousness of Christ by Faith," *Works*, 14:61).

144 Edwards, *Notes on Scripture*, *Works*, 15:66–67. See "Miscellanies" No. 726 for a Trinitarian application of this language (*Works*, 18:353).

145 Edwards, "Miscellanies" No. 714, *Works*, 18:345.

146 Edwards, "Faith," *Works*, 21:417.

is: a "depending on,"[147] the "trusting in,"[148] an "approving of,"[149] a "being drawn to,"[150] a "thirst," a "desiring," a "submitting" and a "receiving."[151] Edwards's list goes on and on. One lengthy definition, however, proves worthy of special attention.

[55.] Justifying faith is the soul's sense and conviction of the reality, the excellency and sufficiency of Jesus Christ as Savior, with the soul's answerable entire inclination, entirely an answerable inclining of the heart towards him, and application of itself to him, entirely inclining him and moving the heart to him.[152]

True faith, Edwards knew, moves the will with the renewed inclinations of the new birth.

In his sermon "God Glorified in Man's Dependence," Edwards further qualified his definition of faith with a call for evangelical humility. That is, saving faith requires one to see God as he really is and himself as he truly is: lost and without hope.

Faith is a sensibleness of what is real in the work of redemption; and as we do wholly depend on God, so the soul that believes doth entirely depend on God for all salvation, in its own sense, and act. Faith abases man, and exalts God; it gives all the glory of redemption to God alone. It is necessary in order to saving faith, that man should be emptied of himself, that he should be sensible that he is "wretched, and miserable, and poor, and blind, and naked" [Revelation 3:17].[153]

147 Edwards, "Faith," *Works*, 21:417.
148 Edwards, "Faith," *Works*, 21:419.
149 Edwards, "Faith," *Works*, 21:420.
150 Edwards, "Faith," *Works*, 21:421.
151 Edwards, "Faith," *Works*, 21:422–423.
152 Edwards, "Faith," *Works*, 21:428.
153 Edwards, "God Glorified in Man's Dependence," *Works*, 17:213.

Saving faith gives God all the glory.

If Edwards truly hoped to establish the doctrine of justification by faith alone[154] and protect it from theological challenge, he knew that he must prove that faith was in no way to be considered a work of righteousness acceptable to God upon its own merits. For that reason, Edwards contended that faith must be the condition, not the cause, of salvation. "It was not intended that faith was the instrument wherewith God justifies," he wrote, "but the instrument wherewith we receive justification." The believer's faith, he continued, is not an act that justifies but the passive act in which the individual accepts the justification offered. Faith serves as "the instrument" by which we receive Christ and his benefits.[155]

Moreover, it is "fit and congruous," Edwards explained, that God sees the faithful and the object of faith as one in faith. The value that God places on faith is proportional to the value he places on the object of faith—Christ. "God looks on it fit," he wrote, "that he whose heart sincerely unites himself to Christ as his Savior, should be looked upon as united to that Savior, and so having an interest in him." Because God has determined faith to be the appropriate means that one acquires an interest in Christ and his inheritance, "God will neither look on Christ's merits as ours, nor adjudge his benefits to us, till we be in Christ: nor will he look upon us as being in him, without active unition of our hearts and souls to him [by faith]." Thus, according to Edwards's theological construct, justification can be obtained only by faith in the one whom God has deemed worthy because he was truly righteous—Christ.[156]

---

154 Justification results in the application, or imputation, of another's God-pleasing righteousness to one's account, Edwards argued. "God of his sovereign grace is pleased in his dealings with the sinner to take and regard that which indeed is not righteousness, and in one that has no righteousness, so that the consequence shall be the same as if he had righteousness" (Edwards, "Justification by Faith Alone," *Works*, 19:148).

155 Edwards, "Justification by Faith Alone," *Works*, 19:153.

156 Edwards, "Justification by Faith Alone," *Works*, 19:159.

Fallen man has a problem, Edwards reminded his listeners. God, however, has the solution. "Man's soul was ruined by the fall, the image of God was ruined, man's nature corrupted and destroyed, and man became dead in sin," Edwards saw. "The design was to restore the soul of man in conversion and to restore life to it, and the image of God in conversion."[157] In salvation, God renews the fallen man. He undoes the damage done by the Fall. He does so to restore true happiness to the creation and glory to himself.

> As the new nature is from God, so it tends to God as its center; and as that which tends to its center is not quiet and at rest, till it has got quite to the very center, so the new nature that is in the saints never will be at rest, till there is a perfect union with God and conformity to him, and so no separation, or alienation, or enmity remaining. The holy nature in the saints tends to the fountain whence it proceeds, and never will be at rest, till the soul is fully brought to that fountain, and all swallowed up in it.[158]

This new nature, the complete renovation of the fallen man, comes from God that man might return to God and enjoy him and his happiness forever.

A NEW RELATIONSHIP WITH GOD

In salvation God gives fallen man true happiness by giving himself according to the work of the Trinity as revealed in the gospel. He gave of himself sovereignly in the decree of election as God the Father. He gave of himself sacrificially on the cross as God the Son. He gave of himself supernaturally through his indwelling as God the Spirit. Thus, for Edwards, true happiness can be had and enjoyed only when God stands centre stage in the life of the new man.

---

157 Edwards, *A History of the Work of Redemption*, *Works*, 9:124.
158 Edwards, "Striving After Perfection," *Works*, 19:692.

> One design of God in the gospel, is to bring us to make God the object of our undivided respect, that he may engross our regard every way, that whatever natural inclination there is in us, he may be the center of it, and that God may be all in all.[159]

In other words, God saves fallen man that he might bring him into a new and more perfect relationship with himself in all his Trinitarian perfection.

The man of faith enjoys a new relationship, a sweet fellowship with God. From the human perspective, faith is the source of that fellowship and prayer is its means. Those that have faith have fellowship. Those who fellowship with God do so through prayer for "prayer is only the voice of faith."[160]

While Edwards gave several reasons as to why Christians pray, the first and foremost reason for prayer is that it proves the reality of one's faith. It is a sign of true religion.[161] Because God lives in the new man, the new man seeks God.[162] "They want to know more of God, and to know as much of God, and have as much of him in their hearts, and enjoy as much of God as their natures are capable," he claimed.[163] Those that are truly saved want to know and fellowship with God more and more.

Edwards made the same case more generically in *Religious Affections*. When discussing the marks of a true Christian, he mentioned several traits that may or may not denote true faith. In the end, however, he said only one mark belies the presence of saving faith. "Gracious and holy affections have their exercise and fruit in Christian practice."[164] In this, the twelfth and longest sign discussed,

---

159 Edwards, "Miscellanies" No. 510, *Works*, 18:54.

160 Edwards, "Justification by Faith Alone," *Works*, 19:204.

161 Edwards, "The Things That Belong to True Religion," *Works*, 25:573.

162 Edwards, "Keeping the Presence of God," *Works*, 22:526.

163 Edwards, "The Terms of Prayer," *Works*, 19:784.

164 Edwards, *Religious Affections*, *Works*, 2:383.

Edwards argued that "Christian practice is the greatest evidence" of a sincere faith.[165] It is "the proper proof of the true and saving knowledge of God," "the proper evidence of repentance," and "the proper evidence of a saving faith."[166] True faith leads to holy practice of which prayer is chief.

A second reason Edwards offered relates intimately to what was just stated. Those who are saved by God love God. As in human relations, it is necessary for the lover to communicate with the loved. In the case of the Christian's love for God, this love leads the individual to seek God, to please and honour him.[167] The way to honour God, Edwards reasoned, is through prayer.

> Hence how rational is it to suppose, contrary to the prin-
> ciples of the deists, that God ought to be worshipped by
> prayer, confession, praise and thanksgiving, and those duties
> in which we speak to God, and have to do with [him] as a
> properly intelligent being, or one that perceives and knows
> what we say to him; that we ought to show respect to
> him by voluntary acts, as expressions of our thoughts and
> volitions and motions of our hearts, purposely expressed
> before him and directed to him, as all intelligent creatures
> do to all other intelligent beings with whom they are con-
> cerned, or have intercourse.[168]

In prayer, the Christian acknowledges the supremacy and goodness of his God. Worshipful prayer is "a proper acknowledgment of God as the only author of this mercy [salvation]," he said elsewhere.[169] The Christian saved by God's grace and for God's glory comes to God in prayer with love in his heart, gratitude on his mind and worship on his lips.

---

165 Edwards, *Religious Affections*, *Works*, 2:418.
166 Edwards, *Religious Affections*, *Works*, 2:444.
167 Edwards, "Miscellanies" No. 1208, *Works*, 23:139.
168 Edwards, "Miscellanies" No. 749, *Works*, 18:397.
169 Edwards, "Continuing God's Presence," *Works*, 19:403.

The true believer also prays faithfully in obedience to God's desires, fulfilling his saintly duties, the greatest of which is prayer. Because the Christian loves God, he obeys God. Moreover, the true lover of God finds his commands "easy and delightful."[170]

> All the pleasure of love consists in pleasing the beloved. 'Tis the nature of love to rouse and stir to an earnest desire to please, and certainly it must be a great pleasure to have earnest desires satisfied. Now the love of God causes those in whose heart it is implanted more earnestly to desire to please God than anything in the world, causes them heartily to embrace opportunities of pleasing him and sweetly to reflect on it when he knows they have pleased him.[171]

Love for God becomes the source of the Christian's obedience to him.

> The internal duties which God requires are easy and pleasant to those that love God. For love to God itself is a fountain from whence flow all other internal duties and graces, and when this grace is obtained, all the others— repentance, resignation and humiliation, hope, charity, etc., and the exercise of these in meditation—follow naturally and easily of themselves.[172]

Since the Christian loves God, he loves to please him. His obedience to God's commands, while required, are actually quite pleasant because he knows that his obedience brings his lover great pleasure. Knowing that the beloved is pleased pleases the lover. In love, duty becomes joy and the Christian comes to God.

---

170 Edwards, "True Love to God," *Works*, 10:636.
171 Edwards, "True Love to God," *Works*, 10:637.
172 Edwards, "True Love to God," *Works*, 10:638.

Furthermore, God, in his grace, has made the duty of prayer not only pleasurable but profitable as well.

> Seeing therefore you stand in such continual need of the help of God, how reasonable is it that you should continually seek it of him, and perseveringly acknowledge your dependence upon him, by resorting to him, to spread your needs before him, and to offer up your requests to him in prayer....
>
> Consider the great benefit of a constant, diligent, and persevering attendance on this duty. It is one of the greatest and most excellent means of nourishing the new nature, and of causing the soul to flourish and prosper. It is an excellent means of keeping up an acquaintance with God, and of growing in the knowledge of God. It is the way to a life of communion with God. It is an excellent means of taking off the heart from the vanities of the world and of causing the mind to be conversant in heaven. It is an excellent antidote against the poison of the old serpent. It is a duty whereby strength is derived from God against the lusts and corruptions of the heart, and the snares of the world.
>
> It hath a great tendency to keep the soul in a wakeful frame, and to lead us to a strict walk with God, and to a life that shall be fruitful in such good works, as tend to adorn the doctrine of Christ, and to cause our light to shine before others, that they, seeing our good works, shall glorify our Father who is in heaven. And if the duty be constantly and diligently attended, it will be a very pleasant duty.[173]

Thus, Christians are also encouraged by Edwards to pray for spiritual blessings and greater happiness. That is, they should actively seek the

---

173 Edwards, "Hypocrites Deficient in the Duty of Prayer," in ed. Nichols, *Seeking God*, 371–372.

continued blessing of God, through communion with God, resting not on the past but hoping for the future. In return they experience happiness in the present as they spend time with God in prayer.

To encourage his flock to ever greater faithfulness in their prayers, Edwards joyfully reminded them on a number of occasions that God awaits their prayers, ready to hear. Better yet, not only does God hear the prayers of those whose hearts are right with him, he can answer them. He is sufficient for their every need. Plus, God "begrutches" them nothing as too good for them.[174] "There [is] no happiness that God is unwilling to bestow on {his people} as too good, if it be considered that [he] has thought nothing too much as the means of procuring their happiness."[175] He has purchased them at a great expense, with the blood of his only Son. As they are now, in God's eyes, one with the Son, they enjoy the Father's love the same as he.

> Those that God is pleased to make the objects of his love, let them be who they will, or what they will—never so mean, never so great sinners—they are the objects of a love that is infinitely full and sufficient.
>
> And therefore nothing that they need, nothing that they ask of God, nothing that their desires can extend themselves to, nothing that their capacity can contain, no good that can be enjoyed by them, is so great, so excellent that God begrutches it to them.[176]

Because God loves them, he will pour out his mercy on those that ask of him prayerfully.

Among the other things Edwards taught his people to seek were wisdom,[177] earthly comfort[178] and spiritual pleasures.[179] Christian

---

174   Edwards, "The Terms of Prayer," *Works*, 19:772.
175   Edwards, "The Terms of Prayer," *Works*, 19:777.
176   Edwards, "The Terms of Prayer," *Works*, 19:781.
177   Edwards, "A Spiritual Understanding," *Works*, 14:95.
178   Edwards, "The Pleasantness of Religion," *Works*, 14:104.
179   Edwards, "The Pleasantness of Religion," *Works*, 14:107.

liberty, he said, guarantees them the right to ask for what brings true pleasure. God has opened the spiritual lines of communication that they might use them liberally for their own spiritual benefit. As Edwards counselled, "In the service of God, there is true liberty to do whatever tends most for our own pleasure."[180] Christians are encouraged by God to pray for their own happiness, Edwards reckoned, because God has given them a taste of the sweetness of divine things in salvation and beckons to imbibe ever more. Moreover, those who do not pray deny themselves not only unsought blessings but the pleasure of prayer itself—the means of their ongoing, intimate communion with the God who is the source and goal of their true happiness.

What Edwards hinted at in the reasons given above for prayer, he made explicit as well. Those that do not pray prove they are not truly Christians.

> But how is a life, in a great measure prayerless, consistent with an holy life? To lead an holy life is to lead a life devoted to God; a life of worshipping and serving God; a life consecrated to the service of God. But how doth he lead such a life who doth not so much as maintain the duty of prayer? How can such a man be said to walk by the Spirit and to be a servant of the Most High God?

Edwards's questions were not meant to be rhetorical but pointed accusations aimed at those seated in the pews who professed Christianity with their lips but proved their lack of faith with their silence. The one who claims Christ but does not pray is like a man who lives without breathing. Such a scenario is impossible, Edwards warned. The man who does not pray does not worship God. He denies God's glory. He does not long for friendship with God. He does not love God because he does not know God. "He

---

180 Edwards, "Christian Liberty," *Works*, 10:627.

that lives a prayerless life," Edwards concluded, "lives without God in the world."[181]

SUMMARY

Fallen man finds himself devoid of the love of God, Edwards lamented. He is deprived and depraved, lost forever in the darkness of his own sin. Yet, God, in his infinite grace, elects some to happiness and sends his Spirit savingly to them. Through the power of the Spirit, God regenerates them, giving spiritual life where there was once only death. He changes the fallen man, renovates his soul, breaks the hardness of his heart, lifts the darkness of his mind and frees his will to choose God once again. This the new man does in faith, trusting God's sovereignty, and savouring his Son, and surrendering to the Spirit. God does all these wondrous things, Edwards said, to communicate his happiness to his creature. The proof and the blessing of this regenerative work is that the new man can and does walk with God and talk with God as Adam once did, enjoying God's fellowship in that great duty called prayer.

Conclusion

> God's declared design is to communicate of his own fullness, and to bring men to a conformity to himself in happiness, in such a manner as to show that his goodness or willingness to communicate of his fullness, has no bounds.[182]

Edwards's theology of prayer begins and ends with God. The one who prays must know to whom he is praying. He must recognize the grace of God in the provision of the Mediator who makes prayer possible. And, he must be the recipient of God's own Spirit. Yet, for all the theocentricity of Edwards's theology, he never lost

---

181 Edwards, "Hypocrites Deficient in the Duty of Prayer," in ed. Nichols, *Seeking God*, 365.

182 Edwards, "The Terms of Prayer," *Works*, 19:776.

sight of the fact that man—and a right understanding of who man was created to be, what he has lost in his sin and what he might have again—plays a pivotal role in prayer.

As Edwards sought to encourage and embolden his people in their prayers, he appealed to their human nature. He reminded them that God created man for his glory, with a desire for intimate fellowship. God wished to convey something of his fullness to his creation. In the Garden, Adam enjoyed this fullness; he enjoyed fellowship and happiness that can be found only in a right relationship with God. Somewhere along the way, however, Adam lost sight of God's creative purpose, chose a lesser happiness and abandoned his walk with God. Wholly ruined by Adam's sin, his progeny now run from God rather than walk with him.

God, however, is not deterred. His will will be done. Thus, he determined even before the Fall that he would set things aright again, Edwards said. As he noted in one of his earliest "Miscellanies,"

> I am convinced that God is willing to be reconciled to man, and has a design to advance him to the happiness he was created for, by the tokens of his good will in the creation and common providence; and that he therefore would give us those advantages, which are necessary to a holy life and salvation.[183]

Those advantages that Edwards referred to are God's elective grace, Christ's redemptive mission and the Spirit's regenerative work. After all, Edwards said, the redemption of fallen men "is the chief end [of] all God's designs."[184] Fulfilling his design, God restores men to their proper position and returns the happiness once lost.

In this, all that man can do is trust God. He must place his faith in God, cease his fruitless labours and depend upon Christ's. Those who do so, said Edwards, will be restored. God will communicate

---

183 Edwards, "Miscellanies" No. 132, *Works*, 13:294.
184 Edwards, "The Terms of Prayer," *Works*, 19:775.

his fullness and conform the individual to his happiness, a happiness that is found only in God.[185] Those that have tasted of this happiness can find satisfaction nowhere else. Nothing can satisfy their appetite for the excellency of God or quench their thirst for greater intimacy. God instills these desires at the new birth and stirs them throughout the Christian's life.

So revived, the new man wants "to get near to God."[186] He wants more and more of God until his soul overflows. To that end, the new man, the one who has been truly converted, prays. He takes his petitions to God. He gives voice to a real faith. He rests his hopes in the goodness of his God in whom goodness knows no bounds. "Such is God's goodness," Edwards revelled, "that 'tis with more delight that God bestows great blessings than small ones."[187] For that reason, he added, the new man should take advantage of his privileged status as a child of God and go to him ever more frequently in prayer, seeking his face and asking for greater happiness.

> Therefore let the godly take encouragement from hence in their prayers to come boldly to the throne of grace, and to come frequently. It may well be your delight to you to come to a God that is so ready at all times to hear and to grant whatever you desire that tends to your happiness.[188]

---

185   Edwards, "The Terms of Prayer," *Works*, 19:776.
186   Edwards, "The Terms of Prayer," *Works*, 19:784.
187   Edwards, "The Terms of Prayer," *Works*, 19:785.
188   Edwards, "The Terms of Prayer," *Works*, 19:785.

Chapter 8

Conclusion

Mark Noll once noted that Jonathan Edwards's legacy had been divided. Some students applied his piety to the "revivalist tradition" while others limited his theology to "academic Calvinism." The tragedy, Noll said, is that "there were no successors to his God-entranced worldview."[1] History has cleaved Edwards's piety from his theology and created a Calvinistic curiosity—a preacher who inexplicably held to a system of theology thought to be at odds with practical Christianity.[2]

---

1 Mark Noll, "Jonathan Edwards's Moral Philosophy, and the Secularization of American Christian Thought," *Reformed Journal* 33 (1983):26.

2 Sean Lucas has helpfully explained this tendency in his bibliographical survey. "All too often, the Christian church acts unaware of the academy's best work, while conversely the academy often appears unconcerned about the needs of the church.... Over the past ten years [1993–2003], evangelical publishing houses have produced a mass of books on Edwards that the academy has taken little notice of. Conversely, as the study of Edwards within the academy moves increasingly in trendy directions, church ministers and intelligent laypeople believe the academy's Edwards to be far

Fortunately much has been done to change that misperception in the quarter century since Noll noted his concern. A new generation of pastors and scholars has come to see Edwards as something more than an intellectual freak, an "enigma" as Perry Miller referred to him. They have come to see Edwards as the "extraordinary" man Marsden proclaimed him to be.[3] Some have recognized that "the spiritual always controlled the intellectual in him," that his practice was tied inextricably to his theology.[4] These scholars have extolled the virtue of Edwards as an exemplar, both in heart and mind, as one who "always elevates, always stimulates."[5] Through John Piper, many in the present generation have come to see that Edwards's "soul was great because it was filled with the fullness of God."[6] They have taken Edwards back from the academy and restored him to the church where he always wanted to be. They have reversed the tragedy that was once Edwardsean scholarship.

The effort to rehabilitate Edwards's legacy remains incomplete, however. In spite of the thousands of works and tens of thousands of pages about Edwards that have streamed off the presses, fewer than 100 pages have dared consider one area of Christian thought that Edwards himself thought so vital to the faith: prayer. The present work has sought to rectify that shortcoming and bring Edwards's heart and head, his piety and philosophy, to bear to prove that the two not only can coexist but that they must.

---

from what they themselves find when they read the Northampton divine" [Sean M. Lucas, "Jonathan Edwards Between Church and Academy: A Bibliographic Essay," in *The Legacy of Jonathan Edwards*, eds. D.G. Hart, Sean M. Lucas and Stephen J. Nichols (Grand Rapids: Baker, 2003), 228].

3 Marsden, *Jonathan Edwards: A Life*, 1.
4 Lloyd-Jones, *The Puritans: Their Origins and Successors*, 356.
5 Lloyd-Jones, *The Puritans: Their Origins and Successors*, 366.
6 Piper, *God's Passion for His Glory: Living the Vision of Jonathan Edwards*, 50.

Doctrine

All real and true prayer is the voice of faith.[7]

In "real and true prayer," Edwards maintained, the creature acknowledges God, fulfills his created purpose of glorifying God and enjoys the blessing of God. Therefore, an accurate theology of prayer requires a right understanding of God and man, of the Trinity and man's needs, of divine grace and human faith. As Nichols argued, Edwards anchored "his thoughts on prayer in good theology."[8]

THE FATHER

The character of God drove Edwards's theology. That is no less true of his theology of prayer than his other more well-known notions such as that of the will. Edwards himself argued that prayer arises properly out of one's faith in God for "[t]here is no other way that the heart can look to God, but only looking by faith, by faith seeking the blessing of God, and by faith depending on God for the mercy sought."[9]

Key to Edwards's theology of prayer was the nature of God. It is not enough to pray; one must pray to the right God. To that end, Edwards devoted great attention to God and his attributes. The true God to whom Christians alone pray exhibits the moral quality of absolute goodness or holiness. All that he says or does, all that he loves and gives finds its source in the overflow and outworking of that holiness. God, said Edwards, knows all things including the present and future needs of his people. Moreover, God has the ability to provide all that they need. "[God] can do what he will;" he is all-powerful and sufficient to answer their prayers.

---

7   Edwards, "The Terms of Prayer," *Works*, 19:787.
8   Nichols, *Jonathan Edwards: A Guided Tour of His Life and Thought*, 206.
9   Edwards, "The Terms of Prayer," *Works*, 19:787.

Not only does God hear the prayers of his people and have the wherewithal and ability to answer them, he does just that. God answers prayer. He will not withhold any good from them on account of their relationship with Christ and he stands ready to respond to the prayer of faith. "God is as ready, and more ready, to bestow than we are to ask, and more ready to open than we are to knock."[10] God answers prayer, Edwards said, because of his native goodness. His goodness is "without bounds."[11] Thus, a good God gives good gifts for the good of his people. In the end, God answers prayer to bring his glorious purposes to their righteous ends,[12] the communication of himself and the extension of his glory, and he has appointed prayer as a means to those ends.[13]

When God does answer, he condescends to do so in such a way as to promote greater faith and prayer on the part of the faithful. As Edwards maintained, while it appears "as if" God has been moved by their prayers, in actuality he uses prayer to bring about his predetermined purposes, thus preserving his sovereignty, preparing the human heart to receive his mercy, and promoting the worship of the one true God in further prayer. As Michael Haykin correctly interprets Edwards, "Prayer changes those who pray, preparing them to be the sort of people through whom God can work."[14]

Edwards recognized and freely admitted that God does not answer all prayers. God's silence does not undermine the perfections of God; it proves them. God in his omniscience knows what is best for his people and plan. "It is fit that he should answer prayer, and, as an infinitely wise God, in the exercise of his own wisdom, and not ours." Moreover, by choosing to answer some prayers and pass over others, God demonstrates his sovereignty over all things.[15]

---

10 Edwards, "The Terms of Prayer," *Works*, 19:783.

11 Edwards, "The Terms of Prayer," *Works*, 19:780.

12 Edwards, "Approaching the End of God's Grand Design," *Works*, 25:116.

13 Edwards, "There Is No Goodness in Praying, Though It Be Never So Earnestly, Merely Out of Fear of Misery" (1728), manuscript.

14 Haykin, *Jonathan Edwards: The Holy Spirit in Revival*, 139.

15 Edwards, "The Most High a Prayer-Hearing God," *Works* (Hendrickson), 2:117.

While Edwards joyfully reminded the church in Northampton that the "Most High" is a "God who hears prayer," he never let them forget that they must rightly understand the God to whom they prayed. He is unlike any other god. He is a God "of infinite grace and mercy; a God full of compassion to the miserable, who is ready to pity us under all our troubles and sorrows, to hear our cries, and to give us all the relief which we need; a God who delights in mercy, and is rich unto all that call upon him!"[16]

THE SON

Edwards's theology of prayer savours of a strong Christocentrism as well. Without the person and work of Christ there could be no prayer. Because of Christ, the believer has access to the holy throne of God. "We have a glorious Mediator, who has prepared the way, that our prayers may be heard consistently with the honor of God's justice and majesty," Edwards preached.[17]

In Christ, God has fulfilled his divine purpose of communicating himself and his glory. "Jesus Christ, and that as God-man," Edwards noted, "is the grand medium by which God attains his end, both in communicating himself to the creatures and [in] glorifying himself by the creation."[18] Christ could fulfill this grand task because he himself is God. All the attributes of God were possessed and displayed by Christ. "Everything in the Father, is repeated or expressed again, and that fully, so that there is properly no inferiority."[19] Moreover, Jesus, being fully man as well, fulfills God's covenantal purpose for the human race, complete in his obedience and perfect in his nature. Because Christ, as the incarnate God, possessed the perfect attributes of both God and man, "we have advantage for a far more intimate union and conversa-

---

16 Edwards, "The Most High a Prayer-Hearing God," *Works* (Hendrickson), 2:116.
17 Edwards, "The Most High a Prayer-Hearing God," *Works* (Hendrickson), 2:116.
18 Edwards, "Approaching the End of God's Grand Design," *Works*, 25:117.
19 Edwards, "Miscellanies" No. 1062, *Works*, 20:430.

tion with [God]," Edwards said.[20]

Thanks to the work of Christ, Edwards said, "our prayers may be heard consistently with the honor of God's justice and majesty."[21] Christ's death on the cross has "made the way to the throne of grace open."[22] He has paid man's sin debt and appeased God's wrath. Those who unite with Christ in faith stand justified, declared not guilty by way of Christ's innocence. God sees the believer in the precious light of Christ's perfections not his own failure.

The Christian's present and future happiness are tied to Christ as well. He finds his all, his true happiness in Christ alone. "It is He who clothes them with robes of glory and satisfies the soul with rivers of pleasure."[23] In Christ, he now stands in God's favour, partaking of his love directly. As Edwards argued, all that the Christian seeks and needs God gives out of the abundance of his love for the Son. Better still, Christ now intercedes on the behalf of the faithful, bathing their prayers in his blood. That spiritual reality, said Edwards, offers hope to all who cry out to God. "He hath entered for us into the holy of holies, with the incense which he hath provided," he proclaimed, "and there he makes continual intercession for all that come to God in his name; so that their prayers come to God the Father through his hands."[24]

Thus, for Edwards, prayer necessarily involves the proper understanding and faith in the person and work of Christ. Without Christ man cannot fully know God. Worse still, without Christ man cannot access God. But, through Christ, the faithful stand forgiven in the sight and hearing of God. Therefore, Edwards called his flock to consider the excellency of Christ and place their faith in him for salvation and intercession. "Let us plead with his blood,

---

20 Edwards, "Miscellanies" No. 571, *Works*, 18:110.

21 Edwards, "The Most High a Prayer-Hearing God," *Works* (Hendrickson), 2:116.

22 Edwards, "The Most High a Prayer-Hearing God," *Works* (Hendrickson), 2:116.

23 Edwards, "Christ Is the Christian's All," in *The Puritan Pulpit*, ed. Don Kistler (Morgan, PA: Soli Deo Gloria, 2004), 201.

24 Edwards, "The Most High a Prayer-Hearing God," *Works* (Hendrickson), 2:116.

for our prayers must be purified thereby before God will receive them. Christ has promised that we shall receive whatever we ask in his name."[25]

THE HOLY SPIRIT

As God the Father stands at the headwaters of Edwards's theology of prayer and the Son of God bridges the gap between creature and Creator, the Spirit of God bathes the entire process in the grace of God. He is "the true spirit of prayer."[26] Those in whom the Spirit dwells pray, Edwards believed. They "naturally tend to God in holy breathings and pantings."[27] There is no prayer without the Spirit.

Who is the Holy Spirit? He is, Edwards believed, "the sum of all good."[28] A full-fledged Person of the Trinity—the Spirit is God. He possesses and displays all of the attributes of God. He enjoys an equal measure of glory and honour to that of God and Christ "for he is that divine excellency and beauty [possessed by Father and Son]."[29] Moreover, since the Spirit is God and God is love, the Spirit is love. "The Spirit of God is a spirit of love," Edwards remarked.[30] Love is more than what the Spirit does; love is who the Spirit is. He is that love which flows between Father and Son and between God and man. It is this love, the Spirit of God, that calls man back to God, enables man to love God, and encourages man to talk to God.

In every act of God's self-revelation the Spirit has been involved. The Spirit moved on the waters in the creation. The Spirit inspired the authors of Scripture. The power of the Spirit came upon Mary in the incarnation. While God reveals himself now by the Spirit in common grace directed toward all men, the special work of the Spirit

---

25 Edwards, "Christ's Sacrifice," *Works*, 10:602.

26 Edwards, "Hypocrites Deficient in the Duty of Prayer," in ed. Nichols, *Seeking God*, 359.

27 Edwards, "Hypocrites Deficient in the Duty of Prayer," in ed. Nichols, *Seeking God*, 359.

28 Edwards, "Treatise on Grace," *Works*, 21:188.

29 Edwards, "Discourse on the Trinity," *Works*, 21:135.

30 Edwards, *Charity and Its Fruit*, *Works*, 8:132.

is that of the re-creation. In salvation, the Spirit acts immediately upon the soul of the elect. "'Tis of him that we are in Christ Jesus; 'tis the Spirit of God that gives us faith in him, whereby we receive him, and close with him," Edwards announced.[31] Moreover, in salvation, the Spirit gives more than the ability to believe. He gives himself and takes up permanent residence in the believer. Throughout the believer's subsequent life, the Spirit continues to work, drawing him ever closer to God through Christ. Thus, salvation from beginning to end, from regeneration to glorification, reflects Edwards's theocentric approach to all theology: "all is *of* the Father, all *through* the Son, and all *in* the Holy Ghost."[32]

The Spirit's work does not end with salvation, Edwards reminded his hearers. The Spirit of God plays a vital role in prayer as well. He facilitates the prayer relationship between the believer and God. He steers the Christian through providence and internal urgings toward God's throne. He makes the believer holy and willing. He teaches him how to pray.[33] Christians are to seek to be filled with the Spirit, led by the Spirit and sanctified by the Spirit. With God in them they become more like God. For this they are to pray. "The good, that shall be sought by prayer," Edwards noted, "is God himself."[34] This prayer God always answers.[35]

Edwards's theology of prayer stands or falls with his understanding of the Holy Spirit. Without the Spirit there is no new birth. Without the Spirit there is no spiritual growth. Without the Spirit there is no prayer. But, with the Spirit, come great blessings, the greatest of which is the Spirit himself. In fact, said Edwards, the Spirit is the "sum of all blessings"[36] and should be "the chief subject matter of prayer."[37]

---

31 Edwards, "God Glorified in Man's Dependence," *Works*, 17:201.

32 Edwards, "God Glorified in Man's Dependence," *Works*, 17:212.

33 Edwards, "Christians a Chosen Generation," *Works*, 17:303.

34 Edwards, *An Humble Attempt*, *Works*, 5:315.

35 Edwards, "The Terms of Prayer," *Works*, 19:785.

36 Edwards, "Miscellanies" No. 755, *Works*, 18:404.

37 Edwards, "Suitableness of Union in Extraordinary Prayer," *Works*, 25:203.

MAN

As George Claghorn rightly said, "Personal communion with the Almighty…was to be a hallmark of [Edwards's] theology."[38] He directed everything to that end. He urged his people to come to God. That they might understand the necessity and privilege of prayer, Edwards shined the bright spotlight of his intellect on the nature of man, fallen and restored, and faith. He called the faithful to prayer.

A true appreciation for prayer does not start with what one might get but what one has lost. Man, in his created state, "enjoyed the favor of God and smiles of heaven."[39] Adam, as the federal head of all humanity, was created in the image of God for the purpose of fellowship with God. He was righteous and he was free and he communed with God. "Here is the happiness he had in intercourse with God, for his thus talking with him in this friendly manner," Edwards commented.[40]

Adam, however, opted for something less than the perfect relationship for which he was created. Rather than choosing to love God above all else, Adam allowed his love for self to reign. In a moment of weakness and evil, Adam fell and forever "lost God's favor and smiles."[41] He forfeited all claims to true happiness. Now the descendents of Adam are bound in their sins, wholly ruined and "totally corrupt," heart, mind and will.[42] Whereas Adam once walked with God, his progeny cannot even pray to him.[43] Their prayers, when they do bother, are offered up without proper regard to God and without faith. As such, he said, "'tis no real prayer in the sight of God."[44] Thus, fellowship with God has been broken and happiness lost.

---

38 Claghorn, "Editor's Introduction," *Works*, 16:745.

39 Edwards, "East of Eden," *Works*, 17:334.

40 Edwards, *Notes on Scripture*, *Works*, 15:395.

41 Edwards, "East of Eden," *Works*, 17:335.

42 Edwards, "The Justice of God in the Damnation of Sinners," *Works*, 19:344.

43 Edwards, "It Becomes Saints in Cases of Special Difficulty and Calamity of God's Church, to Betake Themselves in an Extraordinary Manner to Prayer to God" (1750), manuscript.

44 Edwards, "The Terms of Prayer," *Works*, 19:787.

Yet, God offers the gospel as the only means of hope to a fallen world. Though it is freely offered, it is freely rejected. For that reason, God must and does, in his grace, freely elect some to salvation that they might gain what Adam lost. They are chosen for "the highest happiness."[45] God himself brings them to salvation by the regenerative work of the Spirit. Renewed by the Spirit, the elect see the excellency of the Christ and the beauty of God's sovereignty and surrender themselves to divine care.[46] In faith, they believe that Christ is sufficient for their salvation and unite with him actively becoming one with him. In light of this faith in Christ, God deals with the individual not as he deserves but as Christ deserves, as one who is wholly righteous and worthy of God's favour.[47]

With regeneration and justification comes restoration. The believer, trusting in Christ and filled with the Spirit, can once again enjoy the fellowship with God that Adam lost in the Garden. By faith, he looks to God. He exercises and proves his faith in prayer. He approaches the throne of God confident in the blood of Christ, compelled by the Spirit, and convinced that God loves him. He knows and believes that God withholds nothing from those he loves as too good for them.[48] The true lover of God, saved by the love of God, voicing his faith in God, once again "experiences the pleasures of communion with God."[49] In God alone, the believer finally finds true freedom and his long lost happiness, the happiness for which he was created, because in prayer he finds God.

SUMMARY

Edwards's theology of prayer begins and ends with God. In all of his Trinitarian glory, God is the source and sum of all grace. He created

---

45 Edwards, "Miscellanies" No. 702, *Works*, 18:299.

46 Edwards, "Faith," *Works*, 21:428.

47 Edwards, "Justification by Faith Alone," *Works*, 19:148.

48 Edwards, "The Terms of Prayer," *Works*, 19:777.

49 Edwards, "True Love to God," *Works*, 10:640. Those who do not pray prove not to be the elect (Edwards, "Hypocrites Deficient in the Duty of Prayer," in ed. Nichols, *Seeking God*, 365).

for his own glory; he sent his Son for his own glory; he gives his Spirit for his own glory. In saving fallen men, God resumes communion with them that they might glorify and enjoy him forever, that they might seek him and savour him.[50] For that reason, "God ought to be worshipped by prayer."[51]

Application

And so that may still be true which was before asserted, that God always hears the prayer of FAITH.[52]

Knowing why and how one should and can pray was but one part of Edwards's theology of prayer. He believed these things and he lived these things. Moreover, he taught these things to his people so that they would express greater faithfulness in prayer. To that end, every sermon of Edwards included a call to action. Thus, with Martyn Lloyd-Jones we say, "to end [this work] without application would be false to the memory of this great man of God."[53]

While every sermon on prayer contains points of application, one sermon in particular provides a helpful outline of Edwards's thoughts. In the sermon "God's Manner Is First to Prepare Men's Hearts and Then to Answer Their Prayers," Edwards taught his people "how to attend this duty of prayer so that [their] hearts may be prepared for the mercy [they sought]."[54] The directions given there are echoed and fleshed out in many of his other works. Moreover, they provide the present-day reader with a model for

---

50 Edwards saw the glorification of God and man's enjoyment of him as being one and the same (Edwards, "Approaching the End of God's Grand Design," *Works*, 25:116–117). See also, "Nothing upon Earth Can Represent the Glories of Heaven," *Works*, 14:144 n. 7.

51 Edwards, "Miscellanies" No. 749, *Works*, 18:397.

52 Edwards, "The Most High a Prayer-Hearing God," *Works* (Hendrickson), 2:117.

53 Lloyd-Jones, *The Puritans: Their Origins and Successors*, 367.

54 Edwards, "God's Manner Is First to Prepare Men's Hearts and Then to Answer Their Prayers," in ed. McMullen, *The Glory and Honor of God*, 94.

effective prayer that maintains Edwards's theocentric passion.

HUMILITY

Believers must recognize their "need of those spiritual benefits" that they seek. They need to see their present condition for what it is. For those whose hearts are hardened, they need to acknowledge the need for awakening.[55] Those who are weak must cry for strength. Those who lack faith unto salvation need to go to God without distraction.[56] Those who are divided need unity.[57] Recognition alone, however, fails to satisfy the need for preparation. Those who have such needs must ready their hearts for the mercy they seek. Those in sin need a thorough reformation of life.[58] They need to be, he preached on another occasion, "very much in confessing [their] sins to God in [their] prayers."[59]

In doing so, Edwards was not encouraging the church in Northampton to something they could not do. He was not calling for the spiritual renewal that is the work of the Holy Spirit. Rather, he implored them to show that humility that falls only to man—a humility that admits God's greatness and man's weakness. The prayer must come to God readily admitting that he needs God and is ready to meet him.

SINCERITY

The believer must also "be earnest in prayer" and "importunate."[60] Earnestness, he believed, reveals the sincerity of one's humility. The

55 Edwards, "God's Manner Is First to Prepare Men's Hearts and Then to Answer Their Prayers," in ed. McMullen, *The Glory and Honor of God*, 94.

56 Edwards, "God's Manner Is First to Prepare Men's Hearts and Then to Answer Their Prayers," in ed. McMullen, *The Glory and Honor of God*, 94–95.

57 Edwards, "God's Manner Is First to Prepare Men's Hearts and Then to Answer Their Prayers," in ed. McMullen, *The Glory and Honor of God*, 95.

58 Edwards, "God's Manner Is First to Prepare Men's Hearts and Then to Answer Their Prayers," in ed. McMullen, *The Glory and Honor of God*, 96.

59 Edwards, "Conviction and the Uses of Order," *Works*, 19:268.

60 Edwards, "God's Manner Is First to Prepare Men's Hearts and Then to Answer Their Prayers," in ed. McMullen, *The Glory and Honor of God*, 99.

one who prays earnestly prays passionately. He longs for and desires that which is holy and wholly beyond his reach.

Edwards demanded this of himself. In his diary, he remarked that "it is best to be careful in prayer, not to put up those petitions, of which I do not feel a sincere desire." Such prayers are "less sincere, less acceptable to God, and less useful."[61] The persistent widow in Luke 18, Edwards said, exhibited the kind of earnestness that was needed.[62]

Edwards reiterated the call for earnestness with the word "importunate." The importunate prayer is the one who gives "God no rest" till he answers.[63] To ensure that they are eager for God's blessing and desperate for his grace, they must be free of the dullness of heart and "careless prayers" that undermine the sense of urgency needed. To that end, Edwards reminded his hearers that they must be earnest "in wrestling" with the weakness of the flesh as well.[64] Regardless of the vocabulary applied, Edwards knew that "earnest prayer does abundantly more towards preparing the heart than other prayer."[65]

COMMITMENT

The person who is truly earnest will be also "frequent and constant in prayer."[66] He will pray "at all times" and "without ceasing." In this, Edwards was not advocating some sort of pious legalism. The constancy to which Edwards called them was not to be regulated by a rigid schedule or a prescribed set of prayers. He did not encourage them to neglect other religious duties or secular employment.

---

61 Edwards, "Diary," *Works*, 16:773.

62 Edwards, "God's Manner Is First to Prepare Men's Hearts and Then to Answer Their Prayers," in ed. McMullen, *The Glory and Honor of God*, 99.

63 Edwards, "Importunate Prayer for Millennial Glory" *Works*, 22:369.

64 Edwards, "God's Manner Is First to Prepare Men's Hearts and Then to Answer Their Prayers," in ed. McMullen, *The Glory and Honor of God*, 100.

65 Edwards, "God's Manner Is First to Prepare Men's Hearts and Then to Answer Their Prayers," in ed. McMullen, *The Glory and Honor of God*, 100.

66 Edwards, "God's Manner Is First to Prepare Men's Hearts and Then to Answer Their Prayers," in ed. McMullen, *The Glory and Honor of God*, 100.

Rather, he called them to regular versus intermittent prayer.[67] Prayer was to be a constant expression of their faith not just an activity to which they retreated in times of trouble. Prayer is not to be just something they do sporadically but the ongoing outworking of who they are in relationship to God. Those that are most close to God are "at all times to abound in prayer."[68]

PATIENCE

The prayer must commit himself to "earnest prayer to the end."[69] Do not begin, he said, with any thought of "slackening."[70] One must plan to persevere, to commit to a long and arduous season in which God might delay his answers in order to prepare them for greater blessings. To aid the Christian in this task, he suggested, "Consider how much you always stand in need of the help of God."[71] The believer's dependence upon God never decreases; neither should his prayers.

Likewise, when tempted to stop praying for a particular blessing, Edwards reminded his people, never forget that the blessings may be closer than realized.[72] To let up too soon may be to surrender that which was imminent. Edwards further cautioned against thinking too lightly of one's ability to persevere. "Many people," he said, "think they are most unprepared when they are indeed most

---

67 Edwards, "God's Manner Is First to Prepare Men's Hearts and Then to Answer Their Prayers," in ed. McMullen, *The Glory and Honor of God*, 100.

68 Edwards, "The Suitableness of Union in Extraordinary Prayer for the Advancement of God's Church" (1747), Beinecke Rare Book and Manuscript Library, Yale University, New Haven.

69 Edwards, "God's Manner Is First to Prepare Men's Hearts and Then to Answer Their Prayers," in ed. McMullen, *The Glory and Honor of God*, 104.

70 Edwards, "God's Manner Is First to Prepare Men's Hearts and Then to Answer Their Prayers," in ed. McMullen, *The Glory and Honor of God*, 104.

71 Edwards, "Hypocrites Deficient in the Duty of Prayer," in ed. Nichols, *Seeking God*, 371.

72 Edwards, "God's Manner Is First to Prepare Men's Hearts and Then to Answer Their Prayers," in ed. McMullen, *The Glory and Honor of God*, 105.

prepared."[73] God sometimes delays his answers not to prove the believer's faith but to improve it. As he said elsewhere, "Hereby, they will most be likely to find their insufficiency to reach the good they seek of themselves; and how dependent are they on the power, and arbitrary pleasure, of God for the bestowment; and so are best prepared to acknowledge God on it, when bestowed."[74]

GOD-CENTRED

While Edwards did not include an open call for a theocentric approach to prayer in "God's Manner," such advice runs through all of his teaching on the subject. The centrality of God was not ancillary to prayer but the ground of it. As he argued in "It Becomes Saints in Cases of Special Difficulty and Calamity of God's Church, to Betake Themselves in an Extraordinary Manner to Prayer to God," prayer is a beautiful thing in that it reveals and revels in the relationship of the creature to the Creator.

> Thus prayer is a duty incumbent on all mankind but 'tis a duty especially becoming saints. [It] becomes the acquaintance they have with God. [It] becomes that peculiar relation they have to God. [It] becomes that peculiar concern they have with God....[It] becomes the ends for which they are made saints: To glorify God.[75]

Benediction

The accolades shed upon Edwards through the years have always been full of superlatives. Either he was loved or he was loathed.

---

73 Edwards, "God's Manner Is First to Prepare Men's Hearts And Then to Answer Their Prayers," in ed. McMullen, *The Glory and Honor of God*, 105.

74 Edwards, "Blessed Struggle," *Works*, 19:425.

75 Edwards, "It Becomes Saints in Cases of Special Difficulty and Calamity of God's Church, to Betake Themselves in an Extraordinary Manner to Prayer to God" (1750), manuscript.

Either he was the greatest or the worst. Regardless of one's presuppositions concerning Edwards or his theological leanings, all must seriously consider Sereno Dwight's appraisal of Edwards's legacy.

> The number of those men, who have produced great and permanent changes in the character and condition of mankind, and stamped their own image on the minds of succeeding generations, is comparatively small; and, even of this small number, the great body have been indebted for their superior efficiency, at least in part, to extraneous circumstances, while very few can ascribe it to the simple strength of their own intellect. Yet here and there an individual can be found, who, by his mere mental energy, has changed the course of human thought and feeling, and led mankind onward in that new and better path which he had opened to their view.
>
> Such an individual was JONATHAN EDWARDS.[76]

In the end, history has largely agreed, pronouncing Edwards "America's greatest theologian."[77] Other titles have been added along the way: "theologian of the heart"[78] and "theologian of revival,"[79] among others. May it be that as we finish this study Edwards will now be remembered as the theologian of prayer as well.

---

76 Dwight, *Life of Edwards*, 2.

77 Robert W. Jenson, *America's Theologian: A Recommendation of Jonathan Edwards* (New York: Oxford University Press, 1998), 3.

78 Harold P. Simonson, *Jonathan Edwards: Theologian of the Heart* (Grand Rapids: Eerdmans, 1974).

79 Lloyd-Jones, *The Puritans: Their Origins and Successors*, 361.

Bibliography

Primary sources

PUBLISHED

Edwards, Jonathan. *Apocalyptic Writings.* Vol. 5 of *The Works of Jonathan Edwards.* Edited by Stephen J. Stein. New Haven: Yale University Press, 1977.

_____. *Awakening: The Essential Writings of Jonathan Edwards.* Edited by Bernard Bangley. Brewster, MA: Paraclete, 2004.

_____. *Basic Writings.* Edited by Ola E. Winslow. New York: New American Library, 1966.

_____. *The Blank Bible.* Vol. 24 of *The Works of Jonathan Edwards,* in two parts. Edited by Stephen J. Stein. New Haven: Yale University Press, 2006.

_____. *The Blessing of God.* Edited by Michael D. McMullen. Nashville: Broadman & Holman, 2003.

_____. *Catalogue of Books.* Vol. 26 of *The Works of Jonathan Edwards.* Edited by Peter J. Thuesen. New Haven: Yale University Press, [forthcoming].

_____. *Ecclesiastical Writings.* Vol. 12 of *The Works of Jonathan Edwards.* Edited by David D. Hall. New Haven: Yale University Press, 1994.

_____. *Ethical Writings.* Vol. 8 of *The Works of Jonathan Edwards.* Edited by Paul Ramsey. New Haven: Yale University Press, 1989.

_____. *Freedom of the Will.* Vol. 1 of *The Works of Jonathan Edwards.* Edited by Paul Ramsey. New Haven: Yale University Press, 1957.

_____. *The Glory and Honor of God.* Edited by Michael D. McMullen. Nashville: Broadman & Holman, 2004.

_____. *The Great Awakening.* Vol. 4 of *The Works of Jonathan Edwards.* Edited by C.C. Goen. New Haven: Yale University Press, 1972.

_____. *A History of the Work of Redemption.* Vol. 9 of *The Works of Jonathan Edwards.* Edited by John F. Wilson. New Haven: Yale University Press, 1989.

_____. *Images or Shadows of Divine Things.* Edited by Perry Miller. New Haven: Yale University Press, 1948.

_____. *Jonathan Edwards: Containing 16 Sermons Unpublished in Edwards' Lifetime.* Morgan, PA: Soli Deo Gloria, 2004.

_____. *A Jonathan Edwards Reader.* Edited by John E. Smith, Harry S. Stout, and Kenneth P. Minkema. New Haven: Yale University Press, 1995.

_____. *Jonathan Edwards' Resolutions And Advice to Young Converts.* Edited by Stephen J. Nichols. Phillipsburg, NJ: Presbyterian & Reformed, 2001.

_____. *Knowing the Heart: Jonathan Edwards on True and False Conversion.* Edited by William C. Nichols. Ames, IA: International Outreach, 2003.

_____. *Letters and Personal Writings.* Vol. 16 of *The Works of Jonathan Edwards.* Edited by George S. Claghorn. New Haven: Yale University Press, 1998.

_____. *The Life of David Brainerd.* Vol. 7 of *The Works of Jonathan Edwards.* Edited by Norman Pettit. New Haven: Yale University Press, 1985.

_____. *The "Miscellanies": Entry Nos. a–z, aa–zz, 1–500.* Vol. 13 of *The Works of Jonathan Edwards.* Edited by Thomas A. Schafer. New Haven: Yale University Press, 1994.

_____. *The "Miscellanies": Entry Nos. 501–832.* Vol. 18 of *The Works of Jonathan Edwards.* Edited by Ava Chamberlain. New Haven: Yale University Press, 2000.

_____. *The "Miscellanies": Entry Nos. 833–1152.* Vol. 20 of *The Works of Jonathan Edwards.* Edited by Amy Plantinga Pauw. New Haven: Yale University Press, 2002.

_____. *The "Miscellanies": Entry Nos. 1153–1360.* Vol. 23 of *The Works of Jonathan Edwards.* Edited by Douglas A. Sweeney. New Haven: Yale University Press, 2004.

_____. *Notes on Scripture.* Vol. 15 of *The Works of Jonathan Edwards.* Edited by Stephen J. Stein. New Haven: Yale University Press, 1998.

_____. *Original Sin.* Vol. 3 of *The Works of Jonathan Edwards.* Edited by Clyde A. Holbrook. New Haven: Yale University, 1970.

_____. *Praying Together for True Revival.* Edited by T. M. Moore. Phillipsburg, NJ: Presbyterian & Reformed, 2004.

_____. *The Puritan Pulpit: Jonathan Edwards.* Edited by Don Kistler. Morgan, PA: Soli Deo Gloria, 2004.

_____. *Religious Affections.* Vol. 2 of *The Works of Jonathan Edwards.* Edited by John E. Smith. New Haven: Yale University Press, 1959.

_____. *The Salvation of Souls: Nine Previously Unpublished Sermons on the Call of Ministry and the Gospel by Jonathan Edwards.* Edited by Richard A. Bailey and Gregory A. Wills. Wheaton: Crossway, 2002.

_____. *Scientific and Philosophical Writings.* Vol. 6 of *The Works of Jonathan Edwards.* Edited by Wallace E. Anderson. New Haven: Yale University Press, 1980.

_____. *Seeking God: Jonathan Edwards' Evangelism Contrasted with Modern Methodologies.* Edited by William C. Nichols. Ames, IA: International Outreach, 2001.

_____. *Sermons and Discourses, 1720–1723.* Vol. 10 of *The Works of Jonathan Edwards.* Edited by Wilson H. Kimnach. New Haven: Yale University Press, 1992.

_____. *Sermons and Discourses, 1723–1729.* Vol. 14 of *The Works of Jonathan Edwards.* Edited by Kenneth P. Minkema. New Haven: Yale University Press, 1997.

_____. *Sermons and Discourses, 1730–1733.* Vol. 17 of *The Works of Jonathan Edwards.* Edited by Mark R. Valeri. New Haven: Yale University Press, 1999.

_____. *Sermons and Discourses, 1734–1738.* Vol. 19 of *The Works of Jonathan Edwards.* Edited by M. X. Lesser. New Haven: Yale University Press, 2001.

_____. *Sermons and Discourses, 1739–1742.* Vol. 22 of *The Works of Jonathan Edwards.* Edited by Harry S. Stout, Nathan O. Hatch, and Kyle P. Farley. New Haven: Yale University Press, 2003.

_____. *Sermons and Discourses, 1743–1758.* Vol. 25 of *The Works of Jonathan Edwards.* Edited by Wilson H. Kimnach. New Haven: Yale University Press, 2006.

_____. *The Sermons of Jonathan Edwards: A Reader.* Edited by Wilson H. Kimnach, Kenneth P. Minkema, and Douglas A. Sweeney. New Haven: Yale University Press, 1999.

_____. *To All the Saints of God: Addresses to the Church.* Edited by Don Kistler. Morgan, PA: Soli Deo Gloria, 2003.

_____. *To the Rising Generation: Addresses Given to Children and Young Adults.* Edited by Don Kistler. Morgan, PA: Soli Deo Gloria, 2005.

_____. *Typological Writings.* Vol. 11 of *The Works of Jonathan Edwards.* Edited by Wallace E. Anderson, Mason I. Lowance, and David H. Watters. New Haven: Yale University Press, 1993.

_____. *The Works of Jonathan Edwards.* 2 vols. Peabody, MA: Hendrickson, 1998.

_____. *Writings on the Trinity, Grace, and Faith.* Vol. 21 of *The Works of Jonathan Edwards.* Edited by Sang Hyun Lee. New Haven: Yale University Press, 2003.

UNPUBLISHED

Edwards, Jonathan. "Fast for the Pouring Out of the Spirit" (1740). Beinecke Rare Book and Manuscript Library, Yale University, New Haven.

_____. "How True Believers Receive Christ" (1755). Beinecke Rare Book and Manuscript Library, Yale University, New Haven.

_____. "If a People in a Time of Sore Drought Acknowledge God and Turn from Their Sins Which Procure this Judgment, and Go to God Through Christ by Prayer and Supplication, 'Tis the Way for Them Both to Obtain the Temporal Blessing They Need, and Also to Obtain Great Spiritual Blessings that are Far Better" (1730). Beinecke Rare Book and Manuscript Library, Yale University, New Haven.

_____. "If We Would Be in the Way of God's Grace and Blessing, We Must Wait upon Him in His Own Way and in the Use of His Appointed Means" (1729). Beinecke Rare Book and Manuscript Library, Yale University, New Haven.

_____. "It Becomes Saints in Cases of Special Difficulty and Calamity of God's Church, to Betake Themselves in an Extraordinary Manner to Prayer to God" (1750). Beinecke Rare Book and Manuscript Library, Yale University, New Haven.

_____. "One of the Main Subjects of Christian Prayer Ought to be the Advancement of the Interest of Religion in the World" (1749). Beinecke Rare Book and Manuscript Library, Yale University, New Haven.

_____. "A Person That Maintains Grace in Lively Exercise Is as It Were Never Alone" (1752). Beinecke Rare Book and Manuscript Library, Yale University, New Haven.

_____. "Persons Ought to Do What They Can for Their Salvation" (1733). Beinecke Rare Book and Manuscript Library, Yale University, New Haven.

_____. "The Prayers of Saints Is a Great and Principal Means of Carrying on the Great Designs of Christ's Kingdom in the World" (1742). Beinecke Rare Book and Manuscript Library, Yale University, New Haven.

_____. "Sermon on Luke 18:1" (1753). Beinecke Rare Book and Manuscript Library, Yale University, New Haven.

_____. "The Suitableness of Union in Extraordinary Prayer for the Advancement of God's Church" (1747). Beinecke Rare Book and Manuscript Library, Yale University, New Haven.

_____. "That No Religion Is Acceptable to God but That Which Is Done from a True Respect to Him" (n.d.). Beinecke Rare Book and Manuscript Library, Yale University, New Haven.

_____. "There Is No Goodness in Praying, Though It Be Never So Earnestly, Merely Out of Fear of Misery" (1728). Beinecke Rare Book and Manuscript Library, Yale University, New Haven.

_____. "There Is Such a Thing as Conversion" (1740). Beinecke Rare Book and Manuscript Library, Yale University, New Haven.

_____. "Tho a People That Live Under Means Are Wont in General to Seek and Hope for Salvation, Yet 'Tis the Elect Only That Obtains It and the Rest Are Blinded" (1740). Andover Newton Theological School, Newton Centre.

_____. "'Tis in Vain for Any to Expect to Have Their Prayers Heard as Long as They Continue in the Allowance of Sin" (1739). Andover Newton Theology School, Newton Centre.

_____. "'Tis the Duty of God's People to be Much in Prayer for that Great Outpouring of the Spirit That God Has Promised Shall Be in the Latter Days" (1746). Beinecke Rare Book and Manuscript Library, Yale University, New Haven.

_____. "We Are All in Ourselves Utterly Without Any Strength or Power to Help Ourselves" (1735). Beinecke Rare Book and Manuscript Library, Yale University, New Haven.

_____. "When That Wonderful Time of the Outpouring of the Spirit of God Comes That Will Introduce the Glorious Times of the Church on Earth" (1741). Beinecke Rare Book and Manuscript Library, Yale University, New Haven.

Secondary sources

BOOKS

Ahlstrom, Sydney E. *A Religious History of the American People*. New Haven: Yale University Press, 1972.

Aldridge, Alfred O. *Jonathan Edwards*. New York: Washington Square, 1964.

Allen, Alexander V.G. *Jonathan Edwards*. Boston: Houghton Mifflin, 1889.

Ames, William. *The Marrow of Theology*. Grand Rapids: Baker, 1997.

Bakke, Robert O. *The Power of Extraordinary Prayer*. Wheaton: Crossway, 2000.

Brown, Robert E. *Jonathan Edwards and the Bible*. Bloomington: Indiana University Press, 2002.

Calvin, John. *Institutes of Christ Religion*. Edited by John T. McNeill. Translated by Ford L. Battles. Louisville: Westminster John Knox Press, 1960.

The Cambridge Companion to Jonathan Edwards. Edited by Stephen J. Stein. Cambridge: Cambridge University Press, 2006.

Carse, James P. *Jonathan Edwards & the Visibility of God*. New York: Scribner, 1967.

Chai, Leon. *Jonathan Edwards and the Limits of Enlightenment Philosophy*. New York: Oxford University Press, 1998.

Cherry, Conrad. *The Theology of Jonathan Edwards: A Reappraisal*. Bloomington: Indiana University Press, 1990.

Conforti, Joseph A. *Jonathan Edwards, Religious Tradition & American Culture*. Chapel Hill: University of North Carolina Press, 1995.

Crampton, W. Gary. *Jonathan Edwards: An Introduction to America's Greatest Theology/Philosopher*. Morgan, PA: Soli Deo Gloria, 2004.

Crisp, Oliver. *Jonathan Edwards and the Metaphysics of Sin*. Aldershot, England: Ashgate, 2005.

Danaher, William J. *The Trinitarian Ethics of Jonathan Edwards*.

Louisville: Westminster John Knox, 2004.

Daniel, Stephen H. *The Philosophy of Jonathan Edwards: A Study in Divine Semiotics.* Bloomington: Indiana University Press, 1994.

Delattre, Roland A. *Beauty and Sensibility in the Thought of Jonathan Edwards: An Essay in Aesthetics and Theological Ethics.* New Haven: Yale University Press, 1968.

Dodds, Elisabeth D. *Marriage to a Difficult Man: The "Uncommon Union" of Jonathan and Sarah Edwards.* Philadelphia: Westminster Press, 1971.

Dwight, Sereno E. *The Life of President Edwards.* New York: G. & C. & H. Carvill, 1830.

Edwards in Our Time. Edited by Sang H. Lee and Allen C. Guelzo. Grand Rapids: Eerdmans, 1999.

Finney, Charles G. *Lectures on Revival.* Fenwick, MI: Alethea in Heart, 2005.

Gardiner, Harry N. *The Early Idealism of Jonathan Edwards.* [Boston: n.p.], 1900.

Gerstner, Edna. *Jonathan and Sarah: An Uncommon Union.* Morgan, PA: Soli Deo Gloria, 1995.

Gerstner, John H. *Jonathan Edwards: Evangelist.* Morgan, PA: Soli Deo Gloria, 1995.

Gerstner, John H. *Jonathan Edwards: A Mini-Theology.* Morgan, PA: Soli Deo Gloria, 1996.

Gerstner, John H. *The Rational Biblical Theology of Jonathan Edwards.* Powhatan, VA and Orlando, FL: Berea Publications and Ligonier Ministries, 1991.

A God Entranced Vision of All Things. Edited by John Piper and Justin Taylor. Wheaton: Crossway, 2004.

Guelzo, Allen C. *Edwards on the Will: A Century of American Theological Debate.* Middletown, CT: Wesleyan University Press, 1989.

Gura, Philip F. *Jonathan Edwards: America's Evangelical.* New York: Hill and Wang, 2005.

Hambrick-Stowe, Charles E. *The Practice of Piety: Puritan Devotional Disciplines in Seventeenth-Century New England.* Chapel Hill, NC:

University of North Carolina Press, 1985.

Hannah, John D. *To God Be the Glory*. Wheaton: Crossway, 2000.

Haykin, Michael A.G. *Jonathan Edwards: The Holy Spirit in Revival.* Webster, NY: Evangelical Press, 2005.

Haykin, Michael A.G. *A Sweet Flame: Piety in the Letters of Jonathan Edwards*. Grand Rapids: Reformation Heritage, 2007.

Holifield, E. Brooks. *Theology in America: Christian Thought from the Age of the Puritans to the Civil War.* New Haven: Yale University Press, 2003.

Holifield, E. Brooks. *God's Ambassadors: A History of the Christian Clergy in America*. Grand Rapids: Eerdmans, 2007.

Holmes, Stephen R. *God of Grace and God of Glory: An Account of the Theology of Jonathan Edwards.* Grand Rapids: Eerdmans, 2001.

Hopkins, Samuel. *The Life of the Reverend Mr. Jonathan Edwards.* Boston: S. Keeneland, 1765. Reprint, Northampton, MA: Andrew Wright, 1804.

Jenson, Robert W. *America's Theologian: A Recommendation of Jonathan Edwards*. New York: Oxford University Press, 1988.

Jonathan Edwards, A Retrospect. Edited by Harry N. Gardiner. Boston: Houghton, Mifflin, 1901.

Jonathan Edwards at Home and Abroad: Historical Memories, Cultural Movements, Global Horizons. Edited by David W. Kling and Douglas A. Sweeney. Columbia: University of South Carolina Press, 2003.

Jonathan Edwards at 300: Essays on the Tercentenary of His Birth. Edited by Harry S. Stout, Kenneth P. Minkema, and Caleb J.D. Maskell. Lanham, MD: University Press of America, 2005.

Jonathan Edwards: His Life and Influence. Edited by Charles Angoff. Rutherford, NJ: Fairleigh Dickinson, 1975.

Jonathan Edwards: Philosophical Theologian. Edited by Paul Helm and Oliver Crisp. Aldershot, England: Ashgate, 2003.

Lee, Sang H. *The Philosophical Theology of Jonathan Edwards*. Princeton: Princeton University Press, 1988.

Legacy of Jonathan Edwards: American Religion and the Evangelical

Tradition, The. Edited by D.G. Hart, Sean Michael Lucas, and Stephen J. Nichols. Grand Rapids: Baker, 2003.

Lesser, M. X. *Jonathan EDWARDS: A Reference Guide.* Boston: G. K. Hall, 1981.

Lesser, M. X. *Jonathan Edwards: An Annotated Bibliography, 1979-1993.* Westport, CT: Greenwood, 1994.

Lesser, M. X. *The Printed Writings of Jonathan Edwards: A Bibliography.* Princeton: Princeton University Press, 2003.

Lloyd-Jones, D. Martyn. *The Puritans: Their Origins and Successors.* Carlisle, PA: Banner of Truth, 1997.

Lovelace, Richard F. *Dynamics of Spiritual Life: An Evangelical Theology of Renewal.* Downers Grove: InterVarsity, 1979.

Manspeaker, Nancy. *Jonathan Edwards, Bibliographical Synopses.* New York: Edwin Mellen, 1981.

Marsden, George M. *Jonathan Edwards: A Life.* New Haven: Yale University Press, 2003.

Marty, Martin E. *Pilgrims in Their Own Land: 500 Years of Religion in America.* New York: Penguin, 1985.

McClymond, Michael J. *Encounters with God: An Approach to the Theology of Jonathan Edwards.* New York: Oxford University Press, 1998.

McDermott, Gerald R. *Jonathan Edwards Confronts the Gods: Christian Theology, Enlightenment Religion, and Non-Christian Faiths.* New York: Oxford University Press, 2000.

McDermott, Gerald R. *One Holy and Happy Society: The Public Theology of Jonathan Edwards.* University Park: Pennsylvania State University Press, 1992.

McDermott, Gerald R. *Seeing God: Twelve Reliable Signs of True Spirituality.* Downers Grove: InterVarsity, 1995.

McGiffert, Arthur Cushman. *Jonathan Edwards.* New York: Harper & Brothers, 1932.

Miller, Perry. *Errand into the Wilderness.* Cambridge, MA: Harvard University Press, 1956.

Miller, Perry. *Jonathan Edwards.* New York: W. Sloane Associates, 1949.

Miller, Perry. *The New England Mind: From Colony to Province.* Cambridge, MA: Harvard University Press, 1983.

Miller, Perry. *The New England Mind: The Seventeenth Century.* Cambridge, MA: Harvard University Press, 1983.

Moody, Josh. *The God-Centered Life: Insights from Jonathan Edwards for Today.* Vancouver, BC: Regent College Publishing, 2007.

Moody, Josh. *Jonathan Edwards and the Enlightenment: Knowing the Presence of God.* Lanham, MD: University Press of America, 2005.

Morgan, Chris. *Jonathan Edwards & Hell.* Ross-shire, Scotland: Mentor, 2004.

Morimoto, Anri. *Jonathan Edwards and the Catholic Vision of Salvation.* University Park: Pennsylvania State University Press, 1995.

Morris, William S. *The Young Jonathan Edwards: A Reconstruction.* Brooklyn: Carlson, 1991.

Murray, Iain H. *Jonathan Edwards: A New Biography.* Carlisle, PA: Banner of Truth, 1987.

Murray, Iain H. *The Puritan Hope: Revival and the Interpretation of Prophecy.* Carlisle, PA: Banner of Truth, 1971.

Murray, Iain H. *Revival and Revivalism: The Making and Marring of American Evangelicalism, 1750–1858.* Carlisle, PA: Banner of Truth, 1994.

Nichols, Stephen J. *An Absolute Sort of Certainty: The Holy Spirit and the Apologetics of Jonathan Edwards.* Phillipsburg, NJ: Presbyterian & Reformed, 2003.

Nichols, Stephen J. *Heaven on Earth.* Wheaton: Crossway, 2006.

Nichols, Stephen J. *Jonathan Edwards: A Guided Tour of His Life and Thought.* Phillipsburg, NJ: Presbyterian & Reformed, 2001.

Noll, Mark A. *America's God: From Jonathan Edwards to Abraham Lincoln.* Oxford: Oxford University Press, 2002.

Noll, Mark A. *The Old Religion in a New World: The History of North American Christianity.* Grand Rapids: Eerdmans, 2002.

Noll, Mark A. *The Rise of Evangelicalism: The Age of Edwards, Whitefield, and the Wesleys.* Downers Grove, IL: InterVarsity, 2003.

Parkes, Henry B. *Jonathan Edwards, the Fiery Puritan.* New York: Minton, Balch & Company, 1930.

Parrish, Archie and R.C. Sproul. *The Spirit of Revival: Discovering the Wisdom of Jonathan Edwards.* Wheaton: Crossway, 2000.

Pauw, Amy Plantinga. *The Supreme Harmony of All: The Trinitarian Theology of Jonathan Edwards.* Grand Rapids: Eerdmans, 2002.

Piper, John. *God's Passion for His Glory: Living the Vision of Jonathan Edwards, with the Complete Text of the End for Which God Created the World.* Wheaton: Crossway, 1998.

The Princeton Companion to Jonathan Edwards. Edited by Sang H. Lee. Princeton: Princeton University Press, 2005.

The Puritans. Edited by Perry Miller and Thomas H. Johnson. New York: American Book, 1938.

Simonson, Harold. *Jonathan Edwards, Theologian of the Heart.* Grand Rapids: Eerdmans, 1974.

Smith, John E. *Jonathan Edwards: Puritan, Preacher, Philosopher.* Notre Dame: Notre Dame University Press, 1992.

Stein, Stephen J. *Jonathan Edwards's Writings: Text, Context, Interpretation.* Bloomington: Indiana University Press, 1996.

Sprague, William B. *Lectures on Revivals of Religion.* Birmingham, AL: Sovereign Ground Christian Books, 2005.

Storms, C. Samuel. *Signs of the Spirit: An Interpretation of Jonathan Edwards' Religious Affections.* Wheaton: Crossway, 2007.

Storms, C. Samuel. *Tragedy in Eden: Original Sin in the Theology of Jonathan Edwards.* Lanham, MD: University Press of America, 1985.

Stout, Harry S. *The New England Soul: Preaching and Religious Culture in Colonial New England.* New York: Oxford University Press, 1986.

Sweeney, Douglas A. *Nathaniel Taylor, New Haven Theology, and the Legacy of Jonathan Edwards.* Oxford: Oxford University Press, 2003.

Tappan, Henry P. *A Review of Edwards's "Inquiry into the Freedom of the Will."* New York: J. S. Taylor, 1839.

Tracy, Patricia J. *Jonathan Edwards, Pastor: Religion and Society in Eighteenth Century Northampton.* New York: Hill and Wang, 1980.

Turnbull, Ralph G. *Jonathan Edwards, the Preacher.* Grand Rapids: Baker, 1958.

Turretin, Francis. *Institutes of Elenctic Theology*, 3 volumes. Edited by James T. Dennison, Jr. Translated by George M. Giger. Phillipsburg, NJ: P & R Publishing, 1992.

Walton, Brad. *Jonathan Edwards, Religious Affections, and the Puritan Analysis of True Piety, Spiritual Sensation, and Heart Religion.* Lewiston, NY: Edwin Mellen, 2002.

Westra, Helen. *The Minister's Task and Calling in the Sermons of Jonathan Edwards.* Lewiston, NY: Edwin Mellen, 1986.

Winslow, Ola E. *Jonathan Edwards, 1703–1758: A Biography.* New York: Macmillan, 1940.

Yarbrough, Stephen R., and John C. Adams. *Delightful Conviction: Jonathan Edwards and the Rhetoric of Conversion.* Westport, CT: Greenwood, 1993.

Zakai, Avihu. *Jonathan Edwards' Philosophy of History: The Re-Enchantment of the World in the Age of Enlightenment.* Princeton: Princeton University Press, 2003.

ARTICLES

Beck, Peter. "The Fall of Man and the Failure of Jonathan Edwards." *Evangelical Quarterly* 79 (2007): 209-225.

Cherry, Conrad. "The Puritan Notion of the Covenant in Jonathan Edwards' Doctrine of Faith." *Church History* 34 (1965): 328–341.

Coleman, Robert E. "Jonathan Edwards: A Man Swallowed up in God." *Christian Education Journal* 11 (1990): 87–93.

Davies, R.E. "Jonathan Edwards, Theologian of the Missionary Awakening." *Evangel* 17 (1999): 1–8.

Ehrat, Christopher. "Jonathan Edwards' Treatise Concerning Religious Affections and Its Application to Prayer." *Crux* 24 (1988): 11–16.

Gilpin, W. Clark. "'Inward, Sweet Delight in God': Solitude in the Career of Jonathan Edwards." *Journal of Religion* 82 (2002): 523–538.

Haroutunian, Joseph. "Jonathan Edwards: Theologian of the Great Commandment." *Theology Today* 1 (1944): 361–377.

Haykin, Michael A.G. "Jonathan Edwards and His Legacy." *Reformation & Revival* 4 (1995): 65–86.

Holmes, Stephen R. "Strange Voices: Edwards on the Will." In *Listening to the Past: The Place of Tradition in Theology.* Grand Rapids: Baker, 2002: 86–107.

Kidd, Thomas S. "'The Very Vital Breath of Christianity': Prayer and Revival in Provincial New England." *Fides et Historia* 36 (2004): 19–33.

Kreider, Glenn R. "'God Never Begrutches His People Anything They Desire': Jonathan Edwards and the Generosity of God." *Reformation & Revival Journal* 12 (2003): 71–91.

_____. "Jonathan Edwards's Theology of Prayer." *Bibliotheca Sacra* 160, no. 640 (2003): 434–456.

Lewis, Paul. "'The Springs of Motion': Jonathan Edwards on Emotions, Character, and Agency." *Journal of Religious Ethics* 22 (1994): 275–297.

Logan, Samuel T., Jr. "The Doctrine of Justification in the Theology of Jonathan Edwards." *Westminster Theological Journal* 46 (1984): 26–52

Lucas, Sean M. "'A Man Just Like Us': Jonathan Edwards and Spiritual Formation for Ministerial Candidates." *Presbyterion* 30 (2004): 1–10.

Marsden, George M. "Jonathan Edwards, the Missionary." *Journal of Presbyterian History* 81 (2003): 5–17.

McClymond, Michael J. "Spiritual Perception in Jonathan Edwards." *Journal of Religion* 77 (1997): 195–216.

Minkema, Kenneth P. "Old Age and Religion in the Writings and Life of Jonathan Edwards." *Church History* 70 (2001): 674–704.

Munk, Linda. "His Dazzling Absence: The Shekinah in Jonathan Edwards." *Early American Literature* 27 (1992): 1–30.

Noll, Mark A. "And the Winner Is…Jonathan Edwards." *Reformed Journal* 39 (1989): 5–6.

Noll, Mark A. "God at the Center: Jonathan Edwards on True Virtue." *Christian Century* 110 (1993): 854–858.

Noll, Mark A. "Jonathan Edwards's Moral Philosophy, and the Secularization of American Christian Thought." *Reformed Journal* 33 (1983): 22–28.

Penner, Myron B. "Jonathan Edwards and Emotional Knowledge of God." *Direction* 30 (2001): 63–75.

Schafer, Thomas A. "Jonathan Edwards and Justification by Faith," *Church History* 20 (1950): 212–222

Schafer, Thomas A. "The Role of Jonathan Edwards in American Religious History." *American Theological Library Association Summary of Proceedings* 21 (1967):153–165.

Stein, Stephen J. "'For Their Spiritual Good': The Northampton, Massachusetts, Prayer Bids of the 1730s and 1740s." *William and Mary Quarterly* 37 (1980): 261–285.

Vetö, Miklos. Translated by Michael J. McClymond. "Spiritual Knowledge According to Jonathan Edwards." *Calvin Theological Journal* 31 (1996): 161–181.

Waanders, David W. "Pastoral Sense of Jonathan Edwards." *Reformed Review* 29 (1976): 124–132.

Wainwright, William J. "Jonathan Edwards and the Sense of the Heart." *Faith and Philosophy* 7 (1990): 43–62.

Westra, Helen P. "'Above All Others': Jonathan Edwards and the Gospel Ministry." *American Presbyterians* 67 (1989): 209–219.

Westra, Helen P. "Jonathan Edwards and the Scope of Gospel Ministry." *Calvin Theological Journal* 22 (1987): 68–90.

Westra, Helen P. "Jonathan Edwards on 'Faithful and Successful Ministers'." *Early American Literature* 23 (1988): 281–290.

DOCTORAL PROJECT

Bakke, Robert O. "The Concert of Prayer: Back to the Future?" D.Min. project, Gordon-Conwell Theological Seminary, 1991.

Index

Other titles available from Joshua Press…

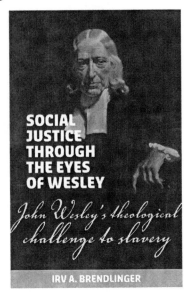

A messenger of grace

A study of
the life and thought
of Abraham Booth
By Raymond A. Coppenger

ABRAHAM BOOTH, a spiritual
giant in eighteenth-century
Baptist life, was a leading London pastor and theologian.
Deeply respected for his living
faith, wise counsel, evangelistic
zeal and perceptive writing, his
influential life and thought are
awakened for a new audience.

ISBN 978–1-894400-31–2

Social justice through the eyes of Wesley

John Wesley's theological
challenge to slavery
By Irv Brendlinger

JOHN WESLEY was the first
Christian leader of world
renown to take a decisive stand
against slavery. With wide-
ranging analysis and depth, this
book shows how Wesley's convictions compelled him to
labour tirelessly for abolition.

ISBN 978–1-894400-23–7

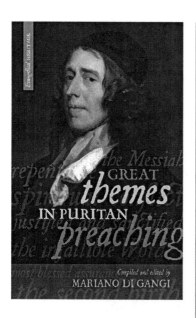

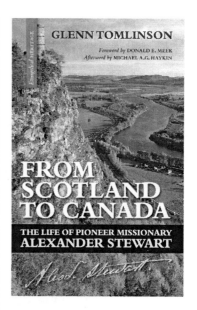

Great themes in Puritan preaching

*Compiled and edited
by Mariano Di Gangi*

DRAWING FROM a gold mine of Puritan writings, this book provides a taste of the riches of Puritan theology and its application to life. This title will whet your appetite and stir your faith to greater views of Christ, his Person and his work.

ISBN 978-1-894400-26-8 (HC)
ISBN 978-1-894400-24-4 (PB)

From Scotland to Canada

*The life of
pioneer missionary
Alexander Stewart*

By Glenn Tomlinson

ALEXANDER STEWART'S story is one of persistent zeal for the extension of God's kingdom and a fervent desire to do what he could to bring the gospel to a young country, founding the first Baptist church in York (Toronto). His pioneer heart left a deep mark on Canada.

ISBN 978-1-894400-29-9

Other titles available from Joshua Press…

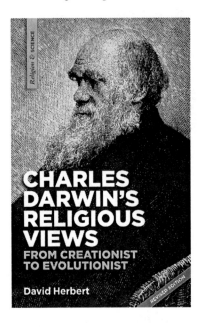

Charles Darwin's religious views
From creationist to evolutionist
By David Herbert

THIS BOOK is a spiritual biography that focuses primarily on the religious experiences of Charles Darwin's life. Its intent is to demonstrate how Darwin's rejection of the Bible led him to adopt the naturalistic assumptions that were foundational to his belief in evolutionism.

"A fascinating and important study of Charles Darwin, one of the most significant figures in our time. The book is a tour de force in its analysis of the creation-science debate, as well as an insightful account of the man himself."—DEREK THOMAS

JOSHUA PRESS
ISBN 978–1-894400-30-5

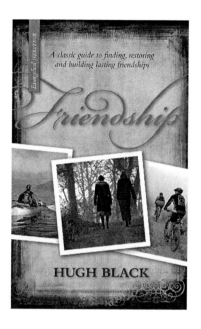

Friendship

By Hugh Black

THE HIGH IDEAL to which friendship was held by the ancient writers seems to be an obsolete sentiment today. Western society can feel like a cold and lonely place. In this culture of cynicism and malaise, Hugh Black directs our attention to the importance of friendship and the blessing that it can be. He addresses the challenges and responsibilities of friendship, including the consequences of wrecked friendships. In true friendship, accountability and love inspire us to live with more honour, integrity and grace. Ultimately, we see that in Jesus Christ we can have that "higher friendship," which revolutionizes the way we live, the way we think and the things we value.

JOSHUA PRESS

ISBN 978-1-894400-28-2 (HC) / ISBN 978-1-894400-27-5 (PB)

Deo Optimo et Maximo Gloria
To God, best and greatest, be glory

www.joshuapress.com